John Osborne
Plays Two

John Osborne's plays include: *Look Back in Anger* (1956), *Luther* (1961), *Inadmissible Evidence* (1965) and *A Patriot for Me* (1966). His collected prose, *Damn You, England* was published in 1994 and the two volumes of his autobiography, *A Better Class of Person* (1929–1956) and *Almost a Gentleman* (1955–1966) were published in 1981 and 1991 respectively. John Osborne was born in 1929 and died at Christmas 1994.

JOHN OSBORNE
Plays Two

The Entertainer,
The Hotel in Amsterdam,
West of Suez
and *Time Present*

Introduced by the author

faber and faber
LONDON · BOSTON

This collection first published in 1998
by Faber and Faber Limited
3 Queen Square London WCIN 3AU

Photoset by Parker Typesetting Service, Leicester
Printed and bound in England by Mackays of Chatham PLC, Chatham, Kent

2 4 6 8 10 9 7 5 3 1

CONTENTS

INTRODUCTION

'Working with Devine at the Royal Court, I was forced to reassess my ideas. I changed my acting career just when it needed a shot in the arm. My career was becoming predictable, solid and rather dull . . . Archie leapt off the page at me and he had to be mine. I began to steep myself in the old music-hall tradition. It wasn't too difficult because it was there in John's play – that, and so many other things. The play was enormous, a huge canvas. The winds of change were there all right. I was in step with the new wave, in step and marching . . . I will always be grateful for those days and look back on them with affection. Archie Rice: there he stands in the bright spotlight, alone, laughless but smiling. A bowler hat, a cane, eyebrows, a gap in his teeth, and dead eyes . . .'

From *On Acting*, by Laurence Olivier
(Weidenfeld and Nicolson)

Journalists insist that I wrote the part of Archie Rice in *The Entertainer* for Laurence Olivier, just as reference books have it that *Look Back in Anger* was originally titled *On the Pier at Morecambe*. These dumb speculations have a way of perpetuating themselves as fact. The true record may not be of much account but it is hard to justify tampering with it.

One evening in the autumn of 1956, I went on my own to the Chelsea Palace. Max Miller was on the bill. Waiting for him to come on, I watched an act, the highlight of which was an impersonation of Charles Laughton playing Quasimodo. I had seen it before. A smoky green light swirled over the stage and an awesome banality prevailed for some theatrical seconds, the drama and poetry, the belt and braces of music-hall holding up epic. This, the critics would later tell me, was the Brechtian influence on the play.

Music-hall was on its last legs but there were still a few halls in and around London for me to visit, not yet quite defeated by grey, front parlour television. I made notes for the play. I knew I was on to the problem – remembering George Devine's dictum that all problems were technical ones – and I was even confident enough to give it a title. I'd been listening to a record by a trumpet-player called Bunk Johnson. He was something of a legend, whose reputation had been revived by a few enthusiasts who had found him working in the Deep South as a truck driver, old and forgotten. They bought him a new set of teeth and he made a short comeback. One of the tunes he recorded was an old Scott Joplin number, 'The Entertainer'. It was graceful and touching and seemed apt for the play.

Sometime in early February 1957, George telephoned me. He was meticulous about not hectoring writers and so I was surprised when he asked, 'How's the play going, dear boy?' 'All right.' 'How far have you got?' This was most unlike him. He knew my powers of evasion. 'Oh, I've finished the second act. Almost.' 'I see. I hate to ask, but something's just come up. I don't suppose you can tell me if there's a part in it for Laurence?' 'Laurence who?' 'Olivier.'

George persuaded me against all his practice. 'Would you mind awfully if I asked you to let me have the first two acts?' Believing us both wrong, I agreed. Olivier's response was immediate and astonishing. He wanted to play Billy Rice, Archie's father. Letting him read just two acts had confused everyone. A week later I rang Tony Richardson, the director, and told him I had finished. 'Read me the last page,' he said, and I mumbled Archie's last speech down the telephone to his final line, which Olivier found incomprehensible and made devastating. 'Let me know where you're working tomorrow night – and I'll come and see YOU.' It was to be Olivier's face but, I hoped, *my* voice – possibly my own epitaph.

At the beginning of 1957, the muddle of feeling about Suez and Hungary, implicit in *The Entertainer*, was so overheated that the involvement of Olivier in the play seemed as dangerous as exposing the Royal Family to politics. There was some relief that an international event could arouse such fierce, indeed theatrical responses, with lifetime readers cancelling the *Observer* and rallies and abuse everywhere. The season was open for hunting down deceivers and self-deceivers. A special meeting of the English Stage Company was convened to make a decision about the production of *The Entertainer* at the Royal Court. Left and Right became allies. Olivier was an undisputed coup, but an embarrassment also. It was decided to drop the play.

Neville Blond, the Chairman of the ESC and its Council, was a Manchester textile magnate and sometime government adviser on transatlantic trade. His wife, Elaine, was a Marks & Spencer heiress. The pair of them promptly issued an invitation to Council members for lunch at their flat in Orchard Court to discuss the matter. Over the next few years I attended a few parties at Orchard Court, a gloomy mausoleum block behind elaborate wrought ironwork near Selfridges. These were sumptuous spreads given in the manner of a Christmas party for servants and tenant farmers. Mrs Blond would itemize the value of the pictures on the walls and the price per yard for the upholstery. We were not expected to stay long. On that first occasion, she told the Council, 'You'd be barmy not to do the play. With Olivier wanting to act in it!' 'You see,' said Neville, less stridently, 'we owe it to the boy.' In the event, George Harewood's casting vote carried the day. *The Entertainer* would go ahead.

Lord Chamberlain's Office,
St James's Palace, SW1
20th March, 1957

Sir,

The Entertainer

I am desired by the Lord Chamberlain to write to you regarding the above Play and to ask for an undertaking that the following alterations will be made:–

1) Act I, page 11, alter 'ass-upwards.'
2) Page 29, alter 'clappers.'
3) Act II, page 25, a photograph should be submitted of the nude in Britannia's helmet.
4) Page 27, alter 'pouf' (twice).
5) Page 30, alter 'shagged.'
6) Page 36, omit 'Right up to the flies. Right up.'

7) Page 43, omit 'rogered' (twice).
8) Page 44, omit 'I always needed a jump at the end of the day – and at the beginning too usually.'
9) Act III, page 3, alter 'wet your pants.'
10) Page 4, omit 'had Sylvia.'
11) Page 6, alter 'turds.'
12) Page 9, alter 'camp.'
13) A photograph of the nude tableau, page 20, should be submitted.
14) Page 21, omit 'balls.'
15) Scene 12 should be submitted in full.
16) The little song entitled, 'The old church bells won't ring tonight 'cos the Vicar's got the clappers.' Substitute: 'The Vicar's dropped a clanger.'

Any alterations or substitutions should be submitted for approval.

Yours faithfully,
Assistant Controller.

The ESC, the Council and the Lord Chamberlain were contained and we were in business. It was too late for reservations or quibbling. Olivier had to fit Archie in during April for five weeks before his summer commitment to *Titus Andronicus*. The opening was announced and within a few days every seat for the short season had been sold. I was anxious that Olivier should not be tempted into the snare of making Archie funny. It would have been an understandable mistake for an actor unused to little less than worship. As it was, people perpetuated the myth that the character was based on Max Miller. Archie was a man all right and one which most people, especially maidenly middle class reviewers, found unfamiliar and despicable. What could possibly be interesting to the civilized sensibility in the spectacle of a third-rate comic writhing in a dying profession?

Max Miller was a god, certainly to me, a saloon bar Priapus. Archie never got away with anything. Life cost him dearly, always. When he came on, the audience was immediately suspicious or indifferent. Archie's cheek was less than ordinary.

Max didn't have to be nauseatingly lovable like Chaplin. His humanity was in his sublime sauce, Archie's in his hollow desperation. Max got fined £5 for giving them one from the Blue Book and the rest of the world laughed with him. Archie would have got six months and no option.

Olivier took this point from the outset. We all paid visits to the remaining London halls. The Chelsea Palace, the Met in Edgware Road and Collins' in Islington were all about to be swept away. When I wrote that the music-hall was dying, I hadn't been aware that the bulldozers and iron balls were poised quite so close to home. I was especially keen that we should go a few times to Collins', where I had witnessed some of the worst acts imaginable. We missed a Scots comedian called Jack Radcliffe who did a very eerie deathbed scene. I thought the spectacle of a 'dying' comic in a sketch about death performed to an almost comatose audience would help an actor who could hardly have witnessed such a farewell to hope and dignity, let alone taken part in it. We did see a more robust act by a Cockney, Scott Sanders, whose signature tune was 'Rolling round the world, waiting for the sunshine and hoping things will turn out right', which he played on a series of pots and pans hanging on a barrow. He was loud, brisk, seldom funny and looked as if he knew it, hurtling through his act hoarsely before retreating to the pub next door. 'Why have you got that lemon stuck in your ear?' 'You've heard of the man with the hearing aid? Well, I'm the one with the lemonade.'

One of Olivier's central problems was to persuade audiences that such poetic awfulness could be authentic. The pressure of time was no bad thing and we threw ourselves into what was a unique venture for everyone. Soon, though, there were disturbing rumours about the domestic life of Olivier and Vivien Leigh. I was not privy to this, although I hoped that they were not true for the selfish reason of safeguarding my play and protecting it from prurient interest in Britain's most famous and near-royal couple, which would surely divert attention from what was happening in the theatre itself. Vivien's watchful presence at rehearsals was the most dangerous threat to the production's progress and everyone was aware of it. She always sat quickly and quietly, occasionally asking her chauffeur for a light, intent on Olivier. It was, of course, impossible to know what she was feeling and I could only guess at the pain.

Olivier was relishing his front-of-cloth scenes, attaining an astonishing skill at throw away business, like a spastic Jimmy Cagney. One Saturday run-through, about midday, he sprang his first realized version of the scene in which Archie sings the blues and crumples slowly down the side of the proscenium arch. The spring sunshine and the noise of the Sloane Square traffic poured through the open door. A dozen of us watched, astounded. Vivien turned her head towards me. She was weeping. I immediately thought of the chill inflection in Olivier's Archie voice: 'I wish women wouldn't cry. I wish they wouldn't . . .'

From *Almost a Gentleman*, by John Osborne
(Faber and Faber)

THE ENTERTAINER

NOTE

The music hall is dying, and, with it, a significant part of England. Some of the heart of England has gone; something that once belonged to everyone, for this was truly a folk art. In writing this play, I have not used some of the techniques of the music hall in order to exploit an effective trick, but because I believe that these can solve some of the eternal problems of time and space that face the dramatist, and, also, it has been relevant to the story and setting. Not only has this technique its own traditions, it own convention and symbol, its own mystique, it cuts right across the restrictions of the so-called naturalistic stage. Its contact its immediate, vital, and direct.

CHARACTERS

BILLY RICE
JEAN RICE
ARCHIE RICE
PHOEBE RICE
FRANK RICE
WILLIAM (BROTHER BILL) RICE
GRAHAM DODD

CONTENTS

The first performance in Great Britain of *The Entertainer* was given at the Royal Court Theatre, Sloane Square, London, on 10th April 1957 by the English Stage Company. It was directed by Tony Richardson and the decor was by Alan Tagg. The cast was as follows:

BILLY RICE	George Relph
JEAN RICE	Dorothy Tutin
PHOEBE RICE	Brenda de Banzie
ARCHIE RICE	Laurence Olivier
FRANK RICE	Richard Pasco
GORGEOUS GLADYS	Vivienne Drummond
WILLIAM (BROTHER BILL) RICE	Aubrey Dexter
GRAHAM	Stanley Meadows

SETTING: *The action takes place in a large coastal resort. The house where the Rice family live is one of those tall ugly monuments built by a prosperous business man at the beginning of the century. Only twenty-five minutes in the brougham to the front. Now, trolley buses hum past the front drive, full of workers from the small factories that have grown up round about. This is a part of the town the holiday makers never see – or, if they do, they decide to turn back to the pleasure gardens. This is what they have spent two or three hours in a train to escape. They don't even have to pass it on their way in from the central station, for this is a town on its own, and it has its own station, quite a large one, with acres of goods sheds and shunting yards. However, the main line trains don't stop there. It is not residential, it is hardly industrial. It is full of dirty blank spaces, high black walls, a gas holder, a tall chimney, a main road that shakes with dust and lorries. The shops are scattered at the corners of narrow streets. A newsagent's, a general grocer's, a fish-and-chip shop.*

OVERTURE

During the Intermissions, an advertising sheet is lowered.

SCENE ONE

At the back a gauze. Behind it, a part of the town. In front of it, a high rostrum with steps leading to it. Knee-high flats and a door frame will serve for a wall. The sight-lines are preserved by swagging. Different swags can be lowered for various scenes to break up the acting areas. Also, ordinary, tatty backcloth and draw-tabs. There are two doors L. and R. of the apron. The lighting is the kind you expect to see in the local Empire – everything bang-on, bright and hard, or a simple follow-spot. The scenes and interludes must, in fact, be lit as if they were simply turns on the bill. Furniture and props are as basic as they would be for a short sketch. On both sides of the proscenium is a square in which numbers – the turn numbers – appear. The problems involved are basically the same as those that confront any resident stage-manager on the twice nightly circuit every Monday morning of his working-life.

Music. The latest, the loudest, the worst. A gauzed front-cloth. On it are painted enormous naked young ladies, waving brightly coloured fans, and kicking out gaily. Written across it in large letters are the words 'ROCK'N ROLL NEW'D LOOK'.

Behind the up-stage gauze, light picks out an old man. He walks across the stage from L. to R. As he reaches C. he pauses and looks up. There are shouts and screams. The noise of a woman trying to separate two men – her son and her lover perhaps. Cries of 'Oh leave him alone! Don't! Please don't! Leave him alone.' He walks off R. and reappears beside the swagging, walking in C. There is a crash and the sounds of blows. He pauses again, then goes on. The woman screams, loudly this time. He pauses again, turns back, and shouts down over the banister rail 'Do you mind being quiet down there, please.' He pauses, but there is no response. 'Will you *kindly stop making all that noise!' He manages to sound dignified, but he has a powerful voice and the noise stops for a moment. He nods and starts moving. A voice shouts 'Why don't you shut your great big old gob, you poor, bloody old fool!' A woman's sob stabs the end of the sentence and the old man hesitates, turns back and calls over the stairs 'Are you all right, Mrs. —?' A man's voice is heard, urgent and heated. A door bangs, and the noise is muffled. The sobbing is still audible but the situation seems to be more controlled. The old man returns C. and enters through the door-frame.*

BILLY RICE *is a spruce man in his seventies. He has great physical pride, the result of a life-time of being admired as a 'fine figure of a man'. He is slim, upright, athletic. He glows with scrubbed well-being. His hair is just grey, thick and silky from its vigorous daily brush. His clothes are probably twenty-five years old – including his pointed patent leather shoes – but well-pressed and smart. His watch chain gleams, his collar is fixed with a tie-pin beneath the tightly knotted black tie, his brown homburg is worn at a very slight angle. When he speaks it is with a dignified Edwardian*

8

diction – a kind of repudiation of both Oxford and cockney that still rhymes 'cross' with 'force', and yet manages to avoid being exactly upper-class or effete. Indeed, it is not an accent of class but of period. One does not hear it often now.

Take up front gauze.

He walks down C., laying down a folded newspaper, two quart bottles of beer, and a telegram, which he glances at quickly. He crosses to the fore-stage door R., and goes through it singing sonorously but cheerfully:

'Rock of Ages cleft for me
Let me hide myself in thee!'

He reappears in his shirt sleeves pulling on a heavy woollen cardigan over his waistcoat. Still singing, he sits down, pours himself out a glass of beer, and starts to unlace his shoes. He puts these in a box with tissue paper up-stage C. The noise starts up again from downstairs. He drinks from his glass of beer, takes out a nail file and stands cleaning his nails expertly. This is like flicking off the old, imaginary speck of dust. There is a yell from downstairs. BILLY *speaks, gravely, with forethought.*

BILLY: Bloody Poles and Irish!

(*He sits down and puts on his carpet slippers. Front door slams, he takes spectacles from his case and puts them on.*)

I hate the bastards.

(*He unfolds his newspaper, the doorbell is still ringing. He looks irritated, but he has his feet up and is too comfortable to move. He sings cheerfully, as if to drown the noise of the doorbell.*)

Nearer my God to Thee
Nearer to Thee!

(*He listens and then goes on.*)

Even though it be a cross
That raiseth me

(*He picks up the newspaper and peers at it gravely.*)

Still all my song would be
Nearer my God to Thee,
Nearer to Thee!

(*He puts down his paper.*)

(*Standing.*) Why don't they answer the bloody door!

(*He leans his arms on the chair, wondering whether he will have to go after all.*)

Ought to be locked up, some of these people.

(*It looks as though he won't have to go after all, and he settles back cheerfully.*)

Dirty, filthy lot. (*Picks up paper. Pushes paper down suddenly.*)

My God, there's a draught!

(*Gets up and goes to door and looks out.*)

I'll bet they've left the front door open. Born in fields, they are.

(*Takes a rug and arranges it against the door.*)

Probably were born in fields. Animals. (*Back to chair and sits down.*) Like animals. Wild animals.

(*He settles down. Across from up L. comes a young girl.* BILLY *pours himself out some more beer. The girl knocks on the door. He listens.*)

Who is it?

(*The girl knocks again.*)

Who is it? Can't get any peace in this damned house.

GIRL: Is that you, Grandad?

BILLY: What?

GIRL: It's Jean.

BILLY: (*Rising*) Who is it?

JEAN: It's me – Jean.

BILLY: (*Goes to door and stands behind it*) Can't even read the paper in peace. Who?

JEAN: It's your granddaughter.

(JEAN *tries to push the door open but the rug prevents it.*)

BILLY: Just a minute! Just a minute! Hold your horses! (*He bends down.*)

JEAN: Sorry.

BILLY: Hold your horses!

(*He releases the rug and opens the door, revealing* JEAN RICE. *She is about twenty-two, dark, with slightly protruding teeth and bad eyesight. She is what most people would call plain, but already humour and tenderness have begun to stake their small claims around her nose and eyes. Her mouth is large, generous.*)

JEAN: Hello, Grandad.

BILLY: I wondered who the hell it was.

JEAN: I'm sorry.

BILLY: I thought it was some of that mad lot carrying on. Well, come in if you're coming, it's draughty standing about in the doorway. I've only just sat down.

JEAN: (*Coming in*) Did I disturb you, I am sorry.

BILLY: I'd just sat down to read the evening paper. It's a bloody farm-yard this place.

JEAN: Well, how are you?

BILLY: Bloody farm-yard. They want locking up. And you know what now, don't you? You know who she's got upstairs, in Mick's old room, don't you? Some black fellow. It's true. I tell you, you've come to a mad-house this time.

JEAN: You're looking very well. How do you feel?

BILLY: I'm all right. You expect a few aches and pains when you get to my age. Phoebe's at the pictures. I think. She didn't tell me you were coming.

JEAN: I didn't tell her.

BILLY: No, well she didn't say anything. So I wasn't expecting a knock on the door.

JEAN: I only decided to come up this morning.

BILLY: I'd only just sat down to read the evening paper.

JEAN: I'm sorry. I disturbed you.

(*She has picked up her cue neatly. The fact that his evening has been disturbed is established. His air of distracted irritation relaxes and he smiles a little. He is pleased to see her anyway.*)

BILLY: Well, give your Grandad a kiss, come on.

(*She does so.*)

JEAN: It's good to see you.

BILLY: Well, it's nice to see you, my darling. Bit of a surprise. Go on, take your things off.

(*Jean undoes her coat, and throws a packet of cigarettes on the table.*)

JEAN: Got you those.

BILLY: Phoebe won't be long. What she went out for, I don't know.

JEAN: Gone to the pictures has she?

BILLY: She's mad. Oh, that's very kind of you. Very kind. Thank you. Yes, she said she was going early. I don't know why she can't stay in.

JEAN: Well, you know – she's always been like that. She enjoys it.

BILLY: Well, she'll have to learn. She's not a youngster any more. When she gets to my age, she won't want to do it. (*He unwraps the cigarettes and takes out an ivory holder from his waistcoat.*) Oh, this is nice of you. Thank you. Still, if she stays in she only gets irritable. And I can't stand rows. Not any more. (*He stares in front of him.*) No use arguing with Phoebe anyway. Would you like some beer? (*She shakes her head.*) She just won't listen to me. Are you sure you won't? There's a damn great crate out in the kitchen, Frank brought it in this morning.

JEAN: No thanks, Grandad.

BILLY: No, when she gets in that mood, I just go out.

JEAN: Where do you go?

BILLY: I go for a walk. Or I go to the Club. You haven't been to the Club. Oh, I must take you then. It's very quiet, mind you. Except at week-ends. You get some of the wives then. But they're mostly oldtimers like me.

JEAN: Sounds fun.

BILLY: Well, it's somewhere to go when you're fed up with the place. Don't suppose it would appeal much to youngsters like yourself. I expect you go in more for these jazz places.

JEAN: I'd like to go. You must take me.

BILLY: Would you really? Would you? All right. But, I warn you, there's none of your boogie-woogie. How long are you here for?

JEAN: Just the week-end.

BILLY: We'll go tomorrow night. It's a good night, Sunday. I sing them some of the old songs, sometimes, when I feel like it. Haven't done it lately, not for a long time. Don't seem to feel like it.

JEAN: Where's Dad?

BILLY: He's at the theatre. He's playing here – at the Grand this week, you know.

JEAN: Oh, yes, of course.

BILLY: I don't seem to feel like it these days. You get a bit depressed sometimes sitting here. Oh, then there's the Cambridge down the road. I go there, of course. But there's not the old crowd there, you know. What about the news, eh? That's depressing. What d'you make of all this business out in the Middle East? People seem to be able to do what they like to us. Just what they like. I don't understand it. I really don't. Archie goes to that damned place down by the clock tower.

JEAN: The Rockliffe.

BILLY: Yes, the Rockliffe. Every tart and pansy boy in the district are in that place at a week-end. Archie tried to get me there the other day. No thank you. It's just a meat-market.

JEAN: How is Dad?

BILLY: He's a fool.

JEAN: Oh?

BILLY: Putting money into a road-show.

JEAN: I didn't know.

BILLY: Oh, it's another of his cock-eyed ideas. He won't listen to me. He spends half his time in that Rockliffe.

JEAN: I see. What show is it this time?

BILLY: Oh, I don't remember what it's called.

JEAN: Have you seen it?

BILLY: No, I haven't seen it. I wouldn't. These nudes. They're killing the business. Anyway, I keep telling him – it's dead already. Has been for years. It was all over, finished, dead when I got out of it. I saw it coming. I saw it coming, and I got out. They don't want real people any more.

JEAN: No, I suppose they don't.

BILLY: They don't want human-beings. Not any more. Wish he wouldn't get stuck in that Rockliffe. Gets half his posing girls in there if you ask me. (*Warming up.*) Well, why should a family man take his wife and kids to see a lot of third-class sluts standing about in the nude? It's not even as if they got the figures nowadays. They're all skin and bone.

JEAN: (*Smiles*) Like me.

BILLY: Well, you don't stand around with nothing on for everyone to gawp at and God bless you for it. But you never see a woman with a really good figure now. I could tell you something about beautiful women now, I could. And it wasn't all make-up either. They were ladies. Ladies, and you took off your hat before you dared speak to them. Now! why, half the time you can't tell the women from the men. Not from the back. And even at the front you have to take a good look, sometimes.

JEAN: Like the Government and the Opposition.

BILLY: What's that? Like the Government and the Opposition. Don't talk to me about the Government. Or that other lot. Grubby lot of rogues. Want locking up. No, old Archie's a fool. He won't even listen to you. That's why I put up with old Phoebe. She's had to cope I can tell you. But I don't have to tell you. He's going to come a cropper I'm afraid. And pretty soon too. He's bitten off more than he can chew.

JEAN: With this new show you mean. Has he really put money into it?

BILLY: Put money into it! Don't make me laugh! He hasn't got two halfpennies for a penny. It's all credit. Credit, if you please! How he gets it beats me, after that last business. Still, he could always talk, your Dad. And that's about all. Do you know, I spent thousands of pounds on his education. Went to the same school as me. And his brother. Thousands of pounds. He wasn't one of these scholarship people, like you. And where's it got 'em? (*He takes a drink.*) That Rockliffe. They should close the place. Someone should write to the Council about it. I'm surprised nobody hasn't. There's a lot of gentry here, you know – Besides the riff-raff round here. Retired people. They don't want that kind of thing going on. Are you all right? You look as though you've been keeping late nights

or something. What have you been doing with yourself?
Lots of these parties, eh?

JEAN: No, not really.

BILLY: Well, you've got to have a good time while you're
young. You won't get it later on. I'll bet he won't be in till
all hours tonight.

JEAN: Dad?

BILLY: I'm very pleased to see you, Jean. Are you all right?
They're treating you right?

JEAN: Oh, yes.

BILLY: They're doing right by you, I hope. You're not in any
trouble, are you?

JEAN: No, Grandad. I'm not in any trouble.

BILLY: I just wondered why you came up to see us like this
suddenly.

JEAN: Oh, it's just –

BILLY: I'm not asking you to tell me. You do as you like, my
darling. I 'spect you're hungry are you?

JEAN: I ate on the train.

BILLY: You shouldn't have done that. It's extravagant, and all
they give you is a lot of rubbish. You're not extravagant,
are you?

JEAN: I don't think so.

BILLY: No, I didn't think so. You're a good girl, Jean. You'll
get somewhere. I know you'll get somewhere. You're not
like the lot in this house. You'll do something for yourself.
You take after your old grandfather.
(*She smiles at him affectionately.*)
Don't you? Jean, if ever you're in any kind of trouble, you
will come to me now won't you?

JEAN: I will.

BILLY: I mean it. Now look – there's just the two of us here.
Promise me you'll come and tell me.

JEAN: Of course I will, but there's nothing –

BILLY: I'm not fooling about, I'm serious. Phoebe will be back
any minute, and I don't want her to know. I want you to
promise me.

JEAN: I promise you. If there is anything –

BILLY: If it's money, mind –

JEAN: Well I tell you I've just –

BILLY: I've got a few pounds in the Post Office. Not much, mind you, but I've got a few pounds. Nobody knows, so not to say a word, mind.

JEAN: No.

BILLY: Not even the pension people. I don't tell them my business. But, as I say –

JEAN: Grandad, I promise. If I want anything –

BILLY: Probably don't give you much in that job, do they? You tell 'em what you're worth, they're robbers.

JEAN: They pay pretty well.

BILLY: How much was your fare up here? (*He is getting slightly carried away.*)

JEAN: No, Grandad, please – I don't want it.

BILLY: Hold your bloody noise. If I want to give it to you, you shall have it. Here just a minute –

JEAN: Please –

BILLY: What's the matter? Isn't it good enough for you?

JEAN: It isn't that –

BILLY: Well then. Do as you're told and take it. I wouldn't have dared argue with my grandfather. Even at your age. (*Counting out his money.*) Um. Well, I don't seem to have enough just now. How much is it?

JEAN: I don't remember.

BILLY: Of course you remember. Look, there's half a quid. You take that towards it for now, and on Monday I'll go to the Post Office and get it out for you.

JEAN: Darling, you'll need that for the week-end. There's cigarettes and papers, and you're taking me to the Club, remember?

BILLY: Oh. Yes. I'd forgotten that. Well, we'll call it a loan, mind?

JEAN: A loan?

BILLY: Yes, a loan. You know what a loan is.

JEAN: Oh, all right.

BILLY: You mustn't go short. We all need looking after. And you've got to look after your own kind. No use leaving it to the Government for them to hand out to a lot of bleeders who haven't got the gumption to do anything for themselves. I want to look after you, Jean. I do, I do really. You're a good girl and I know you'll do something with your life, you'll *be* somebody. You won't waste it away and be silly.

JEAN: Bless you.

BILLY: Don't waste it. Do something good with it. Don't waste it. Sit down, for God's sake. You look as if you're going to put on your hat and coat and go. Sit down and talk to your Grandad. I don't get much chance to talk to anyone. They think you're a bit soft. Just because you can remember things when they were a bit different. Go on, have a glass.

JEAN: Thank you.

BILLY: Like that barmaid in the Cambridge. I don't go there so much. I've seen her laughing up her sleeve. She thinks I haven't seen her, but I am not soft. She's a common bit of goods, too. Great bosoms sticking out here. As if you want to see that, when you lean over for your drink. Enough to put you off your beer. And she gives short measure. You've got to watch them. They think they can have it over you.

JEAN: What time does the second house finish?

BILLY: I don't know. About eleven I suppose. You'll wait up all night if you wait for him. They wouldn't have employed someone like that in the old days. Like a common prostitute.

JEAN: Perhaps I should go and meet him.

BILLY: Do as you like, my girl. But I shouldn't. They've got a television in that bar now. A television. Now who do you think would want a television in a pub? Blaring away, you can't hear yourself think. D'you know? Do you know I asked them to turn it down, the other night. That cow with the bosom. Well, you'd expect her to be insolent. But then I asked the Gov'nor – Charlie Rowse. He's a pal of mine. I've known him for years. And do you know – he wouldn't hear of it! I don't know what's happening to everyone. I don't. Do you know?

JEAN: (*She isn't listening*) No, Grandad I don't.

BILLY: It makes you sad – sometimes. Old Charlie Rowse of all people. I haven't been able to go in there since, somehow. I got these in the off-licence over the way. (*He looks at her shrewdly.*) I suppose you've no right to expect people to listen to you. Just because you've had your life. It's all over for you. Why should anyone listen to you? (*Pause.*) Have you been drinking?

JEAN: Yes.

BILLY: I always know when a woman's been drinking.

JEAN: I'm sorry.

BILLY: That's all right, my girl. I dare say you know what you're doing. I should put your feet up, and close your eyes. You'll feel better in a minute.

JEAN: I had four gins. Four large gins. I'll be all right. What's the business like?

BILLY: At the theatre? I don't know. I don't ask. But I'll bet there's more in the saloon bar of the Cambridge than he's got in there. I know how you feel, girl. You just relax.

JEAN: I like listening to you. I always have.

BILLY: Yes, you always used to like coming to see me, didn't you? You used to enjoy yourself with me when you were a little girl. You were a pretty little thing. With your dark curls and your little dresses. (*Quickly.*) Not that looks are everything. Not even for a woman. Don't you believe it. You don't look at the mantelpiece when you poke the fire. (*She sits down and leans back.*)
No, I'll say this for Archie – he always saw that you looked nicely turned out. You looked a little picture always. Spent too much I daresay. He was a smart little boy himself. Used to dress them in sailor suits then. He was a pretty little boy. Funny how they all turn out. (*Pause, then softly, sincerely.*) I feel sorry for you people. You don't know what it's really like. You haven't lived, most of you. You've never known what it was like, you're all miserable really. You don't know what life can be like.
(*The light fades, a tatty backcloth descends.*)

SCENE TWO

Front cloth. Darkened stage. Spotlight hits the prompt corner. Music strikes up. ARCHIE RICE *makes his entrance.*

ARCHIE: Good evening, ladies and gentlemen – Archie Rice is the name. Archie Rice. Mrs Rice's favourite boy. We're going to entertain you for the next two and a half hours and you've really had it now. All the exit doors locked. Talking about being locked in, some of these people ought to be locked up. Locked up. They did, honest. I'll give you a case in point. A case in point. My wife – my wife. Old Charlie knows her, don't you, Charlie? Old Charlie knows her. A real road-mender's job she is – isn't she, Charlie? It's all right. I've taken his drill away from him now. I have. Haven't I, Charlie. He's the only boy soprano in the Musicians' Union. I know what you're waiting for. I know what you're waiting for and who isn't? Just keep your peckers up – they'll be on in a minute. You've got to put up with me first. And now – now, to open the show. I'm going to sing a little song I wrote myself. I hope you like it.

> 'Why should I care?
> Why should I let it touch me!
> Why shouldn't I, sit down and try
> To let it pass over me?
> Why should they stare,
> Why should I let it get me?
> What's the use of despair,
> If they call you a square?
> You're long time dead –
> Like my pal Fred,
> So why, oh why should I bother to care?'

(*He goes into his dance routine.*)

> 'Why should I care?
> Why should I let it touch me!
> Why shouldn't I, sit down and try

19

To let it pass over me?
Why should they stare,
Why should I let it get me?
What's the use of despair,
If they call you a square?
If they see that you're blue, they'll – look
     down on you
So why should I bother to care? (Thank
     God I'm normal!)
So why should I bother to care?'

(*Exit.*)

SCENE THREE

The music fades. The backcloth goes up, revealing BILLY, JEAN *and* PHOEBE. PHOEBE *is about sixty, with fair hair that was attractive once, and still has a great deal of care spent on it. Her face is made up, though not very skilfully. She is never still, she never listens – like most of the people in this house. Or, if she is obliged to sit and listen to anyone, she usually becomes abstracted and depressed, sitting on the edge of her chair, twisting her fingers round her hair. Just now, she is flushed, like a child, prepared to be excited.*

PHOEBE: Oh, he will be so glad to see you. (*To* BILLY.) Won't he? But why didn't you let us know? I'd have got you something prepared. Are you sure you won't have something? I've got a bit of York ham in – I bought it this morning. Wouldn't you like a bit of that?

JEAN: No thank you, dear. I told you I just came up on the spur of the moment.

PHOEBE: That's right, you did. But you said something in your letter about going away for the week-end. Did something go wrong?

JEAN: I changed my mind.

PHOEBE: Oh, well it's lovely to see you. Isn't it, Dad? He's pleased. He doesn't have anyone much to talk to. Do you? I say you don't have much chance for talk. He's on his own here half the time. It's not my fault. He won't come to the pictures with me. But you've got to go somewhere, as I say to him. You get bored stiff just sitting indoors. He likes to listen to a play on the wireless sometimes. You *like* a nice play. But I can't sit for long, I'd rather have a spot of pictures.

BILLY: I'm all right.

PHOEBE: Well, I suppose that's sitting down too, but it's not the same somehow, is it? Let's open this, shall we? (*She indicates bottle on the table.*) You shouldn't have bought gin. She's naughty, isn't she?

BILLY: She ought to have more sense – spending her money.

PHOEBE: Never mind, she's big hearted, that's the main thing. Hand me a couple of glasses. You're going to have one with me, aren't you? I don't want one on my own.

JEAN: All right – just a small one.

PHOEBE: Oh, sorry, Dad – do you want one?

BILLY: No thank you.

PHOEBE: Well, this is nice. What a shame – I'd have been in earlier but I stayed and saw a bit of the big picture round again.

BILLY: I know better than to overdo it.

PHOEBE: The picture? Oh, wasn't up to much. But there was that nice fellow in it, what's his name? Oh, he sings sometimes, got very deep set eyes, dark. You'd know who I mean.

JEAN: Is he American or British?

PHOEBE: Oh, I don't know. American I should think.

JEAN: What was the picture called?

PHOEBE: (*Laughs*) Blimey, you should know better than to ask me that! You know what a rotten memory I've got. Well, cheerio! (*She drinks.*) Oooh, that's a nice drop of gin – some of the muck they give you nowadays – tastes like cheap scent. You should hear him going on about the beer. No, they've a lot of rubbish on at the pictures these days. I haven't seen a decent picture for ages. It seems to be all bands or singing. Either that or Westerns. He doesn't mind them so much. But I can't stand all that shooting. It gives me a headache. But I'm dreadful – if there's nothing else on, I still go just the same, don't I? Even if it is just to the bug house round the corner. I get myself six penn'orth of sweets and have a couple of hours whatever's on. I hear they're closing that place down, by the way. Everything's doing badly. That's what I tell Archie. 'Course he gets worried because the business is bad. Still, that's how it is; people haven't got the money, have they? I'm at Woolworth's now, did I tell you? I'm on the electrical counter. It's not bad. Girls are a bit common, that's all. Oh, it is nice to see you. Archie will be so pleased. She looks a bit peaky. Round the face, don't you think? Don't you think she looks a bit peaky?

BILLY: She looks all right.

PHOEBE: I don't suppose she's eating properly. You know what these young girls are. They worry about their figures. So, you didn't go away for the week-end after all?

JEAN: No.

PHOEBE: Graham's all right, is he?

JEAN: Yes, he's all right.

PHOEBE: There's nothing wrong there, is there?

BILLY: Why don't you mind your bloody business? She'll tell you if she wants to.

PHOEBE: All right, I know. She doesn't mind telling me if there's anything, do you?

JEAN: We had a slight disagreement. Nothing more, that's all.

PHOEBE: After all, she may not be my own, but I did help to bring her up a little, didn't I? After all, she's Archie's daughter. Be a bit strange if I wasn't interested whether she was happy or not. Oh, well, dear, don't take any notice. You'll soon make it up. Men are funny. You don't want to take any notice of them.

JEAN: (*Smiling*) Wish I didn't.

PHOEBE: That's right. Have another drink. You'll soon feel better. What did you have a row about? Something silly I'll bet. You haven't broken off your engagement?

JEAN: I don't know. Probably.

PHOEBE: Oh dear, I'm sorry.

JEAN: I went to the Rally in Trafalgar Square last Sunday.

BILLY: You did what?

JEAN: I went to the Rally in Trafalgar Square.

BILLY: What for, for God's sake?

JEAN: Because, Grandad, somehow – with a whole lot of other people, strange as it may seem – I managed to get myself steamed up about the way things were going.

BILLY: And you went to Trafalgar Square?

JEAN: Well she said so didn't she?

BILLY: Well I should think you want your bloody head read!

JEAN: That was more or less Graham's feeling about it. Only he happens to be about fifty years younger than you, and he put it a bit differently. It all really started over something I wanted to do, and then it all came out, lots of things. All kinds of bitterness – things I didn't even know existed.

BILLY: I didn't know you were interested in politics.

JEAN: Neither did I. I've always found the whole thing rather boring.

BILLY: Good God! I've heard some things in my time. This is what comes of giving them the bloody vote. They start breaking their engagements, just because they believe every shiftless lay-about writing for the papers.

PHOEBE: Oh, shut up, just for a minute, Dad. You had a row because of something you wanted to do?

JEAN: Well, it's – oh, it's a complicated story. I think I wrote and told you I was teaching Art to a bunch of Youth Club kids.

PHOEBE: Oh, yes. That was ages ago.

JEAN: Nearly a year. I knew someone who had been doing it – a young man Graham knew. He said it was too much for him, and he couldn't stick it any longer. 'They're little bastards the lot of them,' he said. 'If anyone believes you can teach those monsters to create anything, they're crazy. They're a lot of little bastards.' That's what he said. But – something, something, made me want to have a go at it. There wasn't any money in it. Just a few shillings for a few nights a week. But it was something I knew a little about – thought I knew about. I'd never been good enough to paint

23

myself, but I thought this was something I really could do. Even if it was just battling a gang of moronic teenagers. The Club leader thought I was mad, and so did Graham.

PHOEBE: I can't say I blame him really. It doesn't sound a very nice job at all. Not for a young girl like you, Jean. They sound like a real tough crowd to me.

JEAN: They were. Too tough for either of the young men who had taken them on before.

PHOEBE: Well if they don't want to learn, why do they go for heaven's sake?

JEAN: It was an obligatory class, if they attended one of my classes a week, they could take part in the Club's other activities – the dances and so on. I fought those kids back – and some of them were eight feet tall. Most of the time I've loathed it, and I loathed them. I pretended to myself that I didn't, but I did. I hated them, but I think I was getting somewhere. And now Graham wants me to marry him. Now, before he's qualified but I wouldn't. He doesn't want me to try something for myself. He doesn't want me to threaten him or his world, he doesn't want me to succeed. I refused him. Then it all came out – Trafalgar Square and everything. You know, I hadn't realized – it just hadn't occurred to me that you could love somebody, that you could want them, and want them twenty-four hours of the day and then suddenly find that you're neither of you even living in the same world. I don't understand that. I just don't understand it. I wish I could understand it. It's frightening. Sorry, Phoebe, I shouldn't be drinking your gin. I bought this for you.

BILLY: Well we only need a few pigeons for it to be like Trafalgar Square in here. I've never known such a draughty bloody place. Everybody leaves the windows and doors open. I don't believe that's healthy. I tell you, you come in one door and you get blown out the other.

JEAN: How's young Mick – have you heard from him?

PHOEBE: Oh, yes. Of course. He's out there – you knew that, didn't you?

JEAN: Yes. I knew.

PHOEBE: Archie worries about him. He doesn't say so, but I know he does. It's funny really because they never seemed to hit it off so well, in lots of ways. Not like you and him, or Frank. He's a very sensible boy, young Mick. He's very straight. I've lost some sleep this week, I can tell you.

BILLY: He's a fine boy. When they called him, he went. No arguments, nothing. He just went.

JEAN: (*Suddenly*) And when they called Frank, he refused, and he went to jail for it – for six months. Young Frank full of doubts about himself, and everybody, with a cold in his head half the year, and a weak chest. Lucky to pass C3. Poor Frank. (*To* PHOEBE.) He's not very strong, you always said. You went without to buy him little luxuries to eat, why you wouldn't let him even clean his own shoes. No, you'd do it for him. But he went and said no, and, what's more, he went to jail for it. Oh, he gave in eventually, but he said no for six months of his poor protected life – he said no! I think that's something. You don't have to measure up young Mick against Frank, Grandad. Now, don't look hurt. I'm not getting at you. I love you very much – both of you, but I probably shouldn't have started drinking gin on the train.
(*Pause.*)

PHOEBE: Well, we'll shut up about it now.

BILLY: I just said that Mick was a good boy.

JEAN: He is. He's a very good boy. He's a gallant young nineteen year old who's fighting for us all, who never somehow learnt to say no, who never wanted to, and I hope to God he comes back safely.

PHOEBE: Oh dear, Jean, you think he'll be all right, don't you? I don't know why they send these boys out to do the fighting. They're just kids, that's all. That's all he is, a kid.

BILLY: You can't turn against your own people, Jean. You can't do it.

JEAN: Where is Frank? My own people – who are my people?

PHOEBE: He plays the piano in one of these late-night drinking places. He doesn't seem to know what to do with himself. Since he came out of that place. That damned prison. I'll never forget it. Making him go to prison. I'll never forget it. I can't get over it – ever.

JEAN: Well, it's all over now. Have some more of that gin. I bought it for you.

PHOEBE: I won't. And making him do that job. A boy like him shouldn't be doing it. Hospital porter. D'you know they made him stoke the boilers?

JEAN: Yes. He'd have been better off in the Army – sticking a bayonet into some wog.

PHOEBE: He doesn't say a word to me about it. I wish he hadn't done it all the same. I wonder whether Mick isn't better off after all. I mean – they do look after them, don't they?

JEAN: Oh, yes they look after them all right.

BILLY: Look after them better now than they did, when I was in it. I haven't read the evening paper yet. The Dardanelles – I went through that without a scratch. Not a scratch on me.

JEAN: They're all looking after us. We're all right, all of us. Nothing to worry about. *We're* all right. God save the Queen!

(*Blackout. Draw tabs.*)

SCENE FOUR

Spotlight on ARCHIE *at microphone.*

ARCHIE: I've played in front of them all! 'The Queen', 'The Duke of Edinburgh', 'The Prince of Wales', and the – what's the name of that other pub? Blimey, that went better first house. (*Pause.*) I've taken my glasses off. I don't want to see you suffering. What about these crooners, eh? What about these crooners? I don't know what we're coming to. I don't, honest. Look at the stuff they sing. Look at the songs they sing! 'The Dark Town Strutters' Ball' – it's a lot of rubbish, isn't it? I'll bet you thought I was a rotten act before I come on, didn't you? What about these girls? (*Indicates up stage.*) What about them? Smashin'. I bet you think I have a marvellous time up here with all these posing girls, don't you? You think I have a smashin' time don't you? (*Pause.*) You're dead right! You wouldn't think I was sexy to look at me, would you! No, lady. To look at me you wouldn't think I was sexy, would you! (*Pause.*) You ask him! (*Points to conductor's stand.*) Ask him! (*Staring out at audience.*) You think I'm like that, don't you? You think I am! Well, I'm not. But *he* is! (*Points to conductor's stand again.*) I'd rather have a glass of beer any day! And now I'm going to sing you a little song, a little song, a little song written by the wife's sister, a little song entitled 'The Old Church bell won't ring tonight, as the Verger's dropped a clanger!' Thank you, Charlie.

> 'We're all out for good old number one,
> Number one's the only one for me!
> Good old England, you're my cup of tea,
> But I don't want no drab equality.
> Don't let your feelings roam,
> But remember that charity begins at home.
> For Britons shall be free!
> The National Health won't bring you wealth
> Those wigs and blooming spectacles are
>   bought by you and me.
> The Army, the Navy and the Air Force,
> Are all we need to make the blighters see
> It still belongs to you, the old red, white and
>   blue

(*Drop Union Jack.*)

> Those bits of red still on the map
> We won't give up without a scrap.
> What we've got left back
> We'll keep – and blow you, Jack!
> Oh, number one's the only one for me!
> We're all out for good old number one,
> Yes number one's the only one for me –
> God bless you!

Number one's the only one for me!
Number one's the only one for me!'

(*Exit.*)

SCENE FIVE

BILLY, PHOEBE, JEAN.

BILLY: They were graceful, they had mystery and dignity. Why when a woman got out of a cab, she descended. Descended. And you put your hand out to her smartly to help her down. Look at them today. Have you ever seen a woman get out of a car? Well, have you? I have, and I don't want to see it again, thank you very much. Why I never saw a woman's legs until I was nineteen. Didn't know what they looked like. Nineteen. I was married when I was nineteen, you know. I was only twenty when Archie's brother was born. Old Bill. He's got on, anyway. I remember the first time I set eyes on your grandmother. She was just eighteen. She had a velvet coat on, black it was, black with fur round the edge. They were all the fashion just about then. It was so tight round her figure. and with her little fur cap on and muff, she looked a picture.

(ARCHIE *rushes in, his arms full with a carrier bag and bottles, briskly distracted.* ARCHIE RICE *is about fifty. His hair is brushed flat, almost grey. He wears glasses and has a slight stoop, from a kind of offhand pedantry which he originally assumed thirty years ago when he left one of those minor public day schools in London, which have usually managed to produce some raffish middle class adventurers as well as bank managers and poets. Landladies adore and cosset him because he is so friendly, and obviously such a gentleman. Some of his fellow artists even call him 'Professor' occasionally, as they might call a retired Army Captain 'Colonel'. He smiles kindly at this simplicity, knowing himself to belong to no class and plays the part as well as he knows how. He lightly patronizes his father,*

28

*whom he admires deeply. He patronizes his wife, Phoebe, whom
he pities wholeheartedly. It is this which has prevented him from
leaving her twenty years ago. Or, is it simply because, as many
people would suggest, he lacks the courage? Anyway, he makes
no secret of his perennial affairs with other women – real and
fictitious. It is part of his pity, part of his patronage, part of his
personal myth. He patronizes his elder son Frank, who lacks his
own brand of indulgence, stoicism and bravura, and for whom
he has an almost unreal, pantomime affection. In contrast, his
patronage of his daughter Jean is more wary, sly, unsure. He
suspects her intelligence, aware that she may be stronger than
the rest of them. Whatever he says to anyone is almost always
very carefully 'thrown away'. Apparently absent minded, it is a
comedian's technique, it absolves him seeming committed to
anyone or anything.*)

ARCHIE: Ay, ay, women's legs again! (*To the others.*) That's
what Sterne calls riding your tit with sobriety. I think it was
Sterne, anyway. Or was it George Robey? Um? Hello,
dear, this is nice. (*He kisses* JEAN.) I haven't got my glasses
on. I thought you were the Income Tax man sitting there. I
thought we had shaken him off. All right, are you?

JEAN: Thank you. I have had too much gin waiting for you.

ARCHIE: Never mind, you can have some more in a minute.
You haven't fixed an hotel or anything respectable, have
you?

JEAN: No, but –

ARCHIE: Jolly good. I'm sleeping alone tonight. The back of my
legs ache as it is. You and Phoebe can sleep up in my
room, and I'll kip on the sofa. I've just been talking to our
coloured friend on the stairs.

PHOEBE: He's a student.

ARCHIE: No he's not. He's a ballet dancer.

PHOEBE: (*Astonished*) Is he! (*To* JEAN.) He's a big fellow.

ARCHIE: Playing the Winter Gardens for a fortnight.

BILLY: A ballet dancer!

ARCHIE: He was telling me if you drop your hat outside there
now, you have to kick it down to the promenade before
you can pick it up. (*Pauses quickly, then goes on expertly.*)

They're not all coloured, I saw a couple of 'em on the bus on the way home yesterday. They were talking together all the way, everybody listening. I just got up to press the bell, and a woman shouted out, 'I lost two boys in the war for the likes of you!' I thought she meant me for a moment, so I turned round, and there she was, beating them with her umbrella like crazy.

BILLY: Don't like to see a man dancing like that.

ARCHIE: I was in a show with a couple of male dancers once. And wherever we went, on the Monday night some woman used to complain about their tights bulging. Wherever we went. Every Monday night. I'm sure it was the same woman each time. I used to call her the Camp Follower. Now, what are we going to have? Let's see what we've got. (*Rummages in carrier and pockets.*)

BILLY: There's a telegram come for you.

PHOEBE: Don't you think she's looking a bit peaky.

ARCHIE: Looks all right to me. Needs a drink that's all.

BILLY: (*Beginning to get tired and irritable*) There's a telegram come for you!

ARCHIE: Have you been on the batter, you old gubbins!

BILLY: No I haven't! I've been sitting here talking to Jean.

ARCHIE: I should go to bed if you're tired.

BILLY: I'm not tired – I could see you out any day!

ARCHIE: (*Picks up telegram*) You've been giving him that beastly gin. He sounds like a toast-master with DTs. One of my creditors. It'll wait. (*Throws it back on the table.*) You'd think they'd know better by this time! I've got some gin too – and dubonnet. Old Phoebe likes that don't you, dear! She thinks she's being awfully U when she drinks that, don't you?

PHOEBE: I like it. It seems to suit me. I can't drink gin on its own – not like he can. (*To* ARCHIE.) What's all this for? Was it – was it all right at the theatre?

ARCHIE: No it wasn't all right at the theatre. Monday night there were sixty sad little drabs in, and tonight there were about two hundred sad little drabs. If we can open on Monday night at West Hartlepool, it will be by very reluctant agreement of about thirty angry people, but I'm not thinking about that tonight.

PHOEBE: Oh, Archie!

ARCHIE: Go on, have your dubonnet, dear. Don't get all emotional. Jean, that's yours. Billy, wake up!

BILLY: I am awake!

ARCHIE: Well stop yelling then. You're like one of those television commercials. There's a drink for you.

BILLY: I don't want a bloody drink.

ARCHIE: You look as though you're going to sing a hymn.

BILLY: I'm tired.

ARCHIE: Well that's better – have a drink and go to bed.

BILLY: I haven't seen the evening paper yet.

ARCHIE: Well if you've won the pools, we can read about it in the morning.

BILLY: I don't want to sit here and stagnate even if you do. I want to know what's going on in the world.

ARCHIE: Yes, you're amazingly well informed. (*To the others.*) He's quite well-read for an ignorant old pro.

BILLY: I'm not an ignorant old pro!

ARCHIE: Yes you are, now don't argue and drink up. I'm having a celebration.

BILLY: Celebration! What have you got to celebrate about?

ARCHIE: Oh dear.

BILLY: (*Stands up*) You haven't got a thing you can call your own. And as sure as God made little apples, I'll lay a sovereign to a penny piece, you'll end up in the bankruptcy court again before Christmas, and you'll be lucky if you don't land up in jail as well.

PHOEBE: Get 'im to go to bed, Archie. He's over-tired.

ARCHIE: Go to bed. You're over-tired.

BILLY: I'm not over-tired. I don't relish the idea of another jail-bird in the family.

PHOEBE: Be quiet, Dad. You've had too much to drink.

BILLY: I could drink you lot under the table.

ARCHIE: Oh dear, he's getting religious now.

BILLY: I used to have half a bottle of three star brandy for breakfast –

ARCHIE: And a pound of steak and a couple of chorus girls.
He'll tell you the whole story at the drop of a hat.

BILLY: (*In rage*) I leave chorus girls to *you*!

ARCHIE: Nothing like slicing yourself off a nice piece of bacon.

BILLY: I know what you mean.

ARCHIE: Don't get excited, Father. You'll wake the Poles up.

BILLY: Don't talk to me about that bunch of greasy tom-cats!
One Britisher could always take on half a dozen of that
kind. Or used to. Doesn't look like it now.

ARCHIE: Well never mind, don't spoil the party –

BILLY: I pay my way, which is more than you've ever done.
And I'll tell you that I was educated at one of the finest
schools in England.

ARCHIE: It produced one Field Marshal with strong Fascist
tendencies, one Catholic poet who went bonkers and
Archie Rice.

BILLY: D'you know what James Agate said about me?

ARCHIE: Oh yes – that you and Mrs Pat Campbell were his
favourite female impersonators.

BILLY: You know bloody well what he said.
(ARCHIE *knows by long experience how far he can go and he
manages gently to turn the situation.*)

ARCHIE: We all know what he said, and every word of it was
true.
(BILLY *glares at him, and grabs his glass.*)
Well, as I was saying, before my ignorant old Father
interrupted –

BILLY: There's nothing to be ashamed of in being an old pro.
It's more than you'll ever be. You don't know the meaning
of the word!

PHOEBE: Oh go to bed, Dad – you're getting silly now.

BILLY: You had to have personality to be a comedian then. You
had to *really be somebody*!

ARCHIE: The reason for this little celebration is that tomorrow –
oh it's today now – today is my twentieth anniversary.

PHOEBE: Twentieth anniversary? Anniversary of what?

ARCHIE: The twentieth anniversary of my not paying income
tax. The last time I paid income tax was in 1936.

BILLY: They'll get you all right, they always get you in the end. You see!

ARCHIE: All right, love, you can sing us a hymn later. I think that is a very significant achievement, and I deserve some kind of tribute for it. (*To* JEAN.) Don't you think your old man deserves a tribute?

JEAN: I was just wondering how you came to pay income tax in 1936.

ARCHIE: Bad luck that's all. I was trapped in hospital with a double hernia. Very nasty it was too. Terribly complicated. I even thought all my plans for the future were going to be finished at one point. Anyway, that's another story. I'll tell you sometime. I was lying there on my back, wondering whether draught Bass on its own was enough to make life worth living, when two men in bowlers and rain-coats sprang at me from behind the screens. That was Archie's one downfall. Could have happened to anyone. I think the ward-sister must have tipped them off. She used to tell me she was very spiritual, so she probably did. I'd gone legit, for a while just then, and I'd been in 'The Tale of Two Cities'. When I told her she said, 'Oh, yes I think I've heard of that –' (*To* BILLY.) She was an Irish lady. 'A Tale of Two Cities – isn't it about Sodom and Gomorrah?' (JEAN *smiles.* BILLY *and* PHOEBE *are no longer listening.*) A lady in the pit thought that was quite funny tonight.

PHOEBE: Jean's had an upset with Graham.

ARCHIE: Have you? Oh I'm sorry. I should have asked, shouldn't I? I'm sorry dear. I'm afraid I'm a wee bit slewed. (*Looks round.*) I think everyone is. You are.

PHOEBE: She's broken off her engagement.

ARCHIE: Have you really? Well, I should have thought engagements were a bit suburban for intellectuals like you anyway. You'll be getting a motor-cycle and side-car next.

PHOEBE: Oh stop poking fun at her, Archie. Be sensible. You can see she's upset.

JEAN: I'm not upset, and I haven't made a decision about anything yet. I just came up because I wanted to see you all, and see how you are. And because I miss you.

PHOEBE: Oh, did you really? That's very sweet of you, dear. I appreciate that, I do really.

ARCHIE: She knows I'm not poking fun at her.

PHOEBE: Oh, I wish I knew what's going to happen.

JEAN: Never mind about me. You haven't heard from young Mick?

ARCHIE: No, old Mick can look after himself, he's a boy without problems, that one. I expect he's screwing himself silly. I hope he is anyway. What's happened with you and Graham?

BILLY: Your daughter went to that Trafalgar Square circus last Sunday, if you please!

ARCHIE: Oh, really? Are you one of those who don't like the Prime Minister? I think I've grown rather fond of him. I think it was after he went to the West Indies to get Noel Coward to write a play for him. Still, perhaps only someone of my generation could understand that. Does he bring you out in spots?

PHOEBE: Oh, Christ, I wish I knew what was going to happen to us!

ARCHIE: I feel rather like that about that horrible dog downstairs. It brings me out in a rash every time I look at it. There are three things that do that to me, three things. Nuns, clergymen and dogs.

PHOEBE: I don't want to always have to work. I mean you want a bit of life before it's all over. It takes all the gilt off if you know you've got to go on and on till they carry you out in a box. It's all right for him, he's all right. He's still got his women. While it lasts anyway. But I don't want to end up being laid out by some stranger in some rotten stinking little street in Gateshead, or West Hartlepool or another of those dead-or-alive holes!

JEAN: Phoebe don't upset yourself, please. Let's enjoy ourselves –

PHOEBE: Enjoy myself! D'you think I don't want to enjoy myself! I'm just sick of being with down and outs, I'm sick of it, and people like him.
(*She is crying.*)

ARCHIE: I wish women wouldn't cry. I wish they wouldn't. Try and say something to her, Jean.

JEAN: (*Going to* PHOEBE) Why don't you?

ARCHIE: I wish I could. I only wish I could.

JEAN: (*To Phoebe*) Come on, dear, would you like to go to bed?

PHOEBE: Yes, I think so, dear, if you don't mind. I think I've overdone it a bit. Archie knows what I'm like. I never could stand too much excitement. I think perhaps I got over-excited seeing you. It was such a nice surprise. And I'm probably worrying about young Mick underneath. I keep thinking of all that fighting –

ARCHIE: Get some sleep, love, you'll feel better when you wake up.

PHOEBE: (*Rising*) All right, dear. I'll get along, it's late anyway. Dad should have been in bed hours ago. He'll be awful tomorrow. Make him go to bed, Archie, will you?

ARCHIE: I will. (*To* JEAN.) See her up.

PHOEBE: (*Stopping*) Would you come and say good night to me, Archie?

ARCHIE: Yes. I'm just going to finish my little celebration. It's my anniversary, remember?

PHOEBE: (*Smiles*) He's funny.

(*Exit with* JEAN.)

ARCHIE: (*To* BILLY) Want another before you turn in?

BILLY: No thank you. I have had sufficient.

ARCHIE: Go on you old gubbins. (*Pours out a drink.*) I know that expression. That's your hymn look.

BILLY: You think I won't!

ARCHIE: I'm damn sure you will. All right, let's have a good heart warmer. Then drink up your beer and go to bed.

BILLY: All right, I will.

(*He sits upright and sings.*)

> 'Onward Christian soldiers
> Marching as to war
> With the Cross of Jesus
> Going on before.
> Christ the Royal Master

Fights against the foe
Forward into battle . . .'

(*Jean has come back into the room and Billy is too weary to go on. He starts to move down to his room.*)
Good night, Jean. It was good to see you. We'll have a talk tomorrow.

JEAN: Yes, we will. And you're taking me to the Club, remember.

BILLY: Good night, son.

ARCHIE: Good night, Dad.

(*Exit Billy.*)

JEAN: Dad –

ARCHIE: Yes.

JEAN: You're keeping something to yourself.

ARCHIE: You never miss a thing, do you? Observation – is the basis of all art.

JEAN: What is it? I've had a strange sick feeling in my stomach all day. As if something was going to happen. You know the feeling.

ARCHIE: Yes. I know the feeling. Mick's been taken prisoner. Nobody here seemed to know. It's in the paper actually. There was no point in breaking it tonight. Tomorrow's soon enough. (*He tears open the telegram.*) They usually get these things before the people who really matter. I knew what this must be. (*He hands it to her and picks up the paper.*) He seems to have been shooting up quite a lot of wogs, doesn't he? There's a picture of your friend here too, the one who gives you a rash. He's looking rather serious this time. Perhaps he's worrying about young Mick.

JEAN: I think I will have some of that.

(*He pushes her glass towards her.*)

ARCHIE: Well, Mick wouldn't want us to cut the celebration short. We'll drink to Mick, and let's hope to God he manages. Mick and the income tax man. With you it's Prime Ministers, with me it's dogs. Nuns, clergymen and dogs. Did I ever tell you the greatest compliment I had paid to me – the greatest compliment I always treasure? I

was walking along the front somewhere – I think it was here actually – one day, oh, it must be twenty-five years ago, I was quite a young man. Well, there I was walking along the front, to meet what I think we used to call a piece of crackling. Or perhaps it was a bit of fluff. No that was earlier. Anyway, I know I enjoyed it afterwards. But the point is I was walking along the front, all on my own, minding my own business, (*Pause*) and two nuns came towards me – (*Pause*) two nuns –
(*He trails off, looking very tired and old. He looks across at* JEAN *and pushes the bottle at her.*)

ARCHIE: Talk to me.
(*Curtain.*)

END OF ACT ONE

INTERMISSION

BILLY, PHOEBE *and* JEAN. PHOEBE *is flushed with drink.*

BILLY: I knew they couldn't keep him. They wouldn't dare.

JEAN: Home in a couple of days – I just can't believe it.

BILLY: They wouldn't dare, not even nowadays – cock-eyed bunch they are. I remember 'em from before the war. I was with that show, you remember, Phoebe –

PHOEBE: Well what would they want to keep a boy like that for? That's what I kept asking myself. Can't do them any good. It couldn't do them any good, could it?

BILLY: Grubby lot of rogues. I was a guest at the Ambassadors, you know. Gave me a box of Romeo and Juliet cigars.

JEAN: (*Surrounded by pile of newspapers*) Well, the name of Rice is famous once again.

BILLY: This long they were. Haven't had a cigar like that for years.

PHOEBE: He likes a cigar. I buy those cheroots sometimes. They're only cheap things, but he doesn't mind them, does he?

BILLY: Course I don't mind them. Jeannie gave me some didn't she? What's the matter with you?

PHOEBE: Oh yes I was forgetting.

BILLY: Got a mind like a bloody sieve!

PHOEBE: I was always a dunce at school. I keep thinking of Archie. I'm so afraid that he's going to be disappointed. That everything will go wrong and they won't let Mick come home after all.

BILLY: Pardon me, Phoebe, but you do talk the most almighty rubbish I've ever had to sit and listen to.

JEAN: They've given a formal undertaking.

BILLY: Formal undertaking, my backside – if I thought that boy's future depended on their 'formal undertaking' we could say 'thank you very much and good night'.

PHOEBE: (*Paper in her lap*) We've got an aeroplane standing by all ready to rush him home.

BILLY: 'Formal undertaking' – proper politicians' words they

are. They'd mean damn all if they were said by one of
ours.

JEAN: (*Reading*) 'Bring him home' – in a matter of a few hours
Sergeant Rice should be speeding homewards in a specially
allocated Dakota.

BILLY: They know damn well they daren't do anything else.

JEAN: We're going to have ourselves a hero, you can see that –

BILLY: Any one of us would have done the same thing. There's
nothing wrong with any of us, never has been. You can't
all get to the top. You can't make your own luck. Me, I
was always lucky, always was. Mind you, I was good too.
That Ambassador, Sir Somebody Pearson his name was,
charming, absolutely, the real best type, absolutely the best
type. He told me I was his favourite artist. Barring George
Robey.

PHOEBE: What good would it do them, hanging on to a kid.
That's all he is.

JEAN: This one says –

BILLY: He's lucky. I was always lucky. Mind you, I was good
too.

JEAN: (*Reading*). 'Lieut. Pearson, of Leicester, who had been
with Sergeant Rice until a few minutes before he was
captured, said he must have killed at least seven of the
attackers.'

BILLY: Was that Pearson you said –

JEAN: 'Before he was overwhelmed, "he must have run out of
ammunition" said Pearson. Young Rice wasn't the type to
give up.'
(*Pause.*)

PHOEBE: I don't want Archie to be disappointed, that's all. On
top of everything else. He's had enough of
disappointments. I don't think he ever really gets used to
them.

BILLY: You see, a couple of days, and Mick'll be sitting down
here talking about it.

PHOEBE: I remember once my Mum promised to take us kids
to the pantomime, and then something happened, she
couldn't take us. I don't know what it was, she didn't have

the money I expect. You could sit up in the gallery then for sixpence. Poor old Mum – she took us later, but it didn't seem the same to me. I was too disappointed. I'd been thinking about that pantomime for weeks. You shouldn't build things up. You're always disappointed really. That's Archie's trouble. He always builds everything up. And it never turns out.

BILLY: He's a fool.

PHOEBE: He's too good for them, that's his trouble. People don't appreciate you properly. Let's finish this up shall we? Archie'll bring some more in with him when he comes.

BILLY: It's all over, finished. I told him years ago. But he won't listen. He won't listen to anybody.

PHOEBE: You can't help giving Archie his own way. Not really. No, all they're out for is a cheap thrill. (*To* JEAN.) Come on, have half of this with me. We've all got to – what's the word?

BILLY: I dunno what you're talking about.

JEAN: Compromise?

PHOEBE: She knows what I mean. That's right, dear. You keep on and on, try your best, and then a time comes when you can't go on any longer. It's not giving in – or I suppose it is. It's just being sensible. (*To* JEAN.) Has he said anything to you?

JEAN: What about?

PHOEBE: Oh, about anything. He never tells me anything now, he just tells me not to worry, and says nothing. Frank told me the company only got half salary on Saturday night, and he thinks these scenery people must have caught up with him because –

BILLY: He said he'd bring me back some cigarettes. I could have got them myself by this time. I suppose he's in that Rockliffe.

PHOEBE: Whenever there's a ring at the door, I daren't answer it, in case it's a policeman standing there with another summons.

JEAN: (*Offering cigarettes to* BILLY) Have one of these.

BILLY: That bloody meat market.

PHOEBE: It's not a nice feeling when you can't go and answer the door.

BILLY: There'll be a policeman at the door all right –

PHOEBE: (*Weary, not peevish*) Oh, don't keep interrupting while I'm talking to Jean.

BILLY: (*To* JEAN, *politely*) Thank you, my dear. (*Picks up his newspaper.*)

PHOEBE: I've upset him now.

JEAN: No you haven't. He's just reading. Aren't you, Grandad?

BILLY: Um?

PHOEBE: Oh well, it's no good worrying. Is it? It says in the papers Mick's coming home, and they ought to know about these things, and that's all that really matters. Have a drop of this, dear.

BILLY: No thank you.

PHOEBE: (*To* JEAN) Pour him out a glass. There's one over there. Oh, Dad, he exaggerates everything, don't you? He exaggerates everything, but he's right, you know. He's right about Archie. He hasn't got an enemy in the world who's done him the harm he's done himself.

JEAN: There you are, Grandad.

BILLY: Thank you, Jean. I'll have it later.

JEAN: Don't have it later. Have it now. This is the time to celebrate. Come on then. Let's drink to Mick.

PHOEBE: Yes, we mustn't sit here, getting morbid. We're a bit short on the drink, aren't we? I hope Archie won't be long in that place.

JEAN: Frank's gone with him. He won't be long.

PHOEBE: Oh, Frank'll see he doesn't get home too late. Frank's a sensible boy – sometimes he is anyway. (*To* JEAN.) I think you're the only really sensible one of us lot.

JEAN: Grandad doesn't think so, do you?

BILLY: She's just as bloody daft as the rest of you.

PHOEBE: He's a fool to himself. Always some big idea he's got to make money. A while back it was female impersonators. We were going to make a packet. That's what Archie said anyway. But by the time Archie got started with it it had all petered out. Now it's rock and roll. Oh well. It's like the women. They get tired of him. They come back here a few times, and that's that –

BILLY: Why don't you hold your bloody noise!

PHOEBE: He doesn't like me talking about it. As if she didn't know what's been going on all this time.

BILLY: Well there's no reason to talk about it.

PHOEBE: She's not soft, are you, dear?

BILLY: I don't want to hear about it, and I shouldn't think she does.

PHOEBE: All right, all right.

BILLY: She's used to be with people who know how to behave. She doesn't want to hear about your troubles.

PHOEBE: No of course she doesn't.

BILLY: Well then – the trouble with you people is you don't know how to carry on properly, that's your trouble. Give the girl a chance, she's got her own life to lead.

PHOEBE: I was only telling her –

BILLY: And I'm telling you don't! There's nothing *you* can tell her. So hold your noise –

JEAN: Grandad, please –

BILLY: Why don't you go back to London to your friends?

JEAN: Don't let's argue –

BILLY: We're no good to you –

JEAN: I don't think I want to go back to London –

PHOEBE: I was only talking to her about Archie. You don't want to leave, do you, dear?

JEAN: Of course I don't.

PHOEBE: I was just saying, in the course of ordinary conversation, that Archie wasn't very lucky that's all.

JEAN: Here – (*She has put a small bottle of gin on the table.*)

PHOEBE: And if I mention the women, it was just because it's been the same thing with them. It's never bothered me, that, so much. It never meant a great deal to me, not even when I was young. Still, I suppose men are different. It's more important to them. Oh, look what she's done!

JEAN: I thought I'd better get some in, in case Dad was late.

BILLY: What do you think you're supposed to be – a millionairess?

JEAN: But you're not to have any, till you've had something to
eat first, you've had nothing but tea and cigarettes for
days.
PHOEBE: I couldn't eat anything, dear. Honestly.
JEAN: I'll get something for you.
PHOEBE: No, I couldn't. I couldn't – hold it down.
JEAN: (*Moving*) I'm not going to argue –
PHOEBE: Jean, I've asked you – I can't! I don't want it!
JEAN: But people have got to eat, dear. If you don't have
something –
PHOEBE: (*Laughing slightly*) People have to eat, she says. That's
a good one!
JEAN: You can't carry on, dear.
(*Billy gets up humming 'Rock of Ages' and goes off L.*)
PHOEBE: People have to eat, she says. D'you hear that? Where's
he got to?
JEAN: He's just gone into the kitchen.
PHOEBE: That's not all they have to do. They have to do a
whole lot of things, a lot of things you don't even know
about, and it's nothing to do with being educated and all
that. Why should you know about it?
JEAN: I know, love. Things have been tough. But be sensible,
you've got to keep on.
PHOEBE: Don't tell me to be sensible, Jean.
JEAN: I'm sorry, dear. I didn't mean it like that –
PHOEBE: Don't tell me to be sensible! You're a sweet girl, Jean,
and I'm very fond of you. But you're not even my own
daughter. I wouldn't take that from Mick or Frank, and
they're my own.
JEAN: All right, forget it. We'll forget it. We haven't had our
drink to Mick yet.
PHOEBE: Don't – don't presume too much.
JEAN: Phoebe please – I just –
PHOEBE: Don't presume too much. What's he doing out there?
JEAN: He's probably getting him something to eat, I expect.
PHOEBE: I don't want him messing about out there. He knows I
don't like him going out there. He leaves everything in
such a mess.

JEAN: Here, have this.

PHOEBE: Why doesn't Archie come back? You'd think he'd come back here and celebrate after hearing his son is safe and on his way home. I don't know – you people –

JEAN: Come along, Phoebe, don't let's have a row. And over nothing – it's silly.

PHOEBE: It's not silly. Anyway, who said we're having a row? All I said was I wasn't hungry, and you start getting at me.

JEAN: I wasn't getting at you.

PHOEBE: You people – you're all alike.

JEAN: Believe me, Phoebe. I wasn't –

PHOEBE: I can't eat because I feel sick.

JEAN: Well, all right then.

PHOEBE: You don't know what it's like. You don't know what it's like because we tried to do our best by you. Oh, Archie tried to do his best by you, even if it didn't add up to very much. Not that you weren't a good girl, you worked hard. You deserved it, you've always tried, and you've got what it takes. And that's more than any of us have got, my dear. You're the only one of us who has. You and young Mick. And the old man of course. He had it. Not that it's any use to him now. He's just a has-been, I suppose. Still – it's better to be a has-been than a never-was. His other son's the same – Old Bill. Archie's brother. Not that you'd think he was. Now he's really a big pot. He's really a big pot. There's no flies on brother Bill.

JEAN: (*Trying to turn the conversation*) He's a barrister – that's why you like him so much. He's like that actor on the pictures who's always in a wig and gown in every other –

PHOEBE: I like him because he's a gentleman. He's different from your father, even if they did go to the same posh school and all that. I like him because of the way he treats me. He talks to me beautifully, the way he calls me 'Phoebe'. You should hear the way he calls me 'Phoebe'.

JEAN: I only saw him a couple of times.

PHOEBE: Well, of course you did. He didn't approve of the way Archie carried on. He never did. Sometimes, in the early days he'd come and see us. He always slipped a couple of fivers in my hand before he left, and he'd just say 'Not a word to Archie, now'. I just never used to know what to say to him. We'd always be living in some bloody digs somewhere, and I didn't like him coming. I'd feel awful. He could never bring his wife, and I never knew what to say. Then he and Archie would always have a row over something Archie had been doing. Either he'd lost money, or he was out of work. I remember he came once, and Archie and me didn't have a bean. We'd been living on penny pieces of bacon from the butcher's, and what we got then from the Tribunal. (*She pronounces it Tribbunel.*) You and the boys were staying with the Old Man then. Archie wouldn't take money from his Dad then – perhaps it was professional jealousy, I don't know. Anyway, Bill heard that Archie was in trouble again – I don't remember what it was. But it was something serious this time, I think. Oh, he tried to pass a dud cheque and he'd picked the wrong person or something. That wasn't like Archie, I must admit, because he never did anything really dishonest like that, whatever else he might have done. He must have been drunk. Anyway, Old Bill came over – we were living at Brixton at that time, and the kids in the street made a terrible mess of his car. They didn't see many cars in that street except when it was the doctor. Not that he said a word about it. When we went to the door, and I saw what they'd done to it, I just stood there, I felt so ashamed, and I burst out crying. He patted my arm in that way of his and he just said 'I'm so sorry, Phoebe. I really am. I'm afraid it's always going to be like this'. Well, he got Archie out of whatever it was, and that was that. It wasn't the money, or his helping Archie – although I was grateful for that, of course. It was the way he spoke to me in that quiet gentlemanly way, and the way he patted my arm.

JEAN: Yes, I can see him doing it.

PHOEBE: What do you mean – what do you mean by that remark?

JEAN: Oh nothing, dear. Let's not talk about it –

PHOEBE: What do you mean by that remark?

JEAN: Oh, it's just that I can see brother Bill patting your arm, slipping that ten pounds in your hand, and then driving off to have dinner at his Club. That's all, Phoebe. Now let's not talk about it any more.

PHOEBE: You mean he was just sorry for me, don't you?

JEAN: No, I don't.

PHOEBE: Come on, say it – you mean he was just sorry for me, don't you?

JEAN: I didn't say that and I didn't mean that. Now come on – (*Enter* ARCHIE *with* FRANK. FRANK *is a pale, shy boy of about nineteen. He has allowed himself to slip into the role of* ARCHIE*'s 'feed' because this seems to be a warm, reasonable relationship substitute that suits them both. He is impulsive, full of affection that spills over easily. He is young, and will probably remain so.*)

PHOEBE: I want to know what you meant.

ARCHIE: My dear, nobody can tell you what they mean. You ought to know that by now.

PHOEBE: Shut up a minute, Archie – I'm talking to Jean. She knows what I mean. You know what I meant, don't you?

ARCHIE: Do you know what she means? I wish to God I did. (*To* FRANK.) I can see we should have stayed.

PHOEBE: Shall I tell you something?

JEAN: Phoebe, what are you doing?

PHOEBE: Shall I?

JEAN: It's just that I know exactly how Uncle Bill patted your arm – just in the same way as he'd wait on the men at Christmas when he was in the army. So democratic, so charming, and so English.

ARCHIE: Oh, Bill's all right. Just doesn't understand people like us, that's all. And what's more he doesn't want to. Can't blame him really.

PHOEBE: (*To* JEAN) You don't like him, do you? I knew you didn't like him.

ARCHIE: Like now. Oh, brother Bill wouldn't understand all this at all. He'd be frightfully embarrassed, wouldn't he? Give us over that carrier, Frankie love.

PHOEBE: You can't afford not to like him. You owe him too much.

ARCHIE: Sounds a pretty good reason for not liking anyone, I should say.

PHOEBE: He's something you'll never be.

ARCHIE: And I'm something he'll never be – good Old Bill. He may be successful, but he's not a bad sort. Do you know that my brother Bill has had one wife, no love affair, he's got three charming gifted children. Two of them took honours degrees at Cambridge, and all of them have made what these people call highly successful marriages.

FRANK: What on earth's everybody talking about? Hullo, Jean, love. I thought we were going to have a party.

(*He throws his arms around her and kisses her.*)

ARCHIE: It's perfectly true. I read it in the *Telegraph* today. I got bored reading about young Mick, and there, tucked away in the middle –

JEAN: (*Eagerly*) Don't tell me you read –

ARCHIE: Of course, I read it. How else would I know whether my relations were getting married, or dying, or having babies. As I was saying –

FRANK: Before you were so rudely interrupted.

(*Kissing* JEAN *affectionately once again.*)

ARCHIE: Yes, before that. Young Sonia is getting married.

JEAN: Who to?

ARCHIE: Oh, the son of some industrialist, Capt. Charlie Double-back-Action hyphen-breech loading Gore of Elm Lodge, Shrewkesbury, Glos. Where are all the glasses, for God's sake? Good ole Bill – he's got everything he wants now, including Captain Charlie Double-back-Action Gore.

PHOEBE: Archie, I'm talking to Jean.

ARCHIE: Yes, I thought that's what you were doing. I sized the situation up in a flash.

PHOEBE: Oh, it's easy for people like you to make fun. I left school when I was twelve years old.

ARCHIE: Christ, if she tells me that once more I shall get up on the roof, drunk as I am, I shall get up on the roof and scream. I've never done that before.

PHOEBE: You had to pay sixpence a week then.

FRANK: Leave her alone, you old bastard. Come on, Mum, we're going to have a party.

PHOEBE: I'm talking to Jean.

ARCHIE: Yes, we were in on that. Why don't we all talk to Jean. We don't see much of her. Frank – talk to Jean.

FRANK: Dad –

(*He nods towards* PHOEBE, *distressed to see her like this, but* ARCHIE, *who has come in prepared to be gay, is tired and had begun to give up the situation.*)

ARCHIE: Let's have a drink first. If I'm going to be either very diplomatic, or very tactful, I must have plenty to drink first.

PHOEBE: We had to pay sixpence a week, and most weeks my mother couldn't find it –

ARCHIE: This is a welfare state, my darling heart. Nobody wants, and nobody goes without, all are provided for.

PHOEBE: I was out scrubbing a dining hall for –

ARCHIE: Everybody's all right. Young Mick's all right. Bill's all right. Why, he never even got himself jailed by a lot of wogs. Frank's all right – he won't be stoking boilers much longer, will you, boy?

FRANK: I wish you'd both shut up.

ARCHIE: Jean's all right. She'll make it up with Graham, and forget about silly old Trafalgar Square, and Prime Ministers who look like dogs downstairs. Here you are, dear. (*Offers drink to* PHOEBE.)

PHOEBE: You don't understand –

ARCHIE: I know. Phoebe scrubbed a dining hall floor for five hundred kids when she was twelve years old, didn't you?

PHOEBE: Oh –

ARCHIE: Didn't you? Have you any idea, any of you, have you any idea how often she's told me about those five hundred kids and that dining hall?

FRANK: Oh, shut up.

ARCHIE: Yes, son, I'll shut up. Pass this to Jean. She looks as though she can use it.

(*Rises and gives drink to Jean. Remain standing by D. L. chair.*)

JEAN: I can.

FRANK: You've been away too long. Every night is party night.

ARCHIE: And do you know why? Do you know why? Because we're dead beat and down and outs. We're drunks, maniacs, we're crazy, we're bonkers, the whole flaming bunch of us. Why, we have problems that nobody's ever heard of, we're characters out of something that nobody believes in. We're something that people make jokes about, because we're so remote from the rest of ordinary everyday, human experience. But we're not really funny. We're too boring. Simply because we're not like anybody who ever lived. We don't get on with anything. We don't ever succeed in anything. We're a *nuisance*, we do nothing but make a God almighty fuss about anything we ever do. All the time we're trying to draw someone's attention to our nasty, sordid, unlikely little problems. Like that poor, pathetic old thing there. Look at her. What has she got to do with people like you? People of intellect and sophistication. She's very drunk, and just now her muzzy, under-developed, untrained mind is racing because her blood stream is full of alcohol I can't afford to give her, and she's going to force us to listen to all sorts of dreary embarrassing things we've all heard a hundred times before. She's getting old, and she's worried about who's going to keep her when she can't work any longer. She's afraid of ending up in a long box in somebody else's front room in Gateshead, or was it West Hartlepool?

PHOEBE: What's he talking about?

ARCHIE: She's going to tell you that old brother Bill paid for all your education. That's what she wants to tell you, Jean. That scholarship didn't pay for the things that really mattered, you know. The books, the fares, the clothes, and all the rest of it. Bill paid for that. For all of you. Frank knows that, don't you, Frank? I'm sorry, Phoebe. I've killed your story. Old Archie could always kill anybody's punch line if he wanted.

PHOEBE: She doesn't know about Mick and you and me. I know she doesn't.

ARCHIE: She'll find out. We always find these things out in time. (*To* FRANK *and* JEAN.) She's tired and she's getting old. She's tired, and she's tired of me. Nobody ever gave her two pennyworth of equipment except her own pretty unimpressive self to give anything else to the rest of the world. All it's given her is me, and my God she's tired of that! Aren't you, my old darling? You're tired of that, aren't you?

PHOEBE: (*Fiercely*) I tried to make something of myself. I tried, I really did try. I was nothing much to look at, but what I was I made myself. I was a plain kid – no I wasn't. I wasn't even plain. I was the ugliest bloody kid you ever saw in your life. You've never seen anyone as ugly as I was. But I made something of myself. I did try to do something. I made him want me anyway.

FRANK: Everyone shouts! Please, somebody speak quietly, just for once. Those bloody Poles will be up here in a minute. Let's have a row. It looks as if we're going to have one anyway. But please can we have a *quiet* row!

ARCHIE: It was a long time ago. They knew it was a long time ago. (*To* FRANK.) I wish you'd stop yelling, I can't hear myself shout. Sing one of your songs, there's a good boy. Where's the old man?

JEAN: He's in the kitchen.

ARCHIE: Billy! Come out of there! Who's he got in there? Something you picked up in the Cambridge! Have you ever had it on a kitchen table? Like a piece of meat on a slab. Slicing pieces of bacon. Don't you wish you were back with old Graham? (*To* JEAN.)

PHOEBE: Frank, he's going to bring up one of those women, isn't he? In here, isn't he?

ARCHIE: Leave her alone, son.
     (*Sits L. of D.R. sofa.*)

PHOEBE: Do you think I don't lie awake upstairs, and hear it going on?

ARCHIE: Of course they know. They know what sort of a bastard I am, love. I think they know almost as well as you do. Well, almost as well. She'll be all right, won't you,

love? Where's the old man? (*To* FRANK *and* JEAN.) Now
don't pretend you're not used to it.
(BILLY *appears*.)
There you are, you old has-been! Have you brought us a
slice of bacon in?

BILLY: What's the matter with you lot?

ARCHIE: We're all just waiting for the little yellow van to
come –

BILLY: Did you get my cigarettes?

ARCHIE: Except for Jean. There's still hope for her. You wait,
you old Gubbins, you'll be reading about your grand-
daughters and Mr Graham Thing of Elm Lodge,
Shrewkesbury, Glos. Here you are. (*Tosses cigarettes to*
BILLY *and gives him a drink*.)

PHOEBE: (*To* BILLY) You've been at that cake.

BILLY: What?

PHOEBE: You've been at my cake, haven't you?

BILLY: (*Flushing*) I was hungry –

PHOEBE: That cake was for Mick. It was for Mick, it wasn't for
you.

BILLY: I'm sorry –

PHOEBE: I bought it for Mick. It was for when he comes home.

ARCHIE: Well, never mind.

PHOEBE: What do you mean – never mind!

ARCHIE: Mick wouldn't mind.

PHOEBE: Well I mind! I don't want him in that kitchen. Tell
him to keep out of it. It's not much, and it's not mine, but
I mind very much. Why couldn't you leave it alone?

BILLY: I just fancied –

PHOEBE: Couldn't you leave it alone? It wasn't for you. What's
the matter with you? I feed you, don't I? Don't think you
give me all that much money every week, because you
don't!

ARCHIE: Phoebe, forget it!

PHOEBE: I don't forget, I don't forget anything. I don't forget
anything even if you do.

ARCHIE: We'll buy another one.

PHOEBE: Oh, you'll buy another one! You're so rich! You're

such a great big success! What's a little cake – we'll order a dozen of 'em! I bought that cake, and it cost me thirty shillings, it was for Mick when he comes back, because I want to give him something, something I know he'll like, after being where he's been, and going through what he has – and now, that bloody *greedy* old pig – that old pig, as if he hadn't had enough of everything – he has to go and get his great fingers into it!

(*Unable to top this, she bursts into tears.* BILLY *stands, ashamed and deeply hurt by what she has said, even though he vaguely realizes the condition she is in. He puts down the drink he has been holding, and the cigarette.*)

BILLY: Excuse me, Jean.

(*He crosses down to his room and goes out.*)

PHOEBE: Archie, you haven't got anybody coming tonight, have you?

ARCHIE: I suppose he has had more than any of us, and he's enjoyed it. Good luck to him. All the same, you needn't have done that. No, there's nobody coming.

PHOEBE: Oh, I'm sorry, Archie. Try and forgive me –

ARCHIE: Not that I don't wish there were. But then you know that. Come on love, pull yourself together. That's what we should have done years ago. Pulled ourselves together. Let's pull ourselves together. (*Sings.*) Let's pull ourselves together, together, together. Let's pull ourselves together, and the happier we'll be!

FRANK: That's right chaps – remember we're British!

ARCHIE: That's what everybody does. Perfectly simple. I've always known it. That's what my old brother Bill used to tell me. Now let's fill up and be happy. What about old Mick, eh?

FRANK: Yes, what about old Mick? Don't look so glum, Jean. You know what everybody's like.

JEAN: Do I?

ARCHIE: Never mind, there's no reason why she should, as Phoebe would say. We're all a bit slewed, which means that we're a bit more sub-human even than we usually are. (*To* FRANK.) Isn't that right, you great weedy boiler stoker you! I'll bet the patients in that hospital all freeze to death – he must be saving the National Health thousands.

FRANK: (*To* PHOEBE) Feel all right now?

PHOEBE: Perhaps Jean doesn't want to have a drink, and do you know why?

ARCHIE: No, why?

PHOEBE: Because I don't think she even likes him. I don't think she likes Mick.

ARCHIE: There's no reason why she should. But that won't stop her. Or me. Frank, go in and talk to the old man, and get him to come back. (*Crosses to D.R. proscenium arch.*) We'll try to be a little normal just for once, and pretend we're a happy, respectable, decent family. For Mick's sake. You know, I really think that's what he'd like, somehow. I'm sure he thinks we're rather dreadful. Worse than the wogs really. Don't worry, Jean, you won't have to put up with this kind of thing for long – any more than Mick. And this is Mick's party. Phoebe, let's see you do your dance. (*This is thrown off in the usual casual, studied* ARCHIE *manner.*) She dances jolly well, don't you, you poor old thing. I wonder if she'll make me cry tonight. We'll see. We'll see. Frank, sing us your song.

JEAN: I don't even know what I'm feeling. I don't even know if I do at all.

ARCHIE: Never mind, dear. I didn't know that for years, either. You're a long time dead, Mrs Murphy, let's make it a party, Mick the soldier's coming back, let's just whoop it up!

(*Curtain.*)

SCENE SEVEN

Music. ARCHIE *rises, his face held open by a grin, and dead behind the eyes. Just now and then, for a second or two, he gives the tiniest indication that he is almost surprised to find himself where he is.*

ARCHIE: Here, here! Here, I've just seen a man with a lemon stuck in his ear! A lemon stuck in his ear! So I went up to

him, I said: 'What are you doing with that lemon stuck in your ear?' and he says: 'Well, you know that man with a hearing aid – well, I'm the man with the lemonade.' Thank you for that burst of heavy breathing. You should have heard what James Agate said about *me*! (*Back again.*) But I have a go, lady, don't I? I 'ave a go. I do. You think I am, don't you? Well, I'm not. But *he* is! Here, here! Did I tell you about the wife? Did I? My wife – not only is she stupid, not only is she stupid, but she's cold as well. Oh yes, cold. She may look sweet, but she's a very cold woman, my wife. Very cold. Cold and stupid. She's what they call a moron glacee. Don't clap too hard – it's a very old building. Well, I 'ave a go, don't I? I do – I 'ave a go. Look at me – it's all real, you know. Me – all real, nothing shoddy. You don't think I'm real, do you? Well, I'm not. (*Stumbling.*) I'm not going to deprive you of the treat I know you've all been waiting for. Yes, I'm going to sing to you. I'm going to sing to you a little song, a little song written by myself. I haven't recorded it, so if you like it, you tell 'em. They won't listen, but you tell 'em. A little song called 'My girl's always short of breath, but she don't mind a good blow through.'
(*He sings.*)

Now I'm just an ordinary bloke
The same as you out there.
Not mad for women, I'm not a soak,
I never really care.
I'm what you call a moderate,
I weigh all the pros, and the cons.
I don't push and shove
At the thing they call love,
I never go in for goings on.
Thank God I'm normal, normal, normal.
Thank God I'm normal, I'm just like the rest of you chaps.

Thank God I'm normal,
I'm just like the rest of your chaps,

Decent and full of good sense,
I'm not one of these extremist saps,
For I'm sure you'll agree,
That a fellow like me
Is the salt of our dear old country,
        of our dear old country.

(*Bang on appropriate lighting. Speaking:*)

But when our heritage is threatened
At home or cross the sea.

(*Play 'Land of Hope and Glory'.*)

It's chaps like us – yes you and me,
Who'll march again to victory.
Some people say we're finished,
Some people say we're done.
But if we all stand

(*Spotlight behind gauze reveals a nude in Britannia's helmet and holding a bulldog and trident.*)

By this dear old land,
The battle will be won.
Thank God we're normal, normal, normal.
Thank God we're normal.
We are the country's flower,
And when the great call comes,
Someone will gaze down on us,
And say: They made no fuss –
For this was their finest shower.
Yes, this was their finest shower!
Thank God we're normal, normal, normal,
Thank God we're normal,
Yes, this is our finest shower!

(*Exit* ARCHIE.)

ARCHIE, FRANK, PHOEBE, JEAN, BILLY.

ARCHIE: She'd steal your knickers and sell 'em for dusters.

FRANK: Who?

ARCHIE: Mrs Roberts, No. 7, Claypit Lane, always used to say that.

FRANK: Who are you talking about, you bloody right-wing old poup?

ARCHIE: I'm talking about that blonde bitch in the Cambridge, the one who's always upsetting your Grandad. And don't call me a right-wing old poup.

PHOEBE: I remember Mrs Roberts. She was very nice to us.

ARCHIE: I may be an old poup, but I'm not a right-wing.

FRANK: That's strictly for cigar smokers like Grandad. (*Dancing*.) 'Oh, the end of me old cigar, cigar, the end of me old cigar, I turned 'em round and touched 'em up with the end of me old cigar! The end of me old cigar, cigar, the end of me old cigar –'

ARCHIE: There was a chap at my school who managed to get himself into the Labour Government, and they always said he was left of centre. Then he went into the House of Lords, and they made him an honourable fishmonger. Well, that just about wraps up the Left of Centre, doesn't it?

FRANK: You know, you don't know what you're talking about.

BILLY: I used to have digs in Claypit Lane – ten shillings a week all-in.

PHOEBE: Frank, I thought you were going to sing.

ARCHIE: If you can dodge all the clichés dropping like bats from the ceiling, you might pick up something from me.

FRANK: Well, plenty of others have picked it up from you.

ARCHIE: Just you remember I'm your father.

FRANK: When did you ever remember it?

PHOEBE: Frank! Come on now, be a good boy.

ARCHIE: You want to be more like Jean –

FRANK: She's just not used to us any more. Are you, love? Are you all right?

(*Puts his arm round her.*)

JEAN: I'm all right.

FRANK: Are you really? Bet you'd forgotten what this was like, didn't you?

PHOEBE: Course she hadn't forgotten. She doesn't forget as easy as that, do you dear?

JEAN: No – I don't think so.

FRANK: (*To* PHOEBE) You're feeling better?

PHOEBE: Yes, thank you, dear. Come over here and give me a kiss. (*He does so.*) He's a good boy to me, aren't you, dear? Even when I act a bit daft. We all act a bit daft sometimes, I suppose.

ARCHIE: Except Jean –

JEAN: Will you please stop trying to make me feel as if I were from another planet or something.

PHOEBE: Archie's just pulling your leg, aren't you Archie? I didn't have my Beecham's Pills yesterday. D'you know my mother never had a doctor in her life – except when we were born, of course. And all she ever took was two pennorth of Beecham's, peroxide, and Dutch drops.

JEAN: Peroxide?

FRANK: She used to drink it like Guinness.

PHOEBE: Well, she lived to be ninety-three and never cost the Government a penny. (*To* BILLY.) All right?

BILLY: Yes, thank you, Phoebe.

PHOEBE: (*To* ARCHIE) Put something in his glass, Archie. It's nearly empty.

BILLY: I was just trying to remember the name of the woman.

PHOEBE: What woman?

BILLY: The one in Claypit Lane. She used to give us bacon every morning for breakfast, and she'd melt cheese over it. First time I'd ever had it.

PHOEBE: Don't like anything like that much. Here, did you – pardon my interruption but I just remembered it – did you see that picture of the Duchess of Porth's daughter in the paper today?

FRANK: Should we?

PHOEBE: I wouldn't have seen it. I was only really reading

about Mick, of course, but I couldn't help noticing it. She
looked so fascinating. Did you see it, Archie?

ARCHIE: Oh yes. She was next to Captain Breech-Loading
Gore.

PHOEBE: Didn't you think she looked magnificent?

ARCHIE: I thought she looked like Dad's barmaid in the
Cambridge.

FRANK: Yes – in drag.

PHOEBE: Frank!

ARCHIE: (*Quickly*) Phoebe's very keen on the Duchess of Porth,
aren't you, love? She says she thinks she's natural.

PHOEBE: I suppose it's a bit silly, but I've always taken an
interest in her. Oh, ever since she was quite young. I feel
she must be very nice somehow. (*Pause.*) (*To* ARCHIE.) Is
he all right? (*Nodding to* BILLY.)

ARCHIE: He's all right. You're all right, aren't you?

BILLY: She always used to put cheese over the bacon.

ARCHIE: He's thinking about the landlady in Claypit Lane. You
know, that barmaid in the Cambridge reminds me of a
bloke – (*To* JEAN.) – this'll interest you because it's Prime
Ministers and Dogs – he was Irish, he did a trampoline act
and they called him 'Lady Rosie Bothways'. Actually, he
was a devout sort of a lad. He gave it all up later and went
into Public Relations or something. Well, Rosie knew
more dirty words than you'll hear in any place on any
Saturday night. He could go on for ten minutes without
pausing for breath, or repeating himself once. He was an
artist. But to Rosie the most deadly four-letter word in the
English – or any other – language, was Tory. He'd apply it
to anything, provided he thought it was really bad enough.

BILLY: I'll bet he was bloody Irish.

ARCHIE: I've just said so. Do try and listen.

PHOEBE: I thought Frank was going to sing.

ARCHIE: If you gave him a plate of badly cooked chips, he'd
hold 'em up and say: 'Who done these no-good, blank,
blank, stinking, Tory chips?'

FRANK: You've told that story before.

ARCHIE: I'll bodge you in a minute.

FRANK: I'll bodge *you* in a minute. It's not even a very good
    story.
ARCHIE: When you learn to tell a story as well as I do, you'll be
    all right –
FRANK: I'll never look *old* enough, to tell your stories.
ARCHIE: I think you'd better sing, don't you?
FRANK: All right, all right, I will. I'll sing for Jean, because she
    hasn't heard me. I'm going to sing one of Billy's. It's
    British –
BILLY: What's that? What song?
FRANK: And very religious.
BILLY: What song's he singing?
FRANK: So there's something in it for you all.
    (*He sings and dances.*)

> When you've shouted Rule Britannia,
> When you've sung God Save the Queen,
> When you've finished killing Kruger with
>   your mouth,
> Will you kindly drop a shilling in my little
>   tambourine
> For a gentleman in khaki ordered south.
>
> He's an absent-minded beggar, and his
>   weaknesses are great
> But we informers take him as we find him,
> For he's out on active service, wiping
>   something off a slate
> And he's left a lot of little things behind
>   him.
>
> Cook's son, duke's son, son of a belted earl –
> Fifty thousand horse and foot ordered to
>   Table Bay.
> Each of 'em's doing his country's work –
> And who's to look after the girl?
> Pass the hat for your credit's sake,
>   and pay, pay, pay!

BILLY: Pass the hat for your credit's sake, and pay, pay, pay.

ARCHIE: Not bad for an amateur.

BILLY: Last time I sang that was in a pub, some place in Yorkshire. If you bought a pint of beer, you could get a plateful of Yorkshire Pudding then, as much as you could eat. All for tuppence.

ARCHIE: Come off it, Dad. Nobody ever gave away stuff like that, not even when you remember.

BILLY: I tell you, you got a plate of Yorkshire Pudding –

ARCHIE: You're getting really old.

BILLY: As much as you could eat.

ARCHIE: Your mind's going, Dad. I should sit down.

BILLY: I *am* sitting down.

ARCHIE: Getting feeble.

PHOEBE: Archie – don't tease him.

BILLY: I'm not feeble! I'm not half as bloody feeble as you are – thank God! (*Suddenly sees them smiling at him.*) Thank God I'm not, that's all. You think you can have it over me all right. Give me some of that!

FRANK: When there isn't a girl about you feel so lonely. When there isn't a girl about you're on your only –

ARCHIE: Be quiet a minute, will you? I'm trying to think. Ah! yes. Yes. The girl I love is up in the lavatory, the girl I love is looking down on me.

PHOEBE: No don't do that, Archie. Don't sing it like that! (*To* JEAN *and* FRANK.) He always used to sing that song, didn't you? It was his favourite, I think.

JEAN: You sing it.

PHOEBE: Me – Oh I can't sing. I don't know even if I can remember the words.

FRANK: Go on, love, have a go.

PHOEBE: (*To* ARCHIE) Shall I? (*He nods shortly.*) All right, then. (*She sings:*)

> Oh the boy I love he's up in the gallery
> The boy I love is looking down at me.
> Where is he?
> There he is,
> Waving of his handkerchief,

       Happy as the robin
       That sings on the tree.

JEAN: Thank you, Phoebe. Thank you.

PHOEBE: It sounded bloody awful, I expect.

BILLY: Well, I'm going to bed.

PHOEBE: Going already?

BILLY: (*Going down to his room*) Yes, I only sat up to drink a
toast to young Mick. I'm going to bed before you get those
bloody Poles up here. Good night, everybody.
(*They all call out: 'Goodnight.'*)

PHOEBE: I suppose I ought to go in a minute. I feel a bit tired.
Still, I shan't go in to work tomorrow. Well, I shouldn't
think they'll expect me to, would you?

JEAN: Of course not.

PHOEBE: Probably be too excited to sleep anyway. (*To* JEAN.)
Did I show you the letter I had from Clare?

JEAN: Who's Clare?

ARCHIE: (*To* PHOEBE) I should go to bed, dear.

PHOEBE: Just a minute. I'm going to read her Clare's letter.
Clare's my niece – that's the one in Toronto. I'd better
read it to you, her writing's not very good. She's my
brother John's daughter. They're all over there now, my
brother John as well. They started off in the restaurant
business four years ago with five hundred dollars – that's
their little girl. (*Hands photograph to Jean.*) Now they've got
a hotel in Toronto, and they're going to open another one.

ARCHIE: (*To* JEAN) You don't have to look interested, dear. (*To*
PHOEBE.) She's not interested in all that horse manure
about Canada.

PHOEBE: Of course she's interested. She doesn't mind listening,
do you?

ARCHIE: Why doesn't Frank sing another song?

PHOEBE: I'm only trying to explain to her. They've opened one
in Toronto, and now they're going to open another hotel
in Ottawa. My brother John is managing the one in
Toronto for them, but they want us to go out there, and
for Archie to manage the hotel in Ottawa.

ARCHIE: What do I know about hotels? All I've lived in is digs.
PHOEBE: He gets cross if I mention it.
ARCHIE: For God's sake don't say I get cross if you mention it once more. You've mentioned it, haven't you? And I'm not cross! I just think it's a bloody pointless idea.
JEAN: When did they write this to you?
PHOEBE: About a fortnight now. Oh, she says we needn't make a decision for another month or two.
JEAN: What about the boys?
PHOEBE: They can come too if they want. I don't know about Mick, but Frank likes the idea, don't you?
JEAN: Do you, Frank?
FRANK: Look around you. Can you think of any good reason for staying in this cosy little corner of Europe? Don't kid yourself anyone's going to let you do anything, or try anything here, Jeannie. Because they're not. You haven't got a chance. Who are you – you're nobody. You're nobody, you've no money, and you're young. And when you end up it's pretty certain you'll still be nobody, you'll still have no money – the only difference is you'll be *old*! You'd better start thinking about number one, Jeannie, because nobody else is going to do it for you. Nobody else is going to do it for you because nobody believes in that stuff any more. Oh, they may say they do, and may take a few bob out of your pay packet every week and stick some stamps on your card to prove it, but don't believe it – nobody will give you a second look. They're all so busy, speeding down the middle of the road together, not giving a damn where they're going, as long as they're in the bloody middle! (*Chirpily, almost singing.*) *The rotten bastards!* 'Oh when there isn't a girl about you feel so lonely. When there isn't a girl about you're on your only.'
ARCHIE: Ssh, you'll wake up the Poles.
FRANK: Somebody should wake you up. 'You're on your only!'
ARCHIE: You should go to bed.
FRANK: You and that blonde bitch in the Cambridge. You and her.
Like a monkey up a tree, I don't think! I'm going to bed.

(*He goes out singing, laying an arm on Archie's shoulder, and waving to the others.*)

ARCHIE: Good night, boy.

FRANK: (*Singing*) 'Rock of Ages cleft for me.
 Let me hide myself in thee!'
 (*Exit.*)

ARCHIE: Anyway you can't buy draught Bass in Toronto.

PHOEBE: Here, this is what she says: She talks about us coming out, and paying our fare, etc., and then the job in Ottawa. Experience isn't necessary, it's having your own people. She says: 'We have a twenty-one inch T.V. set, a radio, etc. and now we have a 1956 Chevrolet Bell Air car complete with automatic shift and all the fancy gadgets everyone goes in for over here. I'm quite sure that you and Archie would settle down in no time, and everything would work out fine.' (*She folds the letter up carefully.*) I thought you'd like to hear what she said.

JEAN: Yes, thank you.

PHOEBE: (*After a slight pause.*) Are you staying up much longer, Archie?

ARCHIE: I'm just going.

PHOEBE: I think we're all tired. I can't take all this excitement any more. (*To* JEAN.) Good night, dear. Forgive me being a bit silly, won't you?

JEAN: Forget it. Good night. I shan't wake you up.

PHOEBE: Good night, Archie.

ARCHIE: I'll come up and say good night.

PHOEBE: Thank you, dear. We'll have to find him somewhere to sleep, won't we?

ARCHIE: Mick? Oh, he can bed down here with me.

PHOEBE: Yes, I expect he'll be fagged out, poor kid. Oh, well, he won't be long now.
 (*Exit.*)

ARCHIE: I went to Canada during the war.

JEAN: I remember.

ARCHIE: Couldn't get any draught Bass, not even in Toronto, and they seemed to reckon that was pretty English.
 (*Pause.*) Didn't seem very English to me. Can't get over

you going to Trafalgar Square. Did you really care about all that?

JEAN: I thought I did at the time.

ARCHIE: Like draught Bass and women, eh? Did I ever tell you my nuns story? They just took one look at me – I can remember their white, unhealthy faces, and their little eyes – they took one look at me, and, together, at the same time, quite, quite spontaneously, they crossed themselves. They crossed themselves. And that was the biggest compliment I ever had paid to me in my whole life. Let's have some more of this, shall we?

JEAN: Sure.

ARCHIE: You were having trouble with Phoebe tonight.

JEAN: It was nothing much. She just seemed to suddenly turn on me.

ARCHIE: Your mother caught me in bed with Phoebe. (*Pause.*)

JEAN: I didn't know.

ARCHIE: I don't know what I really expected, but somehow I expected you to say something more than that.

JEAN: What do you expect me to do – hold a rally in Trafalgar Square?

ARCHIE: All my children think I'm a bum. I've never bothered to hide it, I suppose – that's the answer.

JEAN: Perhaps we should go to bed.

ARCHIE: No, stay up for a while. I think we're both in the mood. You'd just been born and your mother found poor old Phoebe and me together. Poor old Phoebe, she's never even enjoyed it very much. Your mother walked out, she walked out just like that. She was what you'd call a person of – a person of principle. She knew how people should behave, and there were no two ways about it. She never forgave me anyway.

JEAN: You didn't love her –

(ARCHIE *is drunk, and he sings and orchestrates his speech as only a drunken man can, almost objectively and fastidiously, like a conductor controlling his own sound.*)

ARCHIE: Yes, I loved her. I was in love with her, whatever that may mean. I don't know. Anyway, a few months later she was dead and that was that. She felt everything very deeply, your mother. Much more deeply than I did. Perhaps we could have worked it out between us. Did I ever tell you the most moving thing that I ever heard? It was when I was in Canada – I managed to slip over the border sometimes to some people I knew, and one night I heard some negress singing in a bar. *Now you're going to smile at this*, you're going to smile your educated English head off, because I suppose you've never sat lonely and half slewed in some bar among strangers a thousand miles from anything you think you understand. But if ever I saw any hope or strength in the human race, it was in the face of that old fat negress getting up to sing about Jesus or something like that. She was poor and lonely and oppressed like nobody you've ever known. Or me, for that matter. I never even liked that kind of music, but to see that old black whore singing her heart out to the whole world, you knew somehow in your heart that it didn't matter how much you kick people, the real people, how much you despise them, if they can stand up and make a pure, just natural noise like that, there's nothing wrong with them, only with everybody else. I've never heard anything like that since. I've never heard it here. Oh, I've heard whispers of it on a Saturday night somewhere. Oh, he's heard it. Billy's heard it. He's heard them singing. Years ago, poor old gubbins. But you won't hear it anywhere now. I don't suppose we'll ever hear it again. There's nobody who can feel like that. I wish to God I could, I wish to God I could feel like that old black bitch with her fat cheeks, and sing. If I'd done one thing as good as that in my whole life, I'd have been all right. Better than all your getting on with the job without making a fuss and all that, or doing something constructive and all that, all your rallies in Trafalgar Square! I wish to God I were that old bag. I'd stand up and shake my great bosom up and down, and lift up my head and make the most beautiful fuss in the world. Dear God, I would. But I'll never do it. I don't give a damn about anything, not even women or

draught Bass. Do you think that you're going to do it?
Well, do you?

JEAN: I don't know. I just really don't know. I'll probably do
exactly the same as you.

ARCHIE: Of course you will. Mind you, you'll make a better job
of it. You're more clever, I think you really feel something
too, in spite of all that Trafalgar Square stuff. You're what
they call a sentimentalist. You carry all your responses
about with you, instead of leaving them at home. While
everyone else is sitting on their hands you're the Joe at the
back cheering and making his hands hurt. But you'll have
to sit on your hands like everyone else. Oh, you think I'm
just a tatty old music hall actor who should be told the
truth, like Old Billy, that people don't wear sovereign cases
and patent leather shoes any more. You know when you're
up there you think you love all those people around you
out there, but you don't. You don't love them, you're not
going to stand up and make a beautiful fuss. If you learn it
properly you'll get yourself a technique. You can smile,
darn you, smile, and look the friendliest jolliest thing in the
world, but you'll be just as dead and smug and used up,
and sitting on your hands just like everybody else. You see
this face, you see this face, this face can split open with
warmth and humanity. It can sing, and tell the worst,
unfunniest stories in the world to a great mob of dead,
drab erks and it doesn't matter, it doesn't matter. It
doesn't matter because – look at my eyes. I'm dead behind
these eyes. I'm dead, just like the whole inert, shoddy lot
out there. It doesn't matter because I don't feel a thing,
and neither do they. We're just as dead as each other. Tell
me, tell me something. I want you to tell me something.
What would you say to a man of my age marrying a girl of
– oh about your age? Don't be shocked. I told you – I
don't feel a thing.

JEAN: You couldn't do a thing like that!

ARCHIE: You've been away from your old Dad a bit too long.
We've never seen much of each other, have we? Well,
never mind.

JEAN: You're not serious! You couldn't do that to Phoebe – not a divorce.

ARCHIE: Children! (*Laughs.*) Children! They're like the bloody music hall. Don't worry about your old man – he's still a bit worried about young Mick. At least, I suppose he is. I told you, nothing really touches me. As the man said, I've paid me one and saxpence – I defy yez to entertain me! Let anyone get up there and give a performance, let them get up, I don't care how good it is. Old Archie, dead behind the eyes, is sitting on his hands, he lost his responses on the way. You wouldn't think I was sexy to look at me, would you? You wouldn't think I was sexy to look at me, would you? Well, I 'ave a go, lady. I 'ave a go, don't I? I do. I 'ave a go. That barmaid in the Cambridge. That barmaid who upset poor old Billy in the Cambridge – I had her! When he wasn't looking . . .

(*Enter* PHOEBE.)

PHOEBE: I thought you'd got somebody here. They called up from downstairs. There's a policeman at the door for you, Archie.

ARCHIE: It's the income-tax man. It's the income-tax man. Tell him I've been expecting him. I've been expecting him for twenty years.

PHOEBE: (*To* JEAN) I thought he had someone in here. What do you think he wants?

ARCHIE: Just me and my daughter Jean. Me and my daughter Jean – by my first love. Why don't you go back to London? Say, aren't you glad you're normal? I've always been a seven day a week man myself, haven't I, Phoebe? A seven day a week man. I always needed a jump at the end of the day – and at the beginning too usually. Just like a piece of bacon on the slab. Well, it's everybody's problem. Unless you're like Mick and have got no problem. Well, he had a problem, but now he's on his way. Yes, that's a boy without problems. I'm a seven day a week man myself, twice a day. Poor old Phoebe, don't look so scared, love. Either they're doing it, and they're not enjoying it. Or else they're not doing it and they aren't enjoying it. Don't look so scared, love. Archie's drunk again. It's only the income tax man!

PHOEBE: Frank's down there –

FRANK: (*In*) The bastards! *The rotten bastards!* They've killed him! They've killed Mick! Those bloody wogs – they've murdered him. Oh, the rotten bastards!

ARCHIE: (*Slowly singing a blues*) Oh, lord, I don't care where they bury my body, no I don't care where they bury my body, 'cos my soul's going to live with God! (*Curtain.*)

END OF ACT TWO

SCENE NINE

Blues. Spot on FRANK *at piano.*

FRANK: Bring back his body, and bury it in England.
　　　Bring back his body, and bury it here.
　　　Bring back his body, in an aeroplane.
　　　But don't ever talk to me.
　　　Those playing fields of Eton
　　　Have really got us beaten.
　　　But ain't no use agrievin'
　　　'Cos it's Britain we believe in.
　　　So bring back his body, and bury it here.
　　　Bring back his body in an aeroplane –
　　　But just don't ever talk to me.

(*Fade.*)

SCENE TEN

BILLY, PHOEBE, JEAN, FRANK, ARCHIE. BILLY *and* PHOEBE *are dressed in black. The others wear black arm bands.*

JEAN: Well, that's that. (*Picks up some newspapers.*) Can anyone tell me what the whole thing added up to? (*Pause.*)

ARCHIE: My aunt always used to say the same thing, 'Well, they gave him a good send off.' Always said it without fail. (*To* BILLY.) Didn't she?

BILLY: Poor old Rosie.

ARCHIE: I used to wonder what would happen if she didn't say it.

BILLY: Old Rosie and me used to have some good times together. Used to go out a lot. Before we were both married.

JEAN: Well, I suppose it gives somebody a kick. Are you all right, Phoebe?

PHOEBE: I'm all right, dear. A bit tired.

BILLY: What a place London was then for having a good time. Best place in the world for a laugh. People were always ready to laugh, to give you a welcome. Best audience in the world.

(*Crosses L.C. Gets chair and sits above table.*)

ARCHIE: I was in a little village in Donegal once. On the Irish fit-ups. (*To* BILLY.) You remember. The morning we arrived there, a man came up to me and said: 'Oh, we're great students of the drama here. Great students of the drama. Our dramatic critics can lick anyone – anyone!' Turned out he was the local blacksmith. He said, he said: 'If you get past an audience here, you'll get past any audience in the world.' It was true too. Think I got a black eye.

BILLY: Some places, they just sit back and stare at you. They just – sit. But, London, that was the place. Old Rosie – she was a beautiful woman. I'm glad she's not here now.

JEAN: (*Grabbing at newspapers*) How can you compete against this stuff?

FRANK: You can't.

JEAN: Why didn't somebody get a picture of you stoking your boilers?

ARCHIE: I don't think Mick would have taken it too seriously.

FRANK: Everybody's tired.

JEAN: Everybody's tired all right. Everybody's tired, everybody's standing about, loitering without any intent whatsoever, waiting to be picked up by whatever they may allow to happen to us next.

ARCHIE: Jesus, don't start getting emotional –

JEAN: I don't expect you to.

ARCHIE: That's right.

JEAN: But Frank's different – at least, I hope he is. You don't have to be afraid, Frank. You needn't worry about being emotional, like my talented fiancé. You won't die of it. You may think you can, but you won't.

ARCHIE: Old Mick was a bit like Graham actually. He seemed to know what he wanted, and where he was going.

JEAN: Did he now, that's interesting –

ARCHIE: I remember he was having an affair with a girl called Sylvia. He was about sixteen at the time.

JEAN: What's the matter with you, Archie?

FRANK: Why don't you leave him alone?

ARCHIE: That's right, why don't you leave your old man alone?

JEAN: Oh, you've been left alone all right!

ARCHIE: Shall I tell you – all my life I've been searching for something. I've been searching for a draught Bass you can drink all the evening without running off every ten minutes, that you can get drunk on without feeling sick, and all for fourpence. Now, the man who could offer me all of that would really get my vote. He really would. Oh, well, I could always make a woman better than I could make a point.

JEAN: You know, Archie, you're a bit of a bastard.

PHOEBE: Jean –

JEAN: You really are – you're a bastard on wheels!

ARCHIE: Because I don't care about anything except draught Bass? Listen, kiddie, you're going to find out that in the end nobody really gives a damn about anything except some little animal something. And for me that little animal something is draught Bass. Now why can't you stop attacking everyone?

JEAN: I can't.

ARCHIE: What do you think you are – a dose of salts?

JEAN: I owe it to myself.

ARCHIE: Well, I never really believed in all that inner cleanliness anyway. Did I leave a bottle of beer in here last night?

PHOEBE: I don't think so, dear.

ARCHIE: If you're not careful, Jean, people will start putting labels on you pretty soon. And then you'll just be nobody. You'll be nobody like the rest of us.

PHOEBE: Frank'll get you some. There's some left in the kitchen. Would you mind, dear?

FRANK: Sure. (*Rises. Crosses L. of chair.*)

PHOEBE: We can't all spend our time nailing our suitcases to the floor, and shin out of the window.

ARCHIE: Scarper the letty.

JEAN: You're like everybody else, but you're worse – you think you can cover yourself by simply not bothering. (*Newspapers.*) You think if you don't bother you can't be humiliated, so you just roar your life out in four-letter words and just hope that somehow the perks will turn up.

FRANK: Leave him alone, he's just as upset as you are! So shut up.

JEAN: I'll give you the Archie Rice story. All right. You want the credit titles first?

ARCHIE: I didn't like the clergyman, anyway. I really hated him. He was as chloe as all get out. Did you notice?

JEAN: You don't fool me. You couldn't fool pussy!

ARCHIE: Go on – insult me, I don't mind. One thing I've discovered a long time ago. Most people never know when they're being insulted. And a whole lot of people make a whole lot of money out of that principle. I'm as dim as a bucket really. You know. I'm no better than the rest of them.

JEAN: Oh now, don't start being humble –

ARCHIE: I *am* humble! I am very humble, in fact. I still have a little dried pea of humility rattling around inside me. I don't think *you* have.

JEAN: And that's just about all.

FRANK: What's the matter with her?

ARCHIE: Don't ask me, son. Don't ask me. I've never solved a problem in my life.

JEAN: You haven't got the nous. You've been too busy hating all those feckless moochers out there in the great darkness, haven't you? You've been really smart. (*To* FRANK.) I'd like you to know the truth about your father.

FRANK: Listen, Jean, Mick's just been buried. He's buried and nobody wants to start talking about it, or having rows.

JEAN: What do you want, two minutes silence? Not only is your father generous, understanding and sympathetic – he doesn't give a damn about anyone. He's two pennorth of nothing.

ARCHIE: Yes, I should say that sums me up pretty well.

JEAN: You don't need to look at me! I've lost a brother too. Why do people like us sit here, and just lap it up, why do boys die, or stoke boilers, why do we pick up these things, what are we hoping to get out of it, what's it all in aid of – is it really just for the sake of a gloved hand waving at you from a golden coach?

PHOEBE: I think I'll go and lie down. (*To* JEAN.) He's always been good to me.

FRANK: Shall I bring you up an aspirin?

JEAN: Nobody listens to anyone.

PHOEBE: Thank you, dear. If you wouldn't mind. (*To* JEAN, *simply*). He's always been good to me. Whatever he may have done. Always.
   (*Exit.*)

FRANK: I'll get you that beer.

BILLY: Always had a decanter on the sideboard at home. I've got the key here.

JEAN: (*To* ARCHIE) You can't do it to her, I won't let you.

BILLY: Yes, here it is.

ARCHIE: He wants to know if I've renewed the ticket. It's all right – I've got another three months on it.

BILLY: Eh? (*To* JEAN.) There.

JEAN: What's this?

BILLY: What's the matter – you want your bloody ears syringed?

FRANK: You want some beer, Grandad?

BILLY: Nobody listens to a bloody word you're saying.

FRANK: I said do you want some beer?

BILLY: That's the trouble nowadays. Everybody's too busy answering back and taking liberties. 'Stead of getting on with it and doing as they're told. No, I'm going to bed. I've got to be out early tomorrow. (*To* ARCHIE.) What time did you say?

ARCHIE: About nine.

FRANK: Where are you going?

BILLY: Your father and I have got some business together. Seemed funny all those people taking off their hats to young Mick today.

FRANK: Most of 'em weren't wearing hats anyway.

BILLY: When I was younger, every man – and every man wore a hat in those days, didn't matter if he was a lord or a butcher – every man used to take his hat off when he passed the Cenotaph. Even in the bus. Nowadays I've watched people just go past it, not even a look. If you took the flags off of it I expect they'd sit down and eat their sandwiches on it.

ARCHIE: I was just thinking of young Mick and Sylvia. She was a nice, attractive little kid. I wonder what she's doing now. I wonder if she's read about him in the papers. Being a national hero and getting killed. I shouldn't think she'd have forgotten him already, would you?

FRANK: I shouldn't think so. Can I have some of your beer?

ARCHIE: Help yourself. I remember being worried about Sylvia. I couldn't get it out of young Mick, and I had an idea she was under-age. It worried me just a bit. I tried to tackle him about it, but he always thought I was a bit of a chump, he did, you know. Oh, I didn't mind. I rather liked it. (*To* JEAN.) He didn't really take me seriously. I hummed and hah'ed, and finally I said: 'Well, look boy, I obviously don't have to tell you to take precautions.' He just grinned like the clappers, and I suddenly felt like some weird old clergyman. So I just said to him: 'Well, anyway, you do know what the age of consent is, don't you?' And he sat there with that great awful grin on his face, and said: 'Sixteen'.

JEAN: Where are you taking Billy tomorrow?

ARCHIE: I think I'll have to go back to Brighton, and become a Beachcomber.

FRANK: (*To* JEAN) Got any aspirins on you? There don't seem to be any.

ARCHIE: Edlins – that was the place. All over Brighton.

JEAN: (*Giving* FRANK *aspirins*) Don't you know what he's trying to do?

ARCHIE: You could get nicely oiled on their draught cider for a few pence.

FRANK: Why don't you leave them alone?

ARCHIE: Haven't had it for years. How much was it?

JEAN: He thinks he's going to divorce her. He thinks he's going to divorce Phoebe. I've seen her – this girl he wants to marry. He's crazy. That's what he is. What's going to happen to her? (*She nods upstairs.*)

FRANK: What's going to happen to any of us. Listen, Jean, love – darling heart, you are not going to change anybody –

JEAN: Have you seen her? I caught them together yesterday. In the Rockliffe. I've seen her all right. She's a professional virgin.

ARCHIE: I wonder what it's like now. (*To* BILLY.) How much did it use to be?

FRANK: I'd better take these (*aspirins*) up to her.

BILLY: What?

ARCHIE: Draught cider, you old gubbins.

BILLY: How the bloody hell should I know? I've never drunk the stuff.

ARCHIE: Yes, it's a bit acid, I suppose.

BILLY: 'Bout a penny, I should say. Penny a pint.

ARCHIE: Be about a bob now, I 'spect. (*Slight pause.*) Might as well drink beer.

JEAN: (*To* ARCHIE) She's pretty, she's spoilt, she's vain, and she's stupid. And her parents are probably stupid. They must be, they must be stupid to produce her – Miss Nothing of 1957.

ARCHIE: That's right.

JEAN: How old is she?

ARCHIE: Twenty.

JEAN: Twenty. They're so stupid, I suppose, they'll even let her marry you?

ARCHIE: You know, I think I've only slept with one passionate woman. What I'd call really passionate. And she was happily married. Her name was Ivy.

JEAN: I suppose you think you'll get them to put up some money for you too?

ARCHIE: That was the idea.

JEAN: You're going to get her to put a ring through your nose, and tell yourself you won't feel it, because nothing matters to you any more, and nobody else does either. You think because you can't get her, nobody else can! What about Phoebe?

ARCHIE: Ivy Williams, that's her name. Mrs Ivy Williams. Mrs Ivy Williams.

BILLY: Well, I'm off. Who're we seeing: Rubens?

ARCHIE: Klein.

BILLY: Charlie Klein. Old Charlie Klein. I was in the first show he ever put on the road, you know that?

ARCHIE: Twelve thirty.

BILLY: He was younger than Jeannie here. I made him a member of the National Sporting Club. It was me who put him up.

ARCHIE: He's a tough bastard.

BILLY: Oh, Charlie should be all right. It was me made him sign up Eddie Drummer. Good artist, Eddie. Been earning a thousand a week for twenty-five years, and just the same. He's a good boy. He's a sort of in-between. He wasn't one of us real old timers, and he wasn't one of these new five-minute wonders with a microphone. They've got no real personality now. He always had style, Eddie, and never any real suggestion of offence in anything he did. We all had our own style, our own songs – and we were all English. What's more, we spoke English. It was different. We all knew what the rules were. We knew what the rules were, and even if we spent half our time making people laugh at 'em we never seriously

suggested that anyone should break them. A real pro is a real man, all he needs is an old backcloth behind him and he can hold them on his own for half an hour. He's like the general run of people, only he's a lot more like them than they are themselves, if you understand me. Well, Eddie's still up there all right. He's still up there. (*To* JEAN.) I always used to say to him, we all used to say: 'Eddie – always be good to the people on the way up, because you may meet them on the way down.' Old Eddie. One of the really great ones, I should say he is. I should say he's probably the last. Yes, I should say he's probably the last.
(*Exit.*)

JEAN: What are you doing, what are you going to do to him? You're not going to put him back into the business?

ARCHIE: Rubens and Klein twelve-thirty tomorrow morning –

JEAN: You're going to kill that old man just to save that no-good, washed-up tatty show of yours –

ARCHIE: It isn't just to save that no-good, tatty show of mine. It's to save your no-good tatty Dad from going to jail. People may not come to see Archie but they may still remember Billy Rice. It's worth a try anyway.

JEAN: Are you going to destroy that too? He's the only one of us who has any dignity or respect for himself, he's the only one of us who has anything at all, and you're going to murder him, you're going to take him down to – who is it – Rubens and Klein tomorrow morning at twelve-thirty, and you're going to let Mr Rubens and Mr Klein sign his death certificate. What are you letting yourself in for now, how on earth did you ever get him to do such a thing? What's happened to him? What's happened to his sense of self preservation?

ARCHIE: He feels he owes it to me.

JEAN: Owes it to you! Owes it to you! Billy doesn't owe you or anyone anything.

ARCHIE: You see, before you got busy lecturing me about inner cleanliness, Billy went and did something. He went and saw my little girl friend's parents, you know, the professional virgin you saw in the Rockliffe. He went and told them I was a married man with three grown-up children. Three acknowledged – anyway, but I don't suppose old Billy needed to mention the rest of them.

JEAN: He scotched it!

ARCHIE: Oh, yes – completely. You see, I hadn't told them about – about Phoebe, and all of you.

JEAN: No, I suppose you wouldn't.

ARCHIE: So you see you weren't wrong, Jeannie, love. Not about Phoebe anyway – old Archie isn't going to get his oats after all.

SCENE ELEVEN

ARCHIE: Ladies and Gentlemen, Billy Rice will not appear tonight. Billy Rice will not appear again. I wish I could sing a song for him – in his place. A farewell. But, unfortunately, I can't. Nobody can. None of us, any way. (*Exit.*)

(*Front Gauze. Funeral cortège with* ARCHIE, PHOEBE, JEAN, FRANK, GRAHAM *and* BROTHER BILL. *They gather round a coffin C. stage, draping over it a Union Jack,* BILLY's *hat, cane, and gloves. In the background, snatches of old songs, wisps of tunes, the stumble of a banjo. Fade to –*)

SCENE TWELVE

Down L. A lime drenches ARCHIE *and* BROTHER BILL. *Down R. lime on* JEAN *and* GRAHAM DODD. BROTHER BILL *looks like a highly successful and distinguished lawyer, and he is.* GRAHAM DODD *may well be like him in thirty years, provided he is successful. There are plenty of these around – well dressed, assured, well educated, their emotional and imaginative capacity so limited it is practically negligible. They have an all-defying inability to associate themselves with anyone in circumstances even slightly dissimilar to their own.* GRAHAM DODD *doesn't need much description. If you*

can't recognize him, it's for one reason only. These two duologues are
independent, but run together.

GRAHAM: Quite honestly, Jean, I don't mean to be rude. I
　　mean, well it is rude to come out and say it, but I can't see
　　what you can possibly have in common with any of them.

JEAN: You can't –

GRAHAM: Well, they're your family and all that, but after all,
　　there does come a point, there does come a point in things –

ARCHIE: He was such a sweet old man. He really was. D'you
　　know who said that? Charlie Klein. Charlie Klein said old
　　Billy was the nicest old man in the business.

GRAHAM: – you just don't have any more responsibility to
　　people.

ARCHIE: And still a first-class performer, Archie. Still a first-
　　class performer!

GRAHAM: – it's your background and you were brought up in it,
　　but there are better, more worthwhile things in life.

ARCHIE: He was one of the great, one of the really great.

JEAN: I'm sorry, Graham. I'm staying with Phoebe. I told you
　　I'd really made up my mind before I left. I can't marry
　　you, and I don't want to any more. Anyway, I've got to
　　stay here. Now that Billy's dead Phoebe needs someone
　　with her. Frank's off to Canada in a couple of weeks –

ARCHIE: Jean thinks I killed him.

BROTHER BILL: You didn't kill him, Archie. You don't kill
　　people that easily. I don't think so.

JEAN: We live differently. You and I don't even draw breath in
　　the same way.

BROTHER BILL: Look, Archie. This is the last time for you. It's
　　got to be Canada. You and Frank and Phoebe can all go
　　out together. Your passages are all booked. I've got them
　　in my pocket here. There's yours. You can go out and start
　　a new life, the three of you.

GRAHAM: Oh, this is just rubbish. You're no different from me.
　　You were in love with me, you said so. We enjoyed
　　ourselves together. We could make a good thing of it. I've
　　got quite a decent career lined up. We would have
　　everything we want. Come back with me, Jean.

ARCHIE: You can't get draught Bass in Toronto. I've tried it.

JEAN: Have you ever got on a railway train here, got on a train from Birmingham to West Hartlepool? Or gone from Manchester to Warrington or Widnes. And you get out, you go down the street, and on one side maybe is a chemical works, and on the other side is the railway goods yard. Some kids are playing in the street, and you walk up to some woman standing on her doorstep. It isn't a doorstep really because you can walk straight from the street into her front room. What can you say to her? What real piece of information, what message can you give to her? Do you say: 'Madam, d'you know that Jesus died on the Cross for you?'

BROTHER BILL: Those tickets are yours, Archie. Now take them. I'll pay up all your debts, I'll settle everything, I'll see that nothing happens.

JEAN: And then the woman, she looks back at you, and she says: 'Oh, yes, I heard all about that.'

ARCHIE: What happens if I don't go?

BROTHER BILL: I'm not doing anything for you to stay here. Archie. Not any more. You'll just have to take the consequences I'm afraid. It's Canada or jail.

ARCHIE: You know, I've always thought I should go to jail. I should think it must be quite interesting. Sure to meet someone I know. D'you know what my landlady in Fulham used to say about you? She used to say: 'He looks like a governor's man.' Always said it – without fail.

GRAHAM: We're all in it for what we can get out of it. Isn't that what your father was supposed to say?

ARCHIE: You can never get anything at this Labour Exchange anyway. They must have more bums in this place than in any other town in England. Oh, well, thanks anyway, just two more performances. It's a pity though – I should have liked to notch up twenty-one against the income-tax man. I'll never make my twenty-first now. It would have been fun to get the key of the door, somehow.

JEAN: Here we are, we're alone in the universe, there's no God, it just seems that it all began by something as simple as sunlight striking on a piece of rock. And here we are. We've only got ourselves. Somehow, we've just got to make a go of it. *We've only ourselves*.

BROTHER BILL: I'm sorry, Archie, but I've given up trying to understand.

(*Fade*.)

SCENE THIRTEEN

Rock-n-Roll. Nude tableau, behind first act gauze. Britannia. Then; the Archie Rice music, the one and only, interrupting the programme. The stage blacks out. A lime picks out the prompt corner, and ARCHIE *makes his entrance. He sings a few bars of 'We're all out for good old Number One'.*

ARCHIE: We're all out for good old Number One

Number One's the only one for me.

Good old England, you're my cup of tea,

But I don't want no drab equality.

Don't let your feelings roam,

But remember that charity begins at home.

What we've got left back

We'll keep – and blow you, Jack.

Number One's the only one for me.

– God bless you.

Number One's the only one for me.

I've just come to tell you about the wife. She's gone back to her husband. She has, straight. Don't clap too hard, we're all in a very old building. Yes, very old. Old. What about *that*? What about *her*, eh – Madam with the helmet on? I reckon she's sagging a bit, if you ask me. She needs some beef putting into her – the roast beef of old England. No, nobody's asking me, never mind. Nice couple of fried eggs, anyway. She's a nice girl, though – a nice girl. Going steady with Charlie here – isn't she, Charlie? (*To the conductor*.) She met him in a revolving door, and they've been going around together ever since. I'm doing me nut, you know that, don't you? I'm doing me nut up here. Nudes, that's what they call them, lady, nudes. Blimey, she's got more clothes on than I have. It's a lot of madam, that's all it is. A lot of madam. Oh, I put a line in there. Never mind, it doesn't matter. I've made a few tumbles in my time. I have, honest. You wouldn't think I was sexy to look at me, would you? No, honestly, you wouldn't, would you, lady. I always reckon you feel stronger after it? (*Sings.*) 'Say, your jelly-roll is fine, but it don't compare with mine!' There's a bloke at the side here with a hook, you know that, don't you? He is, he's standing there. I can see him. Must be the income-tax man. Life's funny though, isn't it? It is – life's funny. It's like sucking a sweet with the wrapper on. Oh, well, we're all in the fertilizer business now, I suppose. Well, I'd rather have a glass of beer any day – I would. You don't believe me, but I would. You think I'm gone, don't you? Go on, say it, you think I'm gone. You think I'm gone, don't you? Well, I am. What's the matter, you feeling cold up there? Before I do go, ladies and gentlemen, I should just like to tell you a little story, a little story. This story is about a man, just a little, ordinary man, like you and me, and one day he woke up and found himself in paradise. Well, he looks up, you see, and he sees a feller standing next to him. It turns out that this feller is a saint or something. Anyway, he's on the welcoming committee. And the feller says to him – the Saint – says to him: 'Well,' he says, 'you're now in paradise.' 'Am I?' he says. 'You are,' says the Saint. 'What's more, you have earned yourself eternal happiness.' 'Have I?' he says. 'You most certainly have,' says the Saint. 'Oh, you're well away,' he says. 'Can't you hear the multitudes? Why, everyone is singing, everyone is joyful. What do you say, my son?' So the little man took a look around him at all the multitudes of the earth, spread out against the universe. So he says to the Saint: 'Well, can I get up where you're standing, and take a proper look?' So the Saint says: 'Of course you can, my son' and makes way for him. And the little man stood up where the Saint was and gazed up at the sight around him. At all the Hosts of Heaven, and all the rest of it. 'All the wonder and the joy of eternity is round about you,' said the Saint. 'You mean, this is all eternity and I'm in Paradise?' 'That is so, my son. Well, what have you to say?' So the little man looks around again for a bit, and the Saint says: 'Well, my son?' 'Well,' he says, 'I've often wondered what I'd say if this ever happened to me. I couldn't think somehow.' And the Saint smiled at him kindly and says again: 'And what *do* you say, my son?' 'Only one thing I can say,' says the little man. And he said it! Well, the Saint looked as if he had been struck across the face by some great hand. The Hosts stopped singing and all the Angels hid their faces, and for a tiny splash in eternity there was no sound at all in Paradise. The Saint couldn't speak for a while, and then he threw his arms round the little man, and kissed him. And he said: 'I love you, my son. With all my soul, I shall love you always. I have been waiting to hear that word ever since I came here.' He's there with his little hook, I can see him. Oh, well, I have a go, don't I? I 'ave a go.

(*The cloth goes up, revealing a dark bare stage. The music starts up softly, and* ARCHIE RICE *stands on the stage in a little round world of light, and swaggers gently into his song:*)

Why should I care
Why should I let it touch me,
Why shouldn't I sit down and cry
To let it pass over me?

(*He begins to falter a little.*)

Why should –
Why should I let it get me –
What's the use of despair?

(*He stops and stares ahead of him. The music goes on, then he picks up.*)

If they see that you're blue
They'll look down on you.

82

(He stares up, then goes on.)

So why oh why should I bother to care?

(PHOEBE appears L. holding a raincoat and hat.)
ARCHIE: Why should I care.
　　　　Why should I let it touch me,
　　　　Why shouldn't I? –

(He stops, the music goes on, as he walks over to PHOEBE, who helps him on with his coat, and gives him his hat. He hesitates, comes back down to the floats.)
You've been a good audience. Very good. A very *good* audience. Let me know where you're working tomorrow night – and I'll come and see *YOU*.
(He walks upstage with PHOEBE. The spotlight is hitting the apron, where ARCHIE has been standing. The orchestra goes on playing: 'Why should I care'; suddenly, the little world of light snaps out, the stage is bare and dark. ARCHIE RICE has gone. There is only the music. Curtain.)

THE HOTEL IN AMSTERDAM

CHARACTERS

HOTEL PORTER
LAURIE
MARGARET
ANNIE
GUS
AMY
DAN
GILLIAN
WAITER

ACT ONE

The drawing-room of a suite in a large, first-class hotel in Amsterdam. It is a fairly cheerful room as such hotel rooms go with bright prints, plenty of low lamps and furnished in a rather friendly combination of thirtyish and tactful Hotel Empire. Three separate bedrooms lead off. The door to the hotel corridor opens and a PORTER *enters with a trolley filled with luggage. He is followed rather tentatively by three couples,* LAURIE *and* MARGARET; GUS *and* ANNIE; *and* DAN *and* AMY. *They are all fairly attractively dressed and near or around forty but none middle-aged. In fact, they are pretty flash and vigorous looking. Perhaps* GUS *and* MARGARET *less so than the others. This is partly because he is dressed a bit more conservatively than the other two men and she is visibly pregnant, though not unattractive. The* PORTER *looks for instructions about the baggage. He looks for the leader and decides on* GUS.

PORTER: Sir?

GUS: I'm sorry?

LAURIE: I think it's the baggage, Gus.

GUS: Oh.

MARGARET: Well, tell him darling.

GUS: No, it's all right. Now, let's see.

ANNIE: Well, don't let's make an operation out of it. Those are ours. There, porter. Those two.

PORTER: Yes, ah but where are we all going to go? We don't, I mean we haven't had a look yet.

LAURIE: Why don't we sort them out and decide afterwards?

MARGARET: Brilliant.

ANNIE: Some men are brilliant, aren't they?

AMY: Can I help?

MARGARET: No. Gus can manage.

GUS: Yes. Well it's just a question of sorting out the rooms isn't it? They're all there.

ANNIE: I should hope so. We're paying enough for them.

MARGARET: Well, don't let him stand there, darling.

GUS: Well, we think we'll have a look at the rooms first and

89

then decide where we're all going and –

ANNIE: That'll take hours with Gus.

MARGARET: No. It won't. Look, porter, just put them all down on the floor and we'll sort them out ourselves.

PORTER: Yes, madam.

GUS: Oh, do you think we should?

LAURIE: Yes, much quicker.

GUS: We'll have to carry it.

LAURIE: That's true. I want a drink really. Have you got any –

GUS: What – a drink? No, but we can order some now.

LAURIE: No. You know. Change. Tip.

GUS: Oh, no, no I haven't. Let's see. No, I used it on the taxi.

LAURIE: Darling?

MARGARET: You know I haven't.

ANNIE: I might have. Did you forget, Laurie?

MARGARET: Of course he didn't. He just didn't like to ask.

ANNIE: Why on earth not?

MARGARET: He's terrified no one's going to speak English.

ANNIE: You don't think they're going to speak Dutch, do you?

LAURIE: I suppose not. She's quite right though. I just feel I ought to and then I dry up. France is worst because it really seems so thick not to.

DAN: Like Americans.

LAURIE: Exactly. And they're so foul, the French I mean. If you do have a bit of a go, they despise you and pretend they don't know. A waiter in Paris actually corrected me saying Vodka once. After all, that's a Russian word.

ANNIE: I shouldn't let it worry you.

LAURIE: Well, it does.

ANNIE: Gus is very good. Bit slow but you're full of initiative always aren't you, darling?

GUS: Yes, I don't think I have that trouble so much. You can usually get someone to understand – especially nowadays.

LAURIE: That's the trouble. Amy, what should we give?

GUS: I looked up the exchange.

AMY: Here.

(*She tips the* PORTER, *who looks neither pleased nor displeased.*)

ANNIE: Thank heavens. Now Laurie can breathe and we can look around.

LAURIE: Just a minute. Do we all want a drink?

MARGARET: You mean: you do.

GUS: I don't know. Do we, darling?

ANNIE: You bet. After that journey. Aeroplanes!

GUS: Margaret?

MARGARET: No. I'm not.

GUS: Of course. Would you like something else?

MARGARET: Just mineral water. Perrier. Something.

GUS: Amy?

LAURIE: I know Amy will and Dan's tongue's dropping out.

MARGARET: You hope.

LAURIE: I can see it from here. Why don't we –

MARGARET: No. It's too expensive.

LAURIE: But we ought to celebrate getting here. After all, we're all in one piece, we're all together, we've escaped and –

ANNIE: Nobody knows we're here.

LAURIE: No one. Absolutely no one.

MARGARET: Well, that's not true.

LAURIE: (*To* PORTER) Don't go. Well, no one who matters or will let on. Amy saw to that, didn't you?

ANNIE: Oh, come on let's order. I'll have a whisky sour.

LAURIE: Oh, isn't that going to be difficult?

ANNIE: Difficult? A whisky sour?

LAURIE: If we all have something different –

GUS: I see what he means.

DAN: Yes. Reinforcements.

LAURIE: Perhaps we could vote on it. All the same thing.

ANNIE: I *have* voted. I'm not being democratic just for convenience.

LAURIE: What about the rest. Amy?

AMY: I really don't mind.

LAURIE: Good girl. And Dan, you'll drink anything. Right? Scotch?

DAN: OK.

LAURIE: Right, then so will I. Gus?

GUS: All right. But don't forget Margaret's Perrier.

LAURIE: Shall I?

ANNIE: We would like one whisky sour, one Perrier water, a
bottle of J. & B. or Cutty Sark. Some ice and some soda.
(*To* LAURIE.) Happy?

LAURIE: Make it two bottles, we'll need them.

ANNIE: And quickly please, if you can.

PORTER: Yes, sir.

GUS: Well now.

ANNIE: Let's look at the room. All right, Margaret?

MARGARET: Fine. Right.

ANNIE: You have first pick.

GUS: Oh, yes.

ANNIE: I don't mind. As long as the bed's big and comfortable.

LAURIE: I do.

MARGARET: You would; spoiled.

LAURIE: Well, let's get it over.

MARGARET: Don't fret, darling. Your drink will be here soon.

LAURIE: God, I hate travelling.

MARGARET: Well, you've arrived. Relax.

LAURIE: Yes, that's true isn't it? I suppose we really have. What
a relief. All those passports and tickets and airport buses
and being bossed about. Air hostesses – I'd love to rape an
air hostess.

GUS: Really? I don't mean about air hostesses. I rather enjoy all
that travel guff.

DAN: You would. Public school.

MARGARET: Now then, Dan, don't be chippy. You're very lucky
to be with your betters.

DAN: I know it. I hate the working classes. That's why I got out.

AMY: You can never get out.

DAN: I did. They're an unlovable, whining, blackmailing
shower.

ANNIE: What's he talking about?

MARGARET: Just being chippy.

LAURIE: Don't keep saying that. You should see *my* horrible
family.

MARGARET: I have and now you're both being chippy.

LAURIE: We're both just saying we've got horrible families and

that you're lucky to have nice, gentle, civilized, moderate
parents like yours. Right, Dan?

DAN: Right.

MARGARET: Oh, my goodness, class solidarity. Anyway, my
mother's not that hot.

LAURIE: She's divine.

MARGARET: Well, you think so. She's just dull and sporty.

LAURIE: She's not. She's extremely attractive and intelligent.

DAN: Not like my mum – scheming old turd.

LAURIE: And your mum's so ugly.

DAN: Telling me.

LAURIE: Funny really because you're not.

ANNIE: He's beautiful.

LAURIE: Mine's got a very mean little face. Celebrates every
effect, plays up all the time, to the gallery, do anything for
anything. Self-involved, bullying.

MARGARET: Oh, come off it.

LAURIE: I suppose you think her face is pitted by the cares of
working class life and bringing up her sons on National
Assistance. Well, it isn't. She has that face there because
there's a mean, grudging, grasping nature behind it.

MARGARET: I don't know why nice men don't like their
mothers.

ANNIE: Gus likes his.

LAURIE: That's because she's probably nice.

ANNIE: She isn't bad.

GUS: No. I suppose she isn't really.

LAURIE: And he's a bit queer too, remember.

ANNIE: That's true.

MARGARET: But you always say you are a bit.

LAURIE: So I am. But not as much as Gus.

AMY: What about Dan?

LAURIE: Well – either less than Gus or me. Or much more.
He's more elusive. I mean Gus is so obvious. Those
clothes. That's real conservatism.

GUS: Are they awful?

MARGARET: You look dishy.

LAURIE: I think my mother *would* have put me off women for

life. I mean just to think of swimming about inside that repulsive thing for nine months.

MARGARET: Please.

LAURIE: But I think when I was quite young I must have decided she was nothing to do with women at all. That's why the real thing was such an eternal surprise.

MARGARET: She'd love this. You usually butter her up.

LAURIE: She doesn't give a twopenny fart. Excuse me – I think I'm going to . . . It's the idea of my mother. Don't worry, I'll tell her before she dies. No. I die. She'll outlive me for years.

DAN: My mother would have made a good air hostess.

LAURIE: Your mother! Listen, my mother should have been Chief Stewardess on Monster's Airlines. She'd have kept you waiting in every bus, withheld information and liquor, snapped at you, and smirked at you meaninglessly or simply just ignored you.

DAN: Have you ever thought of airlines for homosexuals?

LAURIE: I say: what a splendid idea. You could call it El Fag Airlines.

ANNIE: Gus could be a stewardess.

LAURIE: We'd design him a divine outfit. I say I feel better already.

MARGARET: Don't get carried away. The holiday's only just started.

LAURIE: The great escape you mean.

GUS: You mean all the aircrew would be chaps?

DAN: *And* the passengers.

LAURIE: Why don't we start it? Fly El Fag. The airline that floats just for HIM!

GUS: It's not bad is it? I say, we're getting our wind back aren't we? Just starting to feel safe I suppose.

DAN: We're really here.

LAURIE: Really here.

ANNIE: I don't know who's more astonished that we've all scarpered. Us or whether *he* will be.

AMY: K. L. will be *pretty* astonished when he finds out.

MARGARET: Let's face it: so are we.

ANNIE: We do sound a bit amazed at our own naughtiness.

LAURIE: No, we're not.

MARGARET: Yes, we are. Come on. You are.

LAURIE: No, we are relieved, unburdened, we've managed to slough off that monster for a few days. We have escaped, we deserve it, after all this time. Just to be somewhere he doesn't know where any of us are. Can't get near us, call us, ring us, come round, write. Nothing. Nix. For a few blessed days. No K. L. in our lives.

MARGARET: You make it more cowardly than it is.

LAURIE: So what if it is?

ANNIE: No. It isn't. We all deserve to escape. After all, he *is* the biggest, most poisonous, voracious, Machiavellian dinosaur in movies. And we all know what that means.

LAURIE: Quite.

ANNIE: Sorry, Amy. I know he's your boss.

DAN: He seems to be everybody's boss.

AMY: Poor Dan.

ANNIE: Yes. Married to the boss's secretary. That's probably the worst position of all.

MARGARET: You and I are in the same position.

GUS: I suppose we all play different roles to the dinosaur. But they're still roles.

DAN: Amy adores him.

ANNIE: So does everybody. I do. And Margaret does. Gus can't live without him. And Laurie tries to pretend he can.

LAURIE: I can.

ANNIE: I wonder if you will.

LAURIE: I have before and it sure didn't kill me.

MARGARET: I don't think I could bear any more recriminations.

ANNIE: But the rest of us are still supposed to be friends.

GUS: It's difficult isn't it? Perhaps Laurie can come to some understanding.

LAURIE: Not this time, buddy, he's had it.

GUS: I don't know how we'll cope when we get back.

ANNIE: Darling. We've only just arrived.

MARGARET: How amused he'd be. Here we are congratulating

ourselves on escaping from him and we've hardly stopped talking about him since we left Liverpool Street.

LAURIE: I wouldn't feel flattered to hear *what* we've said.

ANNIE: He'd be amused certainly.

LAURIE: Amy, you are sure?

AMY: Absolutely sure.

LAURIE: It would be great if he suddenly walked through that door while we were laughing and joking all together.

AMY: He won't.

GUS: What a thought.

MARGARET: Poor Amy. She's the real Judas amongst us. After all she *is* his secretary. *We're* conspirators.

LAURIE: I don't see that she's been disloyal. So what if she has! That cock's crowed a bit too often for every one of us. *And* everyone else. Those he's victimized at one time or another. Oh, he'll find another spare eunuch knocking around London. The world's full of hustlers and victims all beavering away to be pressed into K. L.'s service. Someone always wants to be useful or flattered or gulled or just plain whipped slowly to death or cast out into the knackers yard by King Sham. Well, let him go ahead and get himself crucified this time. I know him not.

ANNIE: What do you mean?

LAURIE: What I say.

MARGARET: He won't.

GUS: Won't what?

LAURIE: Get himself crucified.

GUS: No, I suppose not.

ANNIE: No.

DAN: Pity.

AMY: He'll be all right. He'll find someone.

GUS: I say, do you know we haven't looked at the view yet. It's rather good.

MARGARET: So it is.

AMY: We're really here.

DAN: I wish you'd stop saying that. Of course we're here. You made all the superb arrangements didn't you?

MARGARET: Yes, thanks, Amy.

LAURIE: Hear, hear. Thank you, Amy.

ANNIE: Well, screw the view, we haven't looked at the rooms yet.

MARGARET: Yes, we must do that now.

ANNIE: Won't K. L. be furious when he can't get hold of you over the weekend? He knows you never go away.

AMY: I said I was staying with some relatives in Yorkshire.

ANNIE: But you're a hopeless liar. You're so transparent.

AMY: I hinted it was really a lover.

LAURIE: Oh, he'd like that. More demolition around the joint.

AMY: Yes, he was rather intrigued. So he didn't ask any questions.

MARGARET: Not even where to get hold of you?

AMY: I said there was no phone. But I'd ring him.

MARGARET: Then won't you have to?

AMY: Well, of course, he'll be furious when I don't. I'll have to say I wasn't well.

LAURIE: That won't wash. He'll ring Dan to stir it up.

AMY: I don't think he'd do that. He wouldn't want to mess things up if he really thinks I've got a lover and Dan doesn't know about it.

ANNIE: Don't fancy your first morning back, with your shorthand pad when your boss has been deprived and rejected of men all weekend and you not on the phone having a bit on the side and not even confiding in him. He'll be *very* hurt.

AMY: Oh, dear. Yes. He will.

LAURIE: So what. Say you had the curse and it ruined the entire rendezvous. That would appeal to him.

AMY: Wouldn't wash. He knows my calendar better than I do.

DAN: Knows your miserable little face, you mean.

MARGARET: Aren't they charming?

ANNIE: Did you know that air hostesses have holy travail with the curse?

LAURIE: Really? Good.

ANNIE: Seriously. To do with the air pressure or something.

LAURIE: Good. Jolly good!

ANNIE: Either don't get it for months on end and worry themselves to death in case they're up the spout . . .

LAURIE: Fancy a pregnant air hostess. Think how high and mighty she'd be. Putting her feet up and pecking at all the customers' canapés.

ANNIE: Or they get it twice a week.

DAN: Do you mind. I feel a pain coming on.

ANNIE: Wish you did. Then you wouldn't jeer at poor little Amy when she's boo-hooing all over K. L.'s office.

DAN: Thank God they don't have women pilots.

GUS: The Russians do.

LAURIE: Remember: never travel on Rusky Airlines. Keep to El Fag.

DAN: Or you might go up front and see a little bundle of Russian misery crying its eyes out over the controls.

LAURIE: All misted up and locking herself in the loo. Worse than seeing a little yellow face turn round and grin at you.

ANNIE: Like the Lost Horizon.

LAURIE: Our bloody drinks are lost. Where is that hopeless Hollander? Do you suppose he understood us?

MARGARET: Of course he understood us. This isn't Bournemouth.
(*Knock*, WAITER *enters.*)

GUS: Ah. There we are. Good evening.

WAITER: Good evening, sir.

MARGARET: Now you can relax.

GUS: I say this is Haig. Didn't you order –

LAURIE: Doesn't matter. It'll take hours. You know what –

GUS: Sure?

LAURIE: Sure. Open it, please, would you?

WAITER: Yes, sir.

GUS: I'm sure he'd change it if we ask him.

MARGARET: Laurie would die. Of embarrassment apart from anything else.

LAURIE: It's all right, leave it. I'll do it.

WAITER: One whisky sour.

ANNIE: Thank God for that. Thank you.

GUS: That's all for the moment. Oh – Perrier? Yes. Here you are, Margaret.

WAITER: Thank you, sir. Good evening.

GUS: Good evening.

(WAITER *goes out.*)

DAN: I don't think he approved of us much.

LAURIE: Did you think so? Yes. I had that feeling.

MARGARET: Thinks we're alcoholics.

LAURIE: I thought he thought the girls were probably OK. But not us.

ANNIE: Perhaps he thinks we're none of us married.

GUS: Oh, yes – having a real mucky weekend, gang bang stuff.

LAURIE: He looked very suspiciously at you.

GUS: Did you think so?

LAURIE: I noticed it. Thought you were a bit effeminate I expect.

GUS: Perhaps he did. I think it's these bloody trousers, darling. You said I should throw them away. They don't do much for me do they?

LAURIE: Nothing desirable.

ANNIE: Darling, you always look rather effeminate. You and Laurie both do. In different ways.

GUS: Ah, but Laurie carries it off somehow. I don't.

MARGARET: Especially to foreigners.

ANNIE: It's part of your masculine charm.

GUS: What do you mean?

ANNIE: Oh, I don't know. A kind of mature softness.

MARGARET: And peacockery.

ANNIE: Yes, a bit uneasy sometimes but gallant and foursquare all the same.

LAURIE: Doesn't sound too bad.

ANNIE: It's lovely.

GUS: You're quite right. I know foreigners think like that. It's hell when I'm in America.

LAURIE: They think I'm Oscar Wilde. It's very flattering.

MARGARET: And don't you play up to it!

LAURIE: Well, I mean you just have to, don't you? It's like they expect to see the Changing of the Guard.

ANNIE: Thank heavens for the charm and femininity of the English male I say.

LAURIE: Well, American women certainly don't have it. Poor sods.

MARGARET: I'll drink to that.

LAURIE: Perrier. Ugh!

MARGARET: I like it.

LAURIE: Everyone's glass charged? Right . . . Well, here we all are.

ANNIE: Here we all are.

LAURIE: Here's to all of us. All friends and all together.

MARGARET: Well, naturally.

LAURIE: No, it's not natural. It's bloody unnatural. How often do you get six people as different as we all are still all together all friends and who all love each other. After all the things that have happened to us. Like success to some extent, making money – some of us. It's not bad.

GUS: Bloody good.

LAURIE: Everyone's married couples nowadays. Thank heaven we're not that.

MARGARET: You're drunk already.

LAURIE: You know what I mean.

MARGARET: Yes.

LAURIE: To us, and may the Good Lord bless and keep us.

ALL: To us.

LAURIE: And preserve us from that dinosaur film producer.

ANNIE: I don't think I can quite drink to that.

GUS: It's a problem.

LAURIE: Well, suit yourselves . . . Ah, that's better.

GUS: Isn't it good?

LAURIE: All right, Amy?

AMY: Fine.

ANNIE: Guilty?

AMY: No. I'm forgetting it until Monday.

ANNIE: I wonder if you will.

LAURIE: Well, give her a chance. Dan?

DAN: Smashing.

ANNIE: You know what: I think people who need people are the ghastliest people in the world.

LAURIE: Absolutely. We all just happened to find one another. At the right time.

ANNIE: It sounds a bit Jewish show biz.

LAURIE: I thought it was a rather tense Anglo-Saxon sentiment myself. I mean you couldn't sing it.

ANNIE: Well, you could. It would be rather mediocre.

LAURIE: I mean you couldn't belt out a rather halting little comment like that. It's not poetic. It's just a smallish statement. About six unusually pleasing people. Well five. God, I'm getting fat.

MARGARET: You've always been fat.

LAURIE: Really? *Have I*? I've deceived myself.

MARGARET: You're very attractive. Pleasing.

LAURIE: More pleasing than K. L?

MARGARET: Yes. Don't know about more attractive.

LAURIE: Hell!

AMY: We really *are* lucky. I mean it's a splendid hotel and a lovely suite.

DAN: Which *you* can't afford.

LAURIE: You don't have to. *I* can. So can Gus. You made all the arrangements. And Dan's going to do all the talking.

AMY: I think they all speak English.

LAURIE: You must admit it's better than that rotten Paris.

ANNIE: I suppose we're all what's called spoiled.

LAURIE: What do you mean: spoiled?

ANNIE: Well, first class hotels, great suites, anything we want to drink.

LAURIE: What's spoiled about that? I'm certainly not spoiled. I work my drawers off and get written off twice a year as not fulfilling my early promise by some philistine squirt drumming up copy, someone who's got as much idea of the creative process as Dan's mother and mine rolled into one lazy minded lump of misery who ever battened off the honest efforts of others.

ANNIE: Writers are born to be reviled.

LAURIE: No they're not. They sit in judgement on themselves all the time without calling in outside help. They need to be loved and cared for and given money.

ANNIE: We all love you and you make lots of money.

LAURIE: Where would K. L. be without me – where *will* he be without me to write his lousy pictures? Pretty all right, I guess. And without Gus to edit them into making sense and cover up his howlers? Of course, I suppose you'll go on doing it.

(*Pause.*)

Well, not this one. Besides, he hates it if I make money. I think he tips off the tax man. We don't live in Switzerland any of us do we? More sense but still . . . Loaded with distinction and not a C.B.E. to go round. When I think of the rotten dollars I've made –

MARGARET: Don't.

ANNIE: And K. L.

LAURIE: Well, lolly doesn't worry him. He spends it. You just round up a few people like Gus and me here, turn them up on the gas and if you suck around the blood counter at the supermarket long enough, you've produced another picture. And you go on doing. What I do, I get out of the air. Even if it's not so hot always, I put my little hand out there in that void, there, empty air. Look at it. It's like being a bleeding conjuror with no white tie and tails. Air . . .

MARGARET: Hot.

LAURIE: It never pays what it costs . . . No. I'm feeling quite relaxed now. Sure you won't drink?

MARGARET: I do keep telling you.

LAURIE: Sorry. Actually, I do speak Italian quite beautifully, don't I, darling?

MARGARET: The accent's good.

LAURIE: Poor vocabulary. But they don't mind if you make it up. They love it. (*All very fast but clear.*) Prego, prego. Si, grazie. Signorina. E machina bella. Grande film con regissori K. L. con attirci Inglesi tutte bellisima. Attrici Inglesi molto ravissante crumpetto di monde. Per che. Me Lauri scritori Inglesi famioso connossori, grosso. Molto experementi, Senza pommodori, si. Oggi declarimento attrice Inglesi crumpetto elegante, insatiabile, splendido lasagne verde antifascisti pesce Anna Magnani Visconti arrividerci con rubato grazie mille, grazie. There, wasn't that good! Allemange basta! Pasta per tute populo. Kosygin pappa mio. Si grappa, per favore.

MARGARET: I think I'm going to sort the rooms out.

LAURIE: Oh, leave it.

MARGARET: I want to unpack.

LAURIE: Oh, all right.

MARGARET: And I expect the others do. Unless they want an Italian lesson.

LAURIE: Shall we go to an Italian restaurant tonight?

GUS: That sounds good. Darling?

ANNIE: Perhaps we should try the local hostelries.

LAURIE: Yes. I expect you're right. I'm too fat for wop food.

MARGARET: Dutch food's rather heavy.

GUS: Enormous portions. Good beer. I've got an information thing here.

ANNIE: Oh heavens – don't start on that already.

GUS: Well, we'll have to make a decision.

LAURIE: I don't see –

GUS: Might have to book a table or something. If we want to get somewhere good.

LAURIE: Yes, I see.

ANNIE: You both make it sound so difficult.

LAURIE: My dear Annie, it *is* difficult. I can't think of anything that comes easily. It's all difficult.

ANNIE: You need one of those things that fortifies the over forties.

LAURIE: I'm not over forty!

MARGARET: Well, you look it.

LAURIE: What are you trying to do to me?

MARGARET: No, you don't. You look like a teenager.

LAURIE: Yes, a plump, middle-aged, played out grotesque.

ANNIE: Never believe in mirrors or newspapers.

LAURIE: I thought I'd got the mirror fixed . . . I need another one after that.

MARGARET: Come on, let's explore this place and see what we've got for our money. Annie?

(ANNIE *follows her. Also* GUS *who looks helpful.*)

LAURIE: Over forties. I heard a disc jockey the other day introducing a pop version of 'Roses of Picardy'. 'Picardy' he said. 'Where's that?' Help . . .

DAN: Do you ever look to see if your birthday's listed in The
   Times?
LAURIE: Always.
DAN: And is it?
LAURIE: They missed me out the year before last. Seemed like
   an obituary only no notice. When you do something, try to
   do something, take a look at someone else's efforts, you
   ask yourself, *I* ask myself: is there something there that
   wasn't there before? Well . . . I picked this damned paper
   up and it seemed I hadn't even been born any more . . . do
   you ever have a little lace curtain in front of your eyes? Like
   little spermy tadpoles paddling across your eyeballs? No?
   Do you think it's drink or eyesight?
DAN: Drink.
AMY: You ought to watch that.
LAURIE: I've been watching it for years. Fascinating. And tell
   me, do you ever either of you, no you wouldn't Amy, but
   you Dan, do you ever wake up with your finger tips all
   tingly and aching?
DAN: No.
LAURIE: Well, do you ever wake up with an awful burn in the
   stomach?
AMY: Yes, he often does.
LAURIE: And then what do you do?
DAN: Get up. Work. Paint if it's light.
LAURIE: This is about five o'clock is it?
DAN: Usually.
LAURIE: And you can actually work can you?
DAN: Not always.
LAURIE: Do you wake up, Amy?
AMY: I usually wake up.
LAURIE: And then?
AMY: I make coffee or give him a glass of milk.
LAURIE: And have a bit of chatter?
DAN: That's it. Until it's time for her to get off to K. L.
LAURIE: I'm afraid I usually need a drink. It's the only thing
   that burns it out. Need to weld my guts with a torch. Then
   about nine, it eases off. I read the post. Try to put off

work. Have a so-called business lunch. That's a good waste of time. Then I know I'll have to sleep in the afternoon.

AMY: Does Margaret get up when you're like that?

LAURIE: She can't – poor old thing. You see she can't get off to sleep. So by the time I'm about to totter about downstairs, reading last night's evening papers, she's only just managed to get off. Especially now.

AMY: When she's pregnant?

(LAURIE *motions her silent at the word*.)

LAURIE: So, I'm afraid we're a bit out of step with sleep. When I was eighteen I used to sleep fourteen hours on Sundays. When my mother would let me.

DAN: My mother made too much noise.

LAURIE: If *only* you can find enough energy. Where do you find it? Where's the spring?

AMY: You're loaded with it. You've got far more than Dan.

LAURIE: No, I haven't. Dan doesn't need energy. He runs perfectly efficiently on paraffin oil. You fill him up once a year and he's alight for another twelve months. With me, I need the super quality high-thing stuff poured into my tank twice a day. Look at K. L. He's unstoppable, you never have to wind him up. He just goes. Like that.

AMY: He gets very worn out.

LAURIE: I should think he does. If I did what he does in a day, I'd be in bed for a month.

DAN: He delegates.

LAURIE: Ah, yes – the operator's alchemy. Where do you get it? He takes it from *us*. We could be giving it to one another. He's been draining our tanks, filling his own. Filling up on all of us, splitting us up.

(MARGARET, ANNE *and* GUS *return*.)

MARGARET: Give what to each other.

LAURIE: A little vitality.

ANNIE: We're all right. And we're on hols. So we can re-charge.

LAURIE: Yes, we've got away.

ANNIE: The rooms are fine. You and Margaret are having that one. Gus and I this one and we decided Amy and Dan would like that one with the view. It's nice.

AMY: Are you sure?

ANNIE: They're all nice. Now we can get our stuff in.

MARGARET: Gus has done nearly all of it already. Gus, you are a darling. Honestly, you two! Letting Gus do all the carrying.

LAURIE: Good for his figure.

MARGARET: Typical.

LAURIE: And bad for my kidneys.

MARGARET: Are you going to help me unpack?

LAURIE: Do you want me to?

MARGARET: No, I don't think so.

LAURIE: I can.

MARGARET: I don't doubt it.

LAURIE: Shall I talk to you while you do it?

MARGARET: No. Talk to Dan and Gus. I might lie down for a bit.

LAURIE: Let me –

MARGARET: Please stay where you are.

ANNIE: Ours won't take a second.

LAURIE: You seem to have brought an awful lot of stuff. What are you going to do? Play golf? Hunt or something?

ANNIE: Mostly Gus's stuff. Medicines, all chemists counter.

DAN: Got my easel?

AMY: Yes.

DAN: Right. Just in case.

(ANNIE *and* MARY *go to rooms.*)

I'll never use it.

LAURIE: Working on your own. I could never live on my own. Oh, I have done. It's been all right for a time. But what about now and then, the steep drop and no one there. And no one to phone or too far away.

DAN: Or too early in the morning.

LAURIE: That's one of the few good things about movies. You do work with others. Bit like the army.

GUS: I suppose we really have made the right selection? Over the rooms?

LAURIE: Who cares? They'll all be the same.

GUS: I just thought Margaret ought to have a nice one. If she's not sleeping.

LAURIE: Gus, I know you mean well but please forget about it. I say, old Amy won't get the sack when she gets back to K. L.?

DAN: No. He relies on her too much.

LAURIE: Do you mind?

DAN: Mind?

LAURIE: I shouldn't think you see much of her. His nibs keeps her at it. Seven days a week.

DAN: He pays her well. More than I earn. It works out.

GUS: Don't think that would suit me.

DAN: Annie can't see all that much of you.

GUS: Oh, a fair bit. He tries to keep me away from her, mind you. You know: don't bother to drive home. Stay here and we can make an early start at breakfast. But I hardly ever do. I need a bit of looking after, I'm afraid. I hate staying in other people's houses. Unprepared and all that. No shaving stuff. Or someone else's. And I don't like really sleeping on my own. Somehow, well the quality of sleep is different. Do you know what I mean?

DAN: I can sleep anywhere.

LAURIE: I think I know. More drink – before they come back?

GUS: Well. It does seem a bit unfair to drink so much in front of Margaret.

LAURIE: It isn't. But just don't say so.

GUS: Oh? All right. Well, here's to all of us. Amsterdam . . . What a brilliant idea of yours. He'd never think of here.

LAURIE: No?

GUS: Not exactly his sort of place I'd have thought. Not much night life.

DAN: Few bank managers dancing with each other and that's it.

MARGARET: (*Off*) Laurie. Would you ring down for some more Perrier for me?

LAURIE: OK darling.

(*He hesitates, looks hopefully at* GUS, *who responds.*)

GUS: I'll do it.

LAURIE: (*Grateful*) Oh, would you? Thanks. (*He pours out for* DAN.)

GUS: (*On phone*) This is room 320. Yes. Oh, yes – room service, please . . . Hullo, can I have two large bottles of Perrier water. And, oh, yes some ice. And a bottle of Cutty Sark. You brought Haig last time. Yes. Thank you. All fixed.

LAURIE: Thanks. And no one's to buy an English newspaper. Right?

DAN: Right. It's not your birthday is it?

LAURIE: I wonder why she didn't ring down herself.

GUS: Unpacking, I suppose . . .

DAN: I was thinking the other day: do you think they make bicycle clips any more?

LAURIE: Hadn't thought of that. No, of course. All those little bare black ankles.

GUS: Bicycle clips . . . I think I've still got mine.

LAURIE: Like Picardy I should think. No one would know. Like those things you used to wear on your sleeves.

DAN: I should hope not.

LAURIE: Well, of course, I never did. I'll bet *you* did.

GUS: What?

LAURIE: Wear those things. Up here.

GUS: No – I don't think so.

LAURIE: Do you have one of those little pocket diaries? You know for appointments and things.

GUS: Yes.

DAN: No.

LAURIE: Well then, Gus. I wonder if this happens to you. You know how just after Christmas and you've got nothing to do except feel ill and miserable and dread those last days of December? If you haven't got to hell out of it. Well, I always start my new diary off before the New Year. Put my licence number in it because I can't remember it. Why *should* I remember it? Then you put in your telephone numbers – I even put my own in. Otherwise I might ring one I had years ago . . . Well, and then there are the names of all those people, not all those people but some people because I don't keep many in there and then you know – every year I sit down and there's not just one I don't put in again, there's four, five, six. I think there are only about eleven in this year – and that includes people like you and

Dan and K. L. *He'll* be out next year. And my agent. And that's about it. Oh, and my mother . . . Hey, what are you all doing in there?

ANNIE: (*Off*) Unpacking!

MARGARET: (*Off*) What do you think?

LAURIE: Well, come back in.

AMY: Coming!

LAURIE: Margaret! We're all missing you. We're on our own.

MARGARET: (*Off*) No, you're not. You're getting stewed.

LAURIE: We're six and there are only three in here.

ANNIE: Bad luck.

LAURIE: We love you. Why have you gone and left us? We came here to be together. And you all disappear off to the bedroom or the bathroom and dolly about with your rollies and skin tonic. Come back in here! You're needed!

GUS: Yes, come back. Annie!

ANNIE: (*Off*) I'm unpacking all your laxatives and pouve juices.

AMY: (*Appearing*) All done! It's a lovely room, Dan. Go and look at the view.

DAN: I will.

LAURIE: You deserve a lovely room, my dear. Come here and give me a kiss. Just for arranging everything if for nothing else ever. Not a hitch.

AMY: It was easy. K. L.'s got a good travel agent.

LAURIE: You didn't use *him*!

AMY: He won't let on. I briefed him.

LAURIE: Good girl. Well, if you lose your job, you'll have to come and work for me. Have a drink. Won't be as exciting as K. L. But you'll get more time off.
(*Knock on door.*)
That's *him*. He's found out where we are. You've bungled it and he got on a plane and did it the quick way.

AMY: Come in.

LAURIE: Scusi, scusi. Momento, momento, tutte in bagno. Basta, per favore.
(WAITER *enters.*)

WAITER: Whisky sour?

LAURIE: No, Cutty Sark.

AMY: Annie, did you order a whisky sour?

ANNIE: (*Off*) Yes. I knew you'd all forget me.

GUS: Why didn't you tell me? I've ordered.

ANNIE: (*Entering from bedroom*) Easier. Thank you.

GUS: I ordered. Cutty Sark. And Perrier. And ice. You won't forget!

WAITER: Very well, sir. (*Goes.*)

GUS: Crossed lines. All right, darling?

ANNIE: Everything's out. Anything from bowels to athlete's foot.

LAURIE: Do you know there really is such a thing as writer's cramp?

ANNIE: Sounds rather comic – like housemaid's knee.

LAURIE: Not funny if you're a housemaid or a writer.

DAN: Have you had it?

LAURIE: Naturally. What's more I get psychosomatic writer's cramp.

AMY: You can type. I've seen you.

LAURIE: The commitment's too immediate. Horrifying. Like kissing someone for the first time and then bingo you're having to slap the breath of life into some rotten little fig of a human being that heaved its way between you five seconds afterwards. Do painters get anything like housemaids?

ANNIE: Aching backs I suppose on murals and things. Do you?

DAN: Not much.

LAURIE: That's because you work at a controlled pace, you see. Everything you do has rhythm, you see. Systematic, consistent. *That's* the thing. Mine's all over the place.

ANNIE: You produce the goods.

LAURIE: Are – but do I then?

ANNIE: Don't fish. You know you do.

LAURIE: But what goods? I ask myself: can anything manufactured out of this chaos and rapacious timidity and scolding carry on really *be* the goods. Should it not be, I ask myself. What do I ask myself, perhaps I shouldn't be rhetorical and clutter conversations with what-do-I-ask-myselfs? Won't the goods be shown up by the way of the manner of their manufacture? How can they become aloof, materials shaped with precision, design, logical detail, cunning, formality. And so on and so on.

ANNIE: And so on. You're not such a bad tailor.

LAURIE: No, I'm not.

ANNIE: There, you *were* fishing.

LAURIE: *And* I provide my own cloth. Any clunkhead can cut. I don't mean in your sense, Gus.

GUS: What? Oh, no – you're right.

ANNIE: I've a feeling we're getting back to K. L. *You* said let's leave him behind. But you won't.

AMY: He will.

GUS: Well, it is difficult you must admit. He rather makes one talk about him.

ANNIE: Perhaps we should go straight back to London and be with him after all.

GUS: Don't suppose he'd have us altogether.

ANNIE: Why were you doing your parliamo Italiano bit?

AMY: He thought it was K. L.

ANNIE: *That* would have fooled him!

GUS: You didn't really did you?

LAURIE: No. Except with him nothing is so awful he couldn't visit it on you.

ANNIE: No one would think you'd been loving friends for ten years.

LAURIE: You can't be loving friends with a dinosaur.

ANNIE: What are you then?

LAURIE: A mouse – what else?

ANNIE: Some mouse. With the soul of a tiger.

LAURIE: A mouse. With the soul of a toothless bear.

ANNIE: What's Gus?

LAURIE: Gus? He's a walking, talking, living dolphin.

ANNIE: Amy?

LAURIE: An un-neurotic fallow-deer.

ANNIE: And Dan?

LAURIE: Dan, he's a bit difficult. Rather cool, absent-minded but observant. Orang-utan.

ANNIE: You're a rather sophisticated mole who keeps pushing

up the earth to contract all her chums in the right place at the right time.

AMY: And Margaret – what's she?

LAURIE: Don't know. That's a difficult one.

GUS: Something frightfully attractive but efficient.

LAURIE: A rather earnest chimpanzee. Practical, full of initiative.

ANNIE: Inquisitive?

GUS: I don't think chimpanzees are very attractive.

ANNIE: Neither are moles.

LAURIE: Oh, yes they are. I'd love a mole for Christmas. Perhaps you can buy rubber ones in Amsterdam.

DAN: I don't think orang-utans and what was it, fallow-deer, are very well matched myself. It's the sort of thing a marriage bureau computer would come up with.

ANNIE: I don't think he was very good at all.

LAURIE: Dinosaur was good.

GUS: That was easy.

ANNIE: And you didn't characterize your dinosaur.

LAURIE: I will.

ANNIE: Don't. We know.

LAURIE: Perhaps he's not the same dinosaur to all of us. It's obvious but it may be his little tiny dinosaur's trade trick.

(MARGARET *enters*.)

MARGARET: Was that the waiter?

GUS: Wrong order. Your Perrier's coming.

MARGARET: You rang down?

LAURIE: Yes. We did.

MARGARET: We?

LAURIE: Gus did. It's the waiter – he likes rough trade, don't you, Gus?

(GUS *grins*.)

It's the beatings at that prep school and scrumming down in the mud and being genuinely liked by the men, no?

GUS: I don't think the waiter's exactly my dish. But I quite like the Dutch I think. Seem rather nice up to now.

ANNIE: We've not taken much of a sample. Taxi drivers, receptionists . . .

LAURIE: Air hostesses. International. But I think we're going to like the Dutch. I think we're going to have a lot of time for the Dutch as my horrible mother says.

ANNIE: Only means nasty contraceptives to me. And chocolate.

LAURIE: What, you mean chocolate coated ones? Oh, I see. Talking about that arse aching subject, somebody told me only very bovine girls can munch away at 'em. Air hostesses are made for the pill, for instance. Will you have a pill with your coffee madam, with the airline's compliments. *They* take them. If you've any temperament at all, you just kick around in your stall like a racehorse. I mean you couldn't *give* the pill to racehorses.

DAN: Well, it would be doping them, wouldn't it?

GUS: I say, this is *good*, isn't it.

ANNIE: Don't say it – we're really here.

LAURIE: Well, we are.

(*Knock at door.*)

ANNIE: Come in.

(WAITER *comes in.*)

(*To* LAURIE) Sorry. I thought we'd had enough of your Italiansprache.

GUS: Ah! Good evening. (*As if he hadn't seen the* WAITER *before.*)

WAITER: Sir. (*He puts things down.*)

(*Pause.*)

GUS: Where would you recommend us all to eat on our first night in Amsterdam?

WAITER: It depends on what you have in mind.

GUS: Well, what we have in mind is absolutely the best, not necessarily the most expensive or the most famous. I mean: what would you suggest?

WAITER: It's difficult, sir. There are many excellent places to dine.

AMY: I've got a typed list here, Gus. More or less in order.

GUS: I just thought he might –

LAURIE: I should forget it.

GUS: What?

LAURIE: Amy's well trained. She always gets out a list of the six-supposed best restaurants for K. L. I've often wondered what he'd have done if his surname had been Youn or Yeo or Yarrow.

GUS: Why?

LAURIE: We'd have called him K. Y.

ANNIE: *You* would.

GUS: What's K. Y.?

LAURIE: Gosh, these prep schools were tough weren't they? Or did you use Matron's vaseline? You *do* like it rough.

GUS: Oh!

(WAITER *goes out.*)

LAURIE: Oh. You know what its legitimate, well intended use is? Cleaning surgical instruments. Well, you remember that assistant K. L. had a couple of years ago . . .

ANNIE: What happened to him?

LAURIE: Stepped on the trap door in front of the desk one day I suppose. Anyway . . .

MARGARET: I don't remember him.

LAURIE: Yes, you do. English faggot he picked up in Hollywood. About thirty-five, all tight pants and white socks and greying hair.

MARGARET: Oh, and that expression . . .

LAURIE: Yes, I think you called him the frozen Madonna. I called him Sibyl. He had a crown of sibillants over his head. He sounded like a walking snake pit. I mean, you could even hear him from one end of the Crush Bar at Covent Garden to the other – *packed*. So, Sibyl told me he went into this chemist and there was this other faggot behind the counter. He says: very dignified: can I have a tube of K.Y. please? The assistant doesn't say a word, wraps up package, gives it to him. Then as he drops his change into his palm, he says . . . 'Have fun.' And Sibyl said 'I looked and said "What? Cleaning my surgical instrument?" '

MARGARET: Now, listen, I think Gus is quite right, we should have a talk about what we're going to do and then make a decision.

ANNIE: That could take hours.

MARGARET: Well, it mustn't. This is our first evening. We've made all this effort to get here and go through all these elaborate conspiracies not to let K. L. know where we are. Amy may have lost her job. *And* we haven't got all that much time.

LAURIE: I wonder where we'll all sit down and do this again.

ANNIE: If you'd said 'when' I'd have belted you.

GUS: Tomorrow. Tomorrow.

MARGARET: Oh, come on. Amy, let's look at your list. I don't think we want to go anywhere too ambitious tonight.

GUS: All right, Margaret?

MARGARET: I just think we've been travelling and getting out of London and we should go somewhere fairly quiet but very nice and – oh, I don't know. What have we got here . . .

GUS: We must go to the Rijksmuseum.

MARGARET: Yes, Gus, but not tonight. Rembrandts are for the morning.

ANNIE: And there's the Stedelijk.

DAN: And those Indonesian places where you get thirty great dishes.

AMY: You're greedy.

MARGARET: This sounds the sort of thing: fairly conservative but attractive seventeenth century surroundings, beautiful tables and candles. That sounds like us. Tonight anyway. Laurie, choose.

LAURIE: They all sound good. Like the waiter said. That one you said looks pretty good.

MARGARET: Annie?

ANNIE: Yes. That sounds what we'd like. Gus doesn't like too much noise. He can't talk *and* eat.

DAN: Anything will do us.

MARGARET: Right. Then let's get the concierge to book a table. As there's six of us. And it may be busy.

LAURIE: I'm on holiday, Amy will do it.

MARGARET: We're all on holiday. Why should she do it?

AMY: I'll go and ring down. Give me the list. (*Goes off to bedroom.*)

GUS: Then we'd better talk about tomorrow. What people want to do. I mean some may just want to sleep or do nothing.

MARGARET: No. I don't think that's right. We should try and all do the same thing. Unless . . . Well, we'll see what everyone says.

ANNIE: I can tell you what everyone will do – just talk. About what to do, where to go, what we should wear to do it. And we'll end up getting drunk at lunchtime in the American Bar and eating in the Hotel Dining Room.

LAURIE: Sounds delightful.

GUS: I suppose it isn't very adventurous.

MARGARET: Annie, you'll have to help me.

LAURIE: We're here – that's adventurous.

ANNIE: We'll talk about tomorrow over dinner.

GUS: I'll bring my guide.

MARGARET: Amy!

AMY: Yes?

MARGARET: I know nobody knows we're here but we might get one call for this room. If we do it'll be for me. Perhaps you should tell them. Save confusion.

LAURIE: For you! But we agreed not to tell *anyone* we were here. Except the blooming nanny and she wouldn't get through. Who did you tell, for God's sake?

MARGARET: Gillian.

LAURIE: What did you go and tell your bloody sister we were here for?

MARGARET: Oh, don't be silly. I told her not to tell anyone we're here.

LAURIE: But what did you tell her *for*? She's not one of us.

MARGARET: Isn't she?

LAURIE: Well, she's not really anything to do with K. L. And, besides, she wouldn't like it. She thinks we're all a bit flippant and middle-aged. Not half as middle-aged as her.

MARGARET: Come on. You like her. It's just that she's been having a bad time lately.

LAURIE: What bad time?

MARGARET: I'm not sure. But this affair she's having –

LAURIE: Oh, fleecing another rich duke of £500 and clenching her fists because she didn't lose her cherry until she was twenty-eight and she doesn't think she gives satisfaction

and she plays Bach fugues all night and doesn't wash her
hair because it's all so difficult. Blimey! I think *I* complain.
She needs a public recognition for the suffering she
undergoes, that's all. Then she'll feel better. She should
get the Golden Sanitary Towel Award. K. L. can give it to
her at the Dorchester with all the past winners present.

MARGARET: Well, I told her if things got too bad to ring me.

LAURIE: You didn't say she could come here?

MARGARET: I said if things got too much, for her, I'd get her a
room.

LAURIE: Oh, lovely for your friends.

MARGARET: I don't think anyone will mind.

LAURIE: Did you ask them?

MARGARET: You don't have to ask friends everything.

LAURIE: Perhaps you do. If she comes out, we can all go home.
Why don't she and K. L. get together?

MARGARET: She's my sister, Laurie. I'm not having anything
happen to her. Just for want of a phone call.

LAURIE: She won't do anything to herself. Not till it's too late.
Like getting laid.

MARGARET: I love her.

LAURIE: You can. Don't expect your friends to.

GUS: Poor girl. What is it?

LAURIE: She's just a star wrecker of other people's coveted,
innocent little weekends, that's all.

GUS: Oh, if she turns up, we'll look after her. She can't spoil
anything. It's all right.

ANNIE: Of course it is. I know how to deal with Gillian. Put her
to bed, that's the best thing.

LAURIE: It's a long way to come to go to bed. I mean, I know
people go to New York for haircuts –

MARGARET: Let's not argue, darling. I'm sure it won't happen.
She doesn't want to worry me.

LAURIE: She wants to worry everybody.

ANNIE: Listen, Laurie, darling. We're together. We've got days
ahead. No one knows where we are. Except your daft
nanny. Now –

GUS: She's right. Oh, I'm sure that restaurant's first class and

tomorrow we'll do just as we like and go round the
Leidseplein and Rembrandtsplein and the discotheques
and clubs . . .

ANNIE: Drink up, Laurie. You'll feel better.

LAURIE: I shall, I shall. I feel better already.

GUS: Old K. L. wouldn't like this at all. He'd have wanted to be
out on the streets by now. Not just sitting around talking.
What *would* he do?

ANNIE: Oh, exhaust a list three times as long as Amy's in half
the time. Play games into the night. Games with victims.

GUS: I mean he'd hate this. Just us: talking among ourselves.

LAURIE: Well, as we're all here because of him, because of him,
let's drink to him. Don't go yet, Amy. Ladies and
gentlemen, to our absent friend.

MARGARET: What's the time?

AMY: Six o'clock.

GUS: He must have rung somebody by now.

MARGARET: Perhaps we should have a little zizz before we go
out to dinner.

ANNIE: Good idea.

GUS: He may not know we're *all* gone yet.

LAURIE: Not together, anyway.

ANNIE: I should think he'll go off to Paris or something.
Anything. And when we get back just manage to make
us feel foolish. We'll just say we went away for the
weekend. Do we have to tell him everything? What am I
saying?

MARGARET: What about Amy?

ANNIE: That's up to her.

LAURIE: Oh, he'll be adroit. But he'll also be maladroit. He
won't be able to resist trying to discover where we've been
and who with.

ANNIE: Perhaps he just won't care. As you said, it's not exactly
his idea of fun. God, he'd be pleased and amused.

LAURIE: Oh, he'll appear to be innocent, rational, ill-used.
Slightly impatient.

GUS: The trouble is he creates excitement.

LAURIE: Not half enough.

GUS: Perhaps we're all second rate and need second rate excitement, sort of heats one's inadequacies.

LAURIE: He takes nothing out of the air round *his* head. Only us. Insinuates his grit into all the available oysters. And if ever any tiny pearls should appear from these tight, invaded creatures, he whips off with them, appropriates them and strings them together for his own necklace. And the pearls have to be switched or changed about. Otherwise the trick, the oyster rustling, would be transparent and the last thing he wants made known is his own function or how he goes about it. Where does he get the damned energy and duplicity? Where? He's tried to split us up but here we are in Amsterdam. He has made himself the endless object of speculation. Useful to him but humiliating for us. Well, no more, my friend. We will no longer be useful to you and be put up and put down. We deserve a little better, not much but better. We have been your friends. Your stock in trade is marked down *and* your blackmailing sneering, your callousness, your malingering, your emotional gun-slinging, your shooting in the dark places of affection. You trade on the forbearance, kindliness and talent of your friends. Go on, go on playing the big market of all those meretricious ambition hankers, plodding hirelings, grafters and intriguers. I simply hope tonight that you are alone – I know you won't be. But I hope, at least, you will feel alone, alone as I feel it, as we all in our time feel it, without burdening our friends. I hope the G.P.O. telephone system is collapsed, that your chauffeur is dead and the housekeeper drunk and that there isn't one con-man, camp follower, eunuch, pimp, mercenary, or procurer of all things possible or one globe trotting bum boy at your side to pour you a drink on this dark January evening . . .

ANNIE: Well – Amen.

GUS: Gosh – it's started to snow.

LAURIE: I think I'm the only one who believed all that. Good, all the better. We can get snowed up.

MARGARET: Well, I'm going to have a zizz.

GUS: Yes. I should. And we can discuss the alts later.

LAURIE: Oh, yes we'll discuss them.

MARGARET: Laurie?

LAURIE: Just finish this.

MARGARET: We don't want to go out too late.

AMY: I'll book the table.

(*They go to their rooms.*)

ANNIE: Think I'll have one too.

LAURIE: Finish your drink first. I am glad it's snowing. How I hate holidays. Those endless, clouded days by the pool even when it's blazing sun. Do you remember doing it? All together – at K. L.'s villa? We drank everything you could think of from breakfast onwards after that vile French coffee. The deadly chink of ice in steaming glasses all day. Luxury, spoiled people. Lounging together, basting themselves with comfort, staring into pools. A swimming pool is a terrible thing to look into on a holiday. It's no past and no future. You can stare into a stream or a river or a ditch. Who wouldn't rather die in a ditch than in a pool? I'm too fat for pools and the pretty girls with their straps down and their long legs just make me long for something quite different. I always want someone to write me long, exhilarating love-letters when I lie there with the others . . . A handwritten envelope by your towel, curling up.

GUS: We didn't get on too well that time, did we? I'm sure it wasn't our fault.

ANNIE: We played too many games – too many bloody games, expected too much of the sun and each other and disappointed K. L. . . .

GUS: He asked us all again.

LAURIE: Yes. I read somewhere that one of those communications people, the men who tell you what it is we're all feeling now because of *the* media, said that marriage and romanticism was out. At least with the young people.

ANNIE: I suppose it was on the way out when we came in.

LAURIE: I wonder where we ought to go to live. All those

sleepy-eyed young mice squealing love, love. Scudding into one another, crawling over each other, eyes too weak for bright light, tongues lapping softly . . . all for love, a boy's tail here, a girl's tail there, litters of them.

DAN: Think I'll take a look at my things. (*He goes out.*)

GUS: Is he all right?

ANNIE: Yes. You know Dan.

LAURIE: I think he may be a very violent man.

GUS: Dan?

LAURIE: Fools make him suffer. So he paints or reads a book.

ANNIE: Or goes into his fallow-deer.

LAURIE: Don't blame him.

GUS: Well, perhaps you'd better come with your whatever-I-was.

ANNIE: Yes.

GUS: So, shall we say seven-forty-five? First drink. Well, not first drink, really.

LAURIE: Nineteen-forty-five hours. First drink.

GUS: Good. Where's my street guide? (*He goes.*)

LAURIE: Ought to have a bath I suppose.

ANNIE: Not sleepy?

LAURIE: Yes. I wish I could live alone. Do you?

ANNIE: No. I never have.

LAURIE: I have sometimes. It can be all right for weeks on end even. But then. You have to crawl out of the well. Just a circle of light and your own voice and your own effort . . . People underestimate Gus I think.

ANNIE: So do I.

LAURIE: Do you think *you* do?

ANNIE: I don't think so.

LAURIE: He doesn't exhilarate you like K. L.?

ANNIE: No.

LAURIE: No. Gus has created himself. Thinks he's nobody, thinks he behaves like it. Result: himself.

ANNIE: Do you think Margaret's all right?

LAURIE: No.

ANNIE: Can I do anything?

LAURIE: She doesn't like being pregnant.

ANNIE: Who does? A few mooish ladies.

LAURIE: She feels invaded, distorted. About to be destroyed.

ANNIE: Why do you both do it then? Was it the same with the others?

LAURIE: I thought we might get pleasure from it. She thought I would get pleasure.

ANNIE: And you haven't?

LAURIE: Perhaps they're like holidays or hotels.

ANNIE: No. Not hotels. You couldn't live without them.

LAURIE: I love Gus very much. I think he really believes most people are better than him . . . I only suspect it.

ANNIE: He loves you.

LAURIE: Good. Try not to be too restless. Don't do that. What were we all doing this time last year? I mean were we all together or separate?

ANNIE: Separate.

LAURIE: I wonder *what* we were doing. We'll have a good evening. I feel better already. The snow's stopped.

ANNIE: Good. Seven-forty-five then. Try and kip. (*She kisses him lightly.*)

LAURIE: I will. And you, Annie. And you.

(*She goes to her room, taking her handbag. The three doors are closed.* LAURIE *looks out of the window.*)

(*Curtain.*)

ACT TWO

The same. Two evenings later. They are all in the sitting room,
looking much more relaxed, enjoying the First Drink of the Evening.

GUS: Well, what's the schedule for this evening?

MARGARET: I don't care.

AMY: Neither do I. Everywhere's been good.

LAURIE: I know. Isn't it weird?

ANNIE: Why shouldn't they be?

GUS: Yes, well if we came up with an absolute dud at this stage
we could hardly complain.

MARGARET: I must say that list of yours has been infallible.

LAURIE: Brilliant.

DAN: All smashing.

GUS: Not a dud. I say, we really have had quite a time, haven't
we? Friday evening seems weeks away. So does K. L. Right
after the first evening. Not a foot wrong. We're jolly lucky.

LAURIE: I mean even that Indonesian place was quite funny.

DAN: Actually, it was a 'lovely feast of colour'.

MARGARET: All those dishes. How many do you think we
actually got through?

AMY: I think Dan had a bit of the whole thirty or whatever it
was.

LAURIE: Still looks as lean and clean as a brass rail.

MARGARET: And we got Laurie round to the Rijksmuseum,
without too much bitterness.

LAURIE: I felt at home in all that non-conformist gothic.

ANNIE: And there *were* the Rembrandts.

LAURIE: Yes. We needed a drink after that. I keep thinking of
him watching his house being sold up. All those objects, all
those pieces and possessions got with sweat, all going. K.
L. would have enjoyed that.

ANNIE: Don't be unfair.

LAURIE: And his child dead. What was his name? Titus?

ANNIE: I liked the place with the bank managers dancing
together.

LAURIE: That's because you danced with that chamber-maid from Hanover.

ANNIE: It seemed only fair. It's a bit churlish to just go and gawp like a tourist. I think you were very mean not to dance.

LAURIE: No one I fancied.

MARGARET: Annie's right. You got frightfully stuffy and absent minded all of a sudden.

LAURIE: I was worried about you and that lady in the black dinner jacket.

MARGARET: You didn't show it. I don't know what I'd have done if Gus hadn't protected me.

ANNIE: She really fancied you, didn't she?

AMY: I'll say. I've never seen anything like it.

DAN: She was just queer for pregnant girls.

MARGARET: I'd have thought that would have put her off.

GUS: Not at all.

ANNIE: What about tonight?

GUS: Yes. We must make a decision.

ANNIE: Where's the list, Amy?

DAN: Let's have a look. What are the alts?

GUS: We've still got lunch tomorrow.

LAURIE: Why don't we stay the extra day?

ANNIE: We've done all that.

MARGARET: Yes. Amy must get back.

LAURIE: But why? I don't see it.

MARGARET: Because she doesn't want to lose her well paid job, which she also likes.

ANNIE: And she has obligations.

LAURIE: What obligations? You don't have obligations to monsters.

DAN: What about this? I don't know . . .

AMY: Why don't we go to the place we went to on the first evening?

LAURIE: That was wonderful.

DAN: At least we know it's first rate.

GUS: You don't think that's being a bit unadventurous do you?

ANNIE: Yes. Let's chance our arm.

LAURIE: Why should we?

MARGARET: I agree. We should try something different.

DAN: What for? Not that I mind.

LAURIE: You girls are so ambitious. Even if it's for others.

GUS: Really escaped, didn't we? I haven't laughed so much for months. Have you, darling? You said last night.

LAURIE: I still think we should go back a day later.

MARGARET: No.

LAURIE: Amy could fix it.

AMY: Of course. Why don't you? I could go. It seems silly when you're having such fun. Dan, you could stay with them.

ANNIE: I think we've voted on that one.

LAURIE: Oh no we haven't. I wonder when we'll all sit down like this again.

MARGARET: Damn it, we've done it enough times before.

ANNIE: Sure, we'll do it again.

LAURIE: Yes. But when? How? Where? How do we arrange it? I don't want to go back to London.

ANNIE: Who does.

LAURIE: No. I mean it. What is there there for any of us? We should all go and live together somewhere.

MARGARET: Where, for instance? Somewhere you didn't have to pick up the phone for room service.

LAURIE: We need a broken down Victorian castle or something, oh with all the plumbing and jazz we wanted. But lots of space around us. Acres of land around us, empty, chipped and scarred still by Roman legions.

ANNIE: Sounds freezing.

LAURIE: What would you prefer, a sonic bang up your lush southern parkland? We could do what we liked, have lots of children.

GUS: There aren't many of us.

LAURIE: We'll think of some others.

ANNIE: But who?

GUS: K. L. would find out about it.

LAURIE: Let him. You'd all come, wouldn't you?

ANNIE: What about staff?

MARGARET: Good question.

DAN: You'd need lots of nannies.

LAURIE: Yes. Well . . . we'd get ex-stewardesses from El Fag Airlines. They're absolutely wonderful nannies. Poor old things will work for absolutely nothing if you get a really rejected one.

AMY: And the rest of the staff?

LAURIE: They must be people we know. People who'd fit in with everyone. I would learn carpentry. I've always wanted to do that. And brick laying. I could work on the house. Gus knows all about electricity. Margaret could drive. Except we wouldn't use the car much. Annie's the great horse expert. We could use them and maybe hunt if we got over our green belt liberal principles. And Dan could, well he could just paint.

GUS: Who do we know?

LAURIE: Well, we ought to make a list. That's one thing, do you realize, we've escaped from Margaret? My relatives and all those layabout people I pay to look after us. So that, the theory being, we are able to do other things, not bother with inessentials because we've *made* it.

ANNIE: I thought your Nannie was good?

MARGARET: She's very good.

LAURIE: Only she doesn't look after *me*. She looks after two creatures who don't even know yet they're being waited on.

ANNIE: I thought you didn't like being waited on.

LAURIE: I don't. But if I pay for it at home I expect it.

AMY: They're only tiny babies.

LAURIE: Darling, don't say 'tiny babies'. All babies are tiny compared to people. Even if they had to be landed like killer sharks, they're still tiny. What I hate about them, it's like my relations and K. L., you always, you're expected to adjust to *their* mood, their convenience, their bad back, or I-don't-know-I'm-just-depressed. What are they going to be like when I ring the bell, when I open their letters. They never anticipate *you*.

ANNIE: Gus never anticipates for himself.

MARGARET: How?

ANNIE: He's always taken by surprise by situations and people's reactions.

MARGARET: Laurie rehearses them all.

GUS: Am I?

ANNIE: He was cutting some trees down just by the pond one day. And he'd keep stepping back. Just about a foot away from the pond. 'You will mind the pond' I'd say to him. 'What? Oh. Yes.' Then he'd do it again. 'Don't forget the pond.' 'No . . . all right' . . . Always a bit surprised. I watched him for two days and then I thought I can't go on. I'll leave him to it. He missed it by inches for a whole morning. And then fell in.

GUS: Yes. That's quite right. I did feel surprised when it happened.

LAURIE: The mistake is to feel guilty. That's always been my mistake. He's driving you about because you're cleverer than he is. And though I say it, he can't even drive as well as I can. That's why he's a servant, she says. Well, why can't he be a good one, I say. I wouldn't want him to wait on me. I don't know though. Why do it at all? There are third rate servants. Perhaps I've got the ones I deserve, like the relatives I deserve.

DAN: As the old saying goes, we're all bloody servants.

LAURIE: You're right. Deliver the goods or the chopper. I suppose that's right. Do we deliver the goods?

ANNIE: If someone's cooked you a meal decently and woken you and been able to smile as well, that would be delivering the goods.

MARGARET: It would.

LAURIE: *Are* we spoiled?

ANNIE: Staying in a luxury hotel on the continent because you're afraid of your servants?

LAURIE: That does make it sound stupid. Very.

GUS: But that wasn't the main reason.

LAURIE: Yes. I just send my nasty relations a cheque. I never see them. They certainly don't want to see me.

DAN: What are they?

LAURIE: Retired rotten, grafting publicans, shop assistants, exwaitresses. They live on and on. Having hernias and arthritic hips and strokes. But they go on: writing poisonous letters to one another. Complaining and wheedling and paying off the same old scores with the same illiterate signs. 'Dear Laurie, thank you very kindly for the cheque. It was most welcome and I was able to get us one or two things we'd had to go without for quite some time, what with me having been off work all this time and the doctor sends me to the hospital twice a week. They tell me it's improving but I can't say I feel much improvement. How are you, old son? Old son? We saw your name in the paper about something you were doing the other day and the people next door said they thought you were on the telly one night but we didn't see it, and Rose won't buy the television papers so we always switch on to the same programme. Rose doesn't get any better, I'm afraid. I brought her a quarter bottle the other day with your kind remittance which served to buck her up a bit. Your Auntie Grace wrote and said she'd heard Margaret was having another baby. That must be very nice for you both. We send our best wishes to you both and the other little ones. Hope you're all well. Must close now as I have to take down the front room curtains and wash them as Rose can't do it any longer, but you know what she is. Bung ho and all the very best. Excuse writing but my hand is still bad. Ever. Your Uncle Ted. P.S. Rose says Auntie Grace said something about a letter from your mother which she sent on but I'm afraid she sent it back unopened. She just refuses to pass any comment. She told me not to say anything about it to you but I thought I'd just – *PASS IT ON TO YOU!*

(*He gestures towards them.*)

Pass *that* on!

MARGARET: Oh, don't talk about them. They're so depressing.

ANNIE: They sound quite funny.

LAURIE: They're not quite funny, Annie. They're greedy, calculating, stupid and totally without questions.

MARGARET: They're just boring.

LAURIE: They're not that even. They're not even boring. Now *I* am boring. I am quite certainly the most boring man you have ever met in your lives. I see you're not going to contradict me so I won't let you.

GUS: As a matter of fact, I was going to contradict you because I am infinitely more boring than you could ever be even on a bad day. Not that I think you could be even then.

MARGARET: You're both drunk.

LAURIE: No, we're not. At least Gus may be a bit. I am just straightforwardly boring. Look, some people when they're drunk are dreadfully boring, especially when they're supposed to be freewheeling and amusing. Now, drink doesn't do that to me. Drink doesn't change one, does it?

ANNIE: Not much.

LAURIE: There you are. I am just as boring drunk as I am sober. There is no appreciable difference. If I could tell you, if I could, how much I bore myself. I am really fed up with the whole subject . . . I am a meagre, pilfering bore.

DAN: Well, don't be a bore and enlarge on it any more.

LAURIE: You're drunk! (*Laughs*.) I say Dan's drunk. We really are having a time . . .

MARGARET: Did you see Terry had married that girl friend of K. L.'s?

ANNIE: Yes.

DAN: Not that horrible Tina Whatsaname?

AMY: The same.

LAURIE: That's the movie business. Where the producer persuades the director to marry *his* crumpet.

MARGARET: He hasn't got a very strong character.

LAURIE: What does that mean?

ANNIE: I think he'll survive her.

LAURIE: I mean K. L.'s got a *strong* character. Hasn't he? Does it mean simply someone who can impose their will on others? Can be politic and full of strategy!

MARGARET: You know what I mean about Terry.

LAURIE: I saw something very interesting the other day. No, somebody told me.

AMY: About air hostesses?

LAURIE: No, about nurses. Is this boring? That's the window sign of a bore. He always says to you at some point, is this boring?

ANNIE: Fascinating.

LAURIE: Yes, well I think it probably is. Because it may affect us all in some way. Well, apparently if you've got the real incurables, the carcinoma or some dance like that going on inside you, the doctors very sensibly start pumping things into you at the right time and make you as thumpingly stupid as possible. Unfortunately, the nursing profession being imperfect, like El Fag Airlines or any other concern contains a considerable and dangerous fifth column of popish ladies in starched collars and cuffs who'll fail to give you your shot of blissful dope come six o'clock. Nothing to call on in the small house but a couple of codeine and an Irish lilt. So, do you know what they do, the clever ones, the doctors? Well, if they should decide they'd rather a patient didn't lie in agony, they insist on a roster of Australian nurses. They're the best. The Aussies. They'll give you enough for you and your horse if you tell 'em. So, if you ever wake up after you've been in hospital for a little while and one day a little cobber voice says to you 'And how are we today, Mr so-and-so?' you know you've scored.

ANNIE: Yes. That's better than the lady pilot.

LAURIE: Annie?

ANNIE: What?

LAURIE: You're called Annie and I'm called Laurie.

ANNIE: What are we supposed to do?

MARGARET: Hadn't you thought of it before?

LAURIE: No. Isn't that odd? Had you?

GUS: Not me. I don't think. Annie mentioned it to me one day.

LAURIE: Dan?

DAN: I've got used to it. The trouble with being spontaneous, or even trying to be, and I think one can, the trouble is it does put you at the mercy of others. That's not the same thing as being a bore.

LAURIE: What do we ever go back to England for? What do we do it for?

ANNIE: I thought you never wanted to come away.

LAURIE: It's the bitchiest place on earth.

MARGARET: That's the name of the place you come from. Now, what have we decided?

GUS: About what?

LAURIE: We haven't decided anything. Um? (*Holds her hand.*)

MARGARET: I mean where are we going for our last night?
    (*Knock on door.*)

LAURIE: You didn't order anything, did you?

GUS: No.

AMY: Probably the maid with all those clean sheets for when we go.

ANNIE: Come in.
    (*The door handle rattles.*)

GUS: No key. Well, if it's K. L., he's too late. We've done it.
    (*He goes to the door, opens it. A girl of about thirty, GILLIAN.*)

LAURIE: Gillian.

MARGARET: Darling.

GILLIAN: I'm sorry. I should have warned you.

MARGARET: (*To her*) My darling, what's the matter? You look ill.

GILLIAN: I didn't have a chance. I'm all right. I couldn't remember how long you were staying.

MARGARET: Why didn't you ring me? Come in and sit down. Take your coat off.

GILLIAN: No. I think I'll keep it on.

LAURIE: Oh, sit down and take the bloody thing off. It's hot in here.

GILLIAN: I'm sorry. I should have rung first. I couldn't find the number.

LAURIE: Just the name of the hotel?

MARGARET: Laurie, give her a drink.

GILLIAN: No, I'll have a Perrier.

LAURIE: Don't tell me *you're* pregnant.

MARGARET: Give her one.

GILLIAN: Just a small one, very small.

LAURIE: Did you bring your own nose dropper?

GILLIAN: Well, how are you? Have you had a good time?

LAURIE: Fanfuckingtastick! Never stopped laughing, have we?

AMY: We've had a marvellous time. Why didn't you come?

GUS: I think you'd have enjoyed it. We've done quite a lot in an easy sort of way, done what we wanted –

LAURIE: After discussion.

GUS: After discussion. And all the places we've been to have been tremendous fun – thanks to Amy's list.

DAN: I liked that place like the Brasserie at Joe Lyons where everyone sang Tipperary – in English.

GUS: Yes, I think you'd have liked it – don't you, darling?

ANNIE: I don't think she'd have liked that place much, Margaret didn't.

GUS: Oh well, Margaret didn't feel so hot for a while.

MARGARET: I just can't stand the smell of beer and all those awful swilling, ugly looking people.

ANNIE: I think the men enjoyed it rather more.

AMY: I loved it.

DAN: You even sang – as usual.

LAURIE: What do you mean – the men liked it?

ANNIE: I mean you sometimes try and fumble your way back to childhood while we watch and get impatient and wait for you to stop.

LAURIE: Perhaps you should try coming along.

ANNIE: Yes. We found two really remarkable restaurants, we discovered a new game, or rather Laurie invented one, and Gus had us in stitches telling us stories about his regiment in the war, with two versions to every story, one tragic and one comic, the tragic one always being comic and the comic one always tragic. Laurie's starting a new airline and Dan's putting out a new scent. They'll tell you.

GILLIAN: I'd like to go to the Rijksmuseum.

LAURIE: There are other things here beside Rembrandt. We needed a drink after him. Drink?

GILLIAN: Thanks.

LAURIE: Too much?

GILLIAN: No fine.

LAURIE: Only I don't want you leaving any because I'm an impoverished writer with a wife, children, useless servants, a family of ageless begging letter writers, a trencherman nanny and three dogs as big as you. I haven't yet found my voice, I write too much not enough, I have no real popular appeal, I take an easy route to solutions –

ANNIE: Stop being paranoid.

LAURIE: Why? If a man is ill he isn't a hypochondriac. And if he's attacked he's –

MARGARET: Oh, shut up, Laurie. Can't you see there's something the matter?

LAURIE: Who with? Annie?

GILLIAN: I told you – honestly – everything's fine. I just thought I'd come suddenly.

MARGARET: Darling, I've known you all my life. Something's very wrong. Do you want to tell me?

LAURIE: Oh, leave her be.

MARGARET: I know her. You don't.

GILLIAN: I wish I *had* come. You all look as if you've had a super time.

LAURIE: I'll bet we do – now. (*To* MARGARET.) You're right – it's not a very convincing performance.

GILLIAN: Tell me what else you've been doing. It does sound good. I've always wanted to come to Amsterdam.
(*She leans forward avidly. The others decline visibly. She has broken the fragile spell.*)
Did you go on the canal?

DAN: Yes.

GILLIAN: And that modern art gallery, whatever it's called. Can't pronounce Dutch. And the harboar, or where is it, where all the tarts sit in the windows looking like dolls. This hotel looks splendid. They were terribly nice downstairs. They seemed to know all about you lot up here. They smiled the moment I said who I wanted. Do you think I can get a room? Perhaps I could get one down the hall. All I need is a little room. I suppose I could come in here with you most of the time. Don't let me interrupt what you're doing. I'll just finish this and change, I think. Perhaps I could have a bath in your room Margaret, if Laurie doesn't mind. What time are you going out? I don't want to hold you up. I needn't unpack. Unless you're dressing up. I could change in your room though and see about the room later. Do you know where you're going tonight?

GUS: We were – just discussing the alts. Perhaps we should go somewhere you'd like.

GILLIAN: Don't change anything because of me. It's my fault for turning up like this. Just do what you would have done by yourselves. Please don't let me change anything . . .

LAURIE: Gillian, for Christ's sake burst into tears . . .

(*Slowly she crumples and they watch her.*)

GILLIAN: Please . . . take no notice. I'll get a room down the hall.

(MARGARET *pulls her arm around her and leads her into her bedroom and closes the door.*)

LAURIE: Drink anyone?

ANNIE: Yes, please.

GUS: Poor girl.

DAN: Just as well we're going tomorrow.

AMY: I wonder what it is.

LAURIE: Oh, either her lover's married and can't or won't get a divorce or he *isn't* married and she can't bring herself to offer herself up to something total. Variations on some crap like that. But I tell you, she's not going to blight our weekend. We've had ourselves something we want to have and we made it work and she's not going to walk in here on the last night and turn it all into a Golden Sanitary Towel Award Presentation.

ANNIE: I'm afraid she's done it.

LAURIE: Well, we mustn't let her. Look, Gus, flip through that list and we'll decide where to go and either she can come with us and put on a happy face or –

ANNIE: Oh, not that.

LAURIE: No, I agree – the miserable one's better. You and Dan can talk to her a bit about the Rembrandts and painting and Dutch domestic architecture and what Marshal McLuhan said to Lévi-Strauss while they were on the job. Otherwise, she can just shut up and leave us to it. Or

Margaret can stay with her arms around her in the
bedroom all evening.

GUS: That's not very fair on poor old Margaret.

LAURIE: Her sister's not being very fair to us.

ANNIE: That's not her fault.

AMY: No. Dan will talk to her and cheer her up. He's good at
that.

LAURIE: Why should he?

DAN: Sure. I don't mind.

ANNIE: Why should we? We do. Listen, Margaret will listen to
her and calm her down. Then we'll take her out with us.
She'll be all right.

LAURIE: But will we be? If I didn't know I'd think it was a last-
minute joke of K. L.'s on us. Blimey, she's turned it into
Agony Junction all right. Look at Gus. Dan, have some
more in there.

GUS: Oh, she's not such a bad girl.

DAN: She's brought London with her . . .

GUS: Perhaps we should go to the place we went on the first
night, anyway.

LAURIE: I suppose so.

GUS: I think she'd like it. It's quiet and the food – did you have
those herrings?

AMY: My chicken in that pastry thing was wild.

LAURIE: Oh, she'll be sick or pushing her food away or leaving
it and pretending she's enjoying it and filling us up with
guilt and damned responsibility. Damn her, we've just got
together again, she's an odd man out, we haven't got time
to take off for her coltish, barren, stiff-upper quivering lips
and, and klart-on. Am I unsympathetic?

ANNIE: Yes.

LAURIE: I'm sorry . . . all of you . . .

DAN: Not your fault.

GUS: Not anybody's fault.

LAURIE: Baudelaire said: can't remember now.

GUS: Someone said the other day: 'What do you do if you
live in San Francisco, you're twenty-one and you go
bald . . .'

LAURIE: He said, I know, 'beauty was something he only
 wanted to see once.'

ANNIE: She's quite attractive.

LAURIE: Gillian?

ANNIE: Um.

GUS: Very.

AMY: Not as much as Margaret.

ANNIE: She's prettier than she thinks, that's the trouble.

LAURIE: She should take some pretty pills. So should I. I'm all
 water. Heavy. Bit of underwater fire like North Sea gas.
 Not much earth or air either . . . What a *precious* remark –
 that's her fault. Did I tell you about the boy with the
 crocodile shoes?

ANNIE: No, but it's too long. I've heard it.

DAN: Tell them the one about the nun in the enclosed order.

GUS: Wish I could remember jokes.

LAURIE: Young nun enters an enclosed order with a strict vow
 of silence. The silence can only be broken once every
 three years with two words. So: after three years the girl
 goes to the Mother Superior, who says: 'Now my child,
 three years have passed since you entered the order. You
 have kept your vow of silence. It is now your privilege to
 say any two words you wish to me.' So the young nun
 pauses painfully, opens her mouth and says:
 'Uncomfortable beds.' So the Mother Superior says,
 'Right, my child, and now you may go back to your work.'
 Three more years pass and she comes before the Mother
 Superior again. 'You have observed the rule of this order
 for three more years. It is your privilege to say two words
 to me – if you wish.' So the nun hesitates and then says:
 'Bad food.' 'Very well, go back to your work, my child.'
 Another three years pass and the nun is brought in front
 of the Mother Superior again. 'Well, my child, three more
 years have passed. Is there anything you wish to say to
 me?' The nun raises her eyes and, after an effort, she
 whispers: 'I want to go home.' 'Well,' says the Mother
 Superior, 'I'm *glad* to hear it. You've done nothing but
 bitch ever since you got here . . .'

ANNIE: Why don't you go in and see how Margaret's
managing?

LAURIE: I don't think I'm what's wanted in there. Margaret will
call if she wants me.

ANNIE: Are you sure?

GUS: Shall I knock?

LAURIE: No, leave them. Did you like her, Amy?

AMY: Gillian? I don't really know her. I felt sorry for her . . .
when she was sitting there trying not to spoil everything.

LAURIE: But doing it pretty well all the same.

DAN: Why did you ask Amy?

LAURIE: Because Amy likes nearly everyone.

ANNIE: You make her sound imperceptive, which she's not.

LAURIE: No. I think she is blessed with loving kindness . . .

DAN: So – we've decided on the first night place? . . . Laurie?

LAURIE: What?

ANNIE: Yes.

GUS: Well, we thought so, Dan. Unless you'd like to suggest
something else. We thought . . .

ANNIE: Discussion.

DAN: Perhaps we'd better start getting ready slowly. Amy?

AMY: Yes. Right. Now.

LAURIE: You two really are a lecherous couple.

AMY: Me?

LAURIE: Me? Yes, you two. You toddle off to the bedroom
every evening twenty minutes before the rest of us.

ANNIE: Good for them.

LAURIE: Perhaps you simply organize these things better. Is
that it, Dan? I'd never thought of it before. Perhaps,
working efficient secretaries make the ideal wives. I mean it
does need fitting in with everything else. How long have
you been married?

AMY: Nine years.

GUS: Marvellous. Is it really?

ANNIE: Nine isn't so long. Some people have golden weddings.

LAURIE: Golden Sanitary Towel Weddings. I think Dan's
pretty formidable. I bet if you looked at his sexual graph of
desire his would be steady, unchanging up there like

Nelson on his column and there'd be mine bumping about among the lions.

DAN: Wish it were true.

LAURIE: Well, get along then.

AMY: Actually, I wanted to write a couple of postcards.

GUS: *Are* you? I don't think you should write postcards from here somehow. I haven't. Deliberately. It seemed like giving evidence that we'd ever been here all of us.

LAURIE: Yes. Well, go and do it, whatever it is. Only don't keep us waiting.

ANNIE: Oh, who kept who waiting last night?

LAURIE: I did.

AMY: See you then.

GUS: Seventeen-forty-five.

(*They go, closing the door behind them. Pause.*)

What'll you do when you get back?

LAURIE: Don't know.

GUS: No, *we* weren't sure. Were we, darling?

LAURIE: I've tried not to think about it.

GUS: Perhaps we should all have dinner the first night back. Where could we go?

LAURIE: I'll ask Margaret.

GUS: That new place you took us to the other week was nice. I wonder if K. L. discovered it.

LAURIE: Hope not.

ANNIE: I expect he has.

GUS: I wonder if he'll ring when we get in.

LAURIE: Sure to.

GUS: Perhaps he'll wait for one of us to ring him.

LAURIE: He can.

GUS: Well, it worked . . . Are you going to work as soon as you get back?

LAURIE: If I can. You?

GUS: I've got to. I should be there tomorrow really. Do you know what you're doing next weekend?

LAURIE: Margaret would know.

GUS: Perhaps we could do something.

LAURIE: Maybe. We'll talk about it on the train . . .

GUS: I think I'll go and have a bath. A *real* bath. I mean. What's the time? Yes, seventeen-forty-five. I'd better book the table hadn't I? Best not disturb Dan.

ANNIE: I'll have one after you.

GUS: What?

ANNIE: A bath, my darling.

GUS: OK. Well, I'll have one first, then I'll run one for you and I can shave while you're in it.

ANNIE: Right.

GUS: You might as well stay and have another drink with old Laurie.

LAURIE: I'm all right. Perhaps she'd like a kip.

ANNIE: Bit late now.

GUS: Do you know what you're going to be wearing this evening?

LAURIE: No. Oh, the same as the first night I expect.

GUS: Yes. I see. I remember. Only it helps me when I make up my mind what to put on. It's that chocolaty mohair kind of thing.

LAURIE: That's the one.

GUS: That's good. Well, fine. See you then.

ANNIE: And, darling – wear your purple tie.

GUS: Are you sure?

ANNIE: It suits you.

GUS: Not too –?

LAURIE: Yes. Divine.

GUS: Oh, all right. Annie gave me that. It's awfully pretty. She's got the most amazing flair and taste in things like men's clothes. In everything, come to that.

LAURIE: Except men.

GUS: Yes. Well, blind spot in us all. I'll call you when I've run the bath, darling. And I'll put some of that oil in, shall I? If there's anything – with Gillian – you know, I can do, give a knock.

LAURIE: Go and have your bath. I want to see you properly turned out for our last night.

GUS: Right.

(*He goes into his room and closes the door. Pause.*)

ANNIE: Are you sure I shouldn't go in to Margaret? Girl stuff.

LAURIE: If you want to.

(*She doesn't move.*)

You haven't been married before, have you?

ANNIE: No.

LAURIE: I have.

ANNIE: It's quite a well known fact.

GUS: Yes. It's like having had a previous conviction . . .

ANNIE: Of course, I lived with people before Gus.

LAURIE: Many?

ANNIE: I don't think so; some would. But I don't think it was inordinate – no. I lived with each one an inordinate time.

LAURIE: I wonder what my other wife thinks of me.

ANNIE: Has she married again?

LAURIE: Twice. I wonder what my name even means to her.

ANNIE: Ever see her?

LAURIE: No. I dread bumping into her somewhere. Even here the other night, I thought I saw her in that smart place.

ANNIE: Why do you dread it?

LAURIE: I don't think she likes me.

ANNIE: Why not?

LAURIE: I imagine I wasn't very kind to her.

ANNIE: Weren't you?

LAURIE: I don't know. I wish I could really remember. I try to. I hope not. But I'm sure I was.

ANNIE: It doesn't mean that *you're* unkind.

LAURIE: Doesn't it?

ANNIE: Oh, come. Just capable of it. Like everyone.

LAURIE: Amy is never unkind.

ANNIE: You don't want to be like Amy.

LAURIE: Don't I?

ANNIE: No . . . It will be all right . . . when we get back.

LAURIE: Yes.

ANNIE: Don't grieve.

LAURIE: Annie. Laurie. I do.

ANNIE: I know.

LAURIE: You live with someone for five, six years. And you begin to feel you don't know them. Perhaps you didn't make the right kind of effort. You have to make choices, adjustments, you have requirements to answer. Then you see someone you love through other eyes. First, one pair of eyes. Then another and more. I was afraid to marry but afraid not to. You see, I'm not really promiscuous. I'm a moulting old bourgeois. I'm not very good at legerdemain affairs . . . Do you like Margaret?

ANNIE: Yes . . . Have you been unfaithful to her?

LAURIE: Yes.

ANNIE: Enjoyable?

LAURIE: Not very.

ANNIE: Often?

LAURIE: No. Not inordinately.

ANNIE: When was the last time?

LAURIE: Six months. Just a few times.

ANNIE: Before that?

LAURIE: Not for ages.

ANNIE: What's ages?

LAURIE: When she was in the nursing home . . .

ANNIE: In the nursing home? You mean, not –

LAURIE: Yes.

ANNIE: I see.

LAURIE: Are you shocked?

ANNIE: No. Surprised . . . Not really.

LAURIE: I thought you might say: men!

ANNIE: You're not men! I'd better go and change.

LAURIE: Gus'll call you. Have some more . . . I've wanted to tell you.

ANNIE: Have you?

LAURIE: No one knows. You won't tell Gus, will you?

ANNIE: I won't tell anyone . . . Why did you want to tell me?

LAURIE: Why? Because . . . to me . . . you have always been the most dashing . . . romantic . . . friendly . . . playful . . . loving . . . impetuous . . . larky . . . fearful . . . detached . . . constant . . . woman I have ever met . . . and I love you . . . I don't know how else one says it . . . one shouldn't . . . and I've always thought you felt . . . perhaps . . . the same about me.

ANNIE: I do.

LAURIE: When we are all away – you are never out of my heart.

ANNIE: Nor you out of mine.

LAURIE: So there it is. It's snowing again . . . I wonder what it'll be like in London.

ANNIE: God knows.

LAURIE: If we were going by plane, I'd say perhaps it'll crash. Or we won't be able to take off.

ANNIE: We'll have longer on the train together.

LAURIE: Together? Yes, and we can all get drunk on the boat.

ANNIE: Perhaps we should change and go on the plane after all. I don't know that I can face the journey with you there . . . sorry. A touch of the Gillians.

LAURIE: A touch of the Annies.

ANNIE: I love you . . . I can never tell you . . .

LAURIE: Thank you for saying it . . . Bless you, Amsterdam. Wouldn't K. L. be furious?

ANNIE: Because it's happened or because he doesn't know?

LAURIE: Both.

ANNIE: I think he'd be envious because it's happened. I fancy he's suspected for a long time.

LAURIE: Do you?

(*She nods.*)

Yes. He doesn't miss much. Do you think Margaret knows?

ANNIE: I think she might. I would.

LAURIE: And Gus?

ANNIE: No.

LAURIE: Good . . . I think we need another . . .

(*He pours for them both. Looks down at her.*)

ANNIE: Don't look at me.

LAURIE: I'm sorry. I shall never be able to come back to this place again.

ANNIE: Which?

LAURIE: Both. The hotel. Amsterdam.

(MARGARET *comes in.*)

ANNIE: How is she?

MARGARET: Oh, she's a little better. Some of it came out and, oh dear, I don't know why some people's lives have to be difficult. I'll tell you about it later. Anyway, she's resting on our bed. I thought she might be able to have a little zizz and then, if she's all right, she can come out with us. If not, I'll stay in with her.

ANNIE: But you can't do that. We must all go out, together, on our last night. You've got to.

MARGARET: Oh, we'll see. We'd better get her a room. Laurie, can you ring down and ask reception if there's a single room down the hall near us she can have?

LAURIE: OK. Like some Perrier?

MARGARET: No, thank you, Laurie, are you all right?

LAURIE: Fine.

MARGARET: No, you're not I can see. He doesn't look well. Does he, Annie?

ANNIE: I think he's just getting a bit sea-sick already.

MARGARET: It's not that. Even Laurie waits till the same day.

LAURIE: Who is it this time?

MARGARET: What? Oh, Gillian. It's too complicated, now.

LAURIE: Nothing's too complicated now.

MARGARET: Darling, I think you started drinking too early. You started right after breakfast . . . Oh, yes, she saw K. L.

LAURIE: Saw him. How?

MARGARET: He asked her round for a drink.

LAURIE: When was this?

MARGARET: Friday.

LAURIE: I never thought he'd ring *her*. She didn't tell him where we'd gone?

MARGARET: Yes, Laurie, I'm afraid she did.

LAURIE: She did! The stupid, dopey mare!

MARGARET: Oh, stop it, Laurie. It doesn't really matter as it's turned out. He didn't ring or *anything* did he?

LAURIE: You mean she told him the hotel, the lot?

MARGARET: You know how clever he is at winkling these things out of people. She said he seemed so concerned about us all, and she was, oh, distraught about her own weekend. He managed to convince her that we'd really want him to know.

LAURIE: Don't tell me she's having an affair with him. They deserve each other. Except he'd spit her out in one bite.

MARGARET: Listen, Laurie, I'm worried about that girl. She's my sister and I love her, and I think she came very close to doing something to herself this weekend.

LAURIE: Don't you believe it. She just models for it. People like her don't go home and do it. They choose a weekend when there's someone likely to come in the flat or they don't take quite enough.

MARGARET: Don't be such a bitch.

LAURIE: Well, I am.

MARGARET: You certainly make the same noises sometimes.

LAURIE: You're sure she didn't spend the weekend with our friend K. L.?

MARGARET: She was all on her own. I should have found out she was feeling like this. I'd have made her come with us.

LAURIE: Nice for us.

MARGARET: Leave her alone. There are some problems you've never had to face.

LAURIE: I should hope so.

(*The telephone in the sitting room rings. They stare at it.*) Who the devil's that?

MARGARET: Well, you'd better answer it.

LAURIE: She hasn't told anyone else where we are?

MARGARET: No. No one. She hasn't spoken to anyone. Well, pick it up.

(ANNIE *does so.*)

ANNIE: Room number . . . what's this one? Three two O. Yes . . . No . . . Just a moment. It's for Amy.

LAURIE: Amy!

ANNIE: Amy! Phone! It's for you.

(*They wait.* AMY *appears putting on her dressing gown.*)

AMY: For me? How do they know?

LAURIE: I'll tell you.

(AMY *picks up the phone.* GILLIAN *appears in the doorway of* MARGARET*'s bedroom.*)

AMY: (*On phone*) Hullo . . . Yes . . . Speaking . . . Oh, hullo, Paul. Yes . . . I see . . . no, wait a moment . . . let me think . . . their number's in a bright green leather book on his desk . . . yes, in the study . . . no, I'll try and get a place earlier . . . no, don't do that . . . Stay there and I'll call you back. (*She puts the phone down.*) That was Paul. K. L.'s chauffeur . . . He's killed himself. He found him half an hour ago.

(*Pause.* DAN *comes in, in dressing gown.*)

LAURIE: How did he find the number?

AMY: It was written on a pad by his desk. By his body.

(LAURIE *starts to pour drinks for them all.*)

I suppose I'd better make some ticket arrangements.

LAURIE: Have a drink first. Here, sit down. Margaret.

(GUS *appears at his door.*)

GUS: Annie? Hullo. I didn't hear someone on the phone, did I?

ANNIE: K. L. has killed himself.

GUS: But how?

AMY: Sleeping pills. Sleeping pills and aspirin.

LAURIE: Come in. Have a drink. You too, Gillian. Dan . . . Sleeping pills, aspirin, bottle of whisky, half a loaf of bread to keep it all down . . . give the housekeeper the weekend off, turn the extension off in your study and lock the front door . . . Well, cheers . . .

(*Silence.*)

AMY: I think I'll talk to them downstairs from my room. Save you having to listen. I expect you'd all like to go back together if I can fix it?

MARGARET: Of course.

DAN: I'll come with you.

(*He follows her to their bedroom door. He says, a little drily:*)

I wonder: if we'll ever come here again?

MARGARET: What – to this hotel?

DAN: To Amsterdam . . .

LAURIE: I shouldn't think so. But I expect we might go somewhere else . . .

(DAN *closes his bedroom door. Curtain.*)

WEST OF SUEZ

CHARACTERS

WYATT GILLMAN	A Writer
FREDERICA	
ROBIN	
EVANGIE	Wyatt's Daughters
MARY	
EDWARD	Frederica's Husband (a pathologist)
ROBERT	Mary's Husband (a teacher)
PATRICK	A Retired Brigadier
CHRISTOPHER	Secretary to Wyatt
ALASTAIR	A Hairdresser
OWEN LAMB	A writer
HARRY	
MRS JAMES	An Interviewer from the Local Newspaper
LEROI	Robin and the Brigadier's Servant
MR DEKKER	American Tourist
MRS DEKKER	American Tourist
JED	American Tourist
TWO ISLANDERS	

First performed at the Royal Court Theatre on 17th August 1971 with the following cast:

WYATT GILLMAN	Ralph Richardson
FREDERICA	Jill Bennett
ROBIN	Patricia Lawrence
EVANGIE	Sheila Ballantine
MARY	Penelope Wilton
EDWARD	Geoffrey Palmer
ROBERT	Frank Wylie
PATRICK	Willoughby Gray
CHRISTOPHER	Nigel Hawthorne
ALASTAIR	Anthony Gardner
OWEN LAMB	Nicholas Selby
HARRY	Peter Carlisle
MRS JAMES	Sheila Burrell
LEROI	Raul Neunie
MR DEKKER	John Bloomfield
MRS DEKKER	Bessie Love
JED	Jeffrey Shankley
ISLANDER	Leon Berton
ISLANDER	Montgomery Matthew

Directed by Anthony Page
Designed by John Gunter
Lighting by Andy Phillips

ACT ONE

The loggia of a trim, attractive villa on a subtropical island, neither Africa nor Europe, but some of both, also less than both. Startling shrubs and trees. Bright, stippled patches, cold, dark places, a whisper of ocean and still heat. Chairs reclining in and out of the sun. FREDERICA *and* EDWARD, *her husband, are sitting beneath a trailing vine. She is just in the sun, her eyes closed, he in the shade, reading a newspaper. Presently, a brownish-coloured servant in a white jacket,* LEROI, *comes over to the table beside them and laboriously puts down a glass of iced orange juice and a long exotic-looking drink in a taller glass.*

EDWARD: Thank you. That's fine.

> (LEROI *stares at the glass, hesitates.*)

Fine. Thanks. (*To* FREDERICA.) Sure you won't have a proper drink?

FREDERICA: Sure. Alcohol and me before lunchtime in this climate just don't go.

> (LEROI *goes.*)

It does something to women, anyway.

EDWARD: Well, there are misfortunes all sides. Nothing else, thanks, Leroi.

FREDERICA: He's gone. Not that he'd hear you.

EDWARD: They really do stand and stare.

FREDERICA: They're not waiters for nothing.

EDWARD: Yes. A sort of ethnic group. While they last.

FREDERICA: We *last*, you mean. It's an odd mixture.

EDWARD: What?

FREDERICA: Them. Lethargy and hysteria.

EDWARD: Oh yes. I've noticed. Perhaps it's being a small island.

FREDERICA: Brutality and sentimentality.

EDWARD: Perched between one civilization and the next.

FREDERICA: Craven but pleased with themselves.

EDWARD: Listen to those birds.

FREDERICA: They're too pleased with themselves as well.

EDWARD: Jolly pretty.

FREDERICA: Not pretty enough. Like those same old native songs they sing every night. And those dreadful instruments. One of the worst things about England.

EDWARD: What?

FREDERICA: Bloody birds. Making a din, first thing you hear.

EDWARD: Only in the country.

FREDERICA: No, in London as well. Wake me up every day.

EDWARD: Don't know what we can do about your sleep.

FREDERICA: Neither do I.

EDWARD: Still, better than aeroplanes.

FREDERICA: Um?

EDWARD: Birds.

FREDERICA: Oh. Don't see why. I rather like the sound of aeroplanes. At least they're useful. I thought I'd be all right, marrying a doctor.

EDWARD: All right for what?

FREDERICA: Oh, everything. Getting to sleep, I suppose.

EDWARD: Well, I have *tried*.

FREDERICA: Oh, you all *try*.

EDWARD: Thanks a hump.

FREDERICA: I think doctors are an oddly narrow lot on the whole.

EDWARD: We try not to give rise to incident.

FREDERICA: Indeed. Don't forget to dispense negatives. Like Civil Servants. I didn't used to think so.

EDWARD: I suppose you're really a bit of a whore about medicine.

FREDERICA: Oh, I'll try anything once.

EDWARD: But not necessarily twice.

FREDERICA: Doctors are to be *used*.

EDWARD: Like bookmakers.

FREDERICA: Right. They never lose . . .

EDWARD: We all lose.

FREDERICA: Some sooner and quicker.

EDWARD: No. That's how we start out.

FREDERICA: Or faster and funnier.

EDWARD: No. Not very funny.

FREDERICA: Oh, I think so. Don't you really?

EDWARD: No.

FREDERICA: I do. What's dull is people who don't know they've lost already. Like Leroi.

EDWARD: That's a misnomer, I must say.

FREDERICA: They're all misnomers, if you ask me. Mr and Miss Nomers . . .

EDWARD: I think you concern yourself a bit too much about sleeping.

FREDERICA: You mean I shouldn't?

EDWARD: No. But –

FREDERICA: But what?

EDWARD: You know what I was going to say, so what's the point?

FREDERICA: Perhaps you might surprise me for once.

EDWARD: I doubt it.

FREDERICA: Now *you* sound pleased.

EDWARD: You shouldn't incite me to repeat myself.

FREDERICA: Then why rise to it?

EDWARD: Why lay it?

FREDERICA: No quarry, no bait, I suppose is that answer.

EDWARD: It's a habit people have when they've lived at close quarters for long. People *can* live without too –

FREDERICA: Much sleep. Like you?

EDWARD: It can be acquired. Or not.

FREDERICA: What do you do instead?

EDWARD: Keep awake?

FREDERICA: And the options?

EDWARD: What you fancy.

FREDERICA: And if there's nothing you fancy?

EDWARD: Do nothing and don't panic.

FREDERICA: Keep the patient in a warm blanket, if possible, with hot sweet tea.

EDWARD: That sort of thing.

FREDERICA: Thanks, doctor. I don't know what we'd do without your medical skill.

EDWARD: Survive, in most cases . . . Sure you won't have something stronger than that?

FREDERICA: Quite sure. What's that flowery thing you've got?

EDWARD: Rum with local flora and fauna.

FREDERICA: Looks disgusting.

EDWARD: It does. Bit cloying and pleased with itself, as you'd say. But quite pleasant. Try a bit.

FREDERICA: No thanks. I've had all the hangovers I want in this place.

EDWARD: Good for boredom.

FREDERICA: You mean I'm bored?

EDWARD: Didn't occur to me . . . Did you mean what you just said?

FREDERICA: What? About birds?

EDWARD: Well, that too . . .

FREDERICA: Why shouldn't I mean it? I didn't realize you were such a bird lover. If one can still use it in the feathered sense.

EDWARD: And about losing . . .

FREDERICA: You think I lie?

EDWARD: No. Only that –

FREDERICA: What? Only?

EDWARD: The ones who make an ethic out of truthfulness do incline to rhetoric.

FREDERICA: You mean I put on a show of feelings I don't have?

EDWARD: Not necessarily.

FREDERICA: Then what?

EDWARD: I don't know.

FREDERICA: Then why say it?

EDWARD: Say what?

FREDERICA: What you said.

EDWARD: I don't remember.

FREDERICA: Then you should. You've a trained, scientific mind.

EDWARD: Only in a very narrow discipline.

FREDERICA: I don't think you could call pathology narrow. Somewhat inhuman and requiring a detachment that's almost unscientific. *If* that's what I mean.

EDWARD: You see. It *is* difficult. So let's not pursue it, shall we?

FREDERICA: 'Let's not pursue it, shall we?' If you really do think you've got the gift of scientific lucidity, you'd better brush up on your English a bit.

EDWARD: Blood and shit.

FREDERICA: A blood and shit man. ‚

EDWARD: That's all I need to look at all day, just as –

FREDERICA: I always remind you.

EDWARD: As you do. Which isn't quite necessary as I'm only too conscious of it.

FREDERICA: Then why should I remind you of it?

EDWARD: Only you and God knows. You wouldn't, or what's even more likely, couldn't, and I don't see much chance of God revealing any of his prime moves or divine intention.

FREDERICA: Oh, that was quite good . . .

EDWARD: What was?

FREDERICA: That sentence. It had almost a syntactical swing about it.

EDWARD: But not quite.

FREDERICA: Not bad though.

EDWARD: 'Syntactical''s a pretty poor word to flash at anyone.

FREDERICA: Don't spar with me.

EDWARD: I wouldn't dream of it. I haven't the equipment.

FREDERICA: You haven't.

EDWARD: Or inclination.

FREDERICA: Or energy.

EDWARD: Or stamina.

FREDERICA: Or interest.

EDWARD: That either.

FREDERICA: Then why are you here then?

EDWARD: To have a refreshing, enhancing holiday with my wife.

FREDERICA: You don't really like holidays . . .

EDWARD: My sister-in-law's very pleasant villa with their family and friends.

FREDERICA: Or anything else for that matter.

EDWARD: That's right, actually. Sometimes, your open-ended tongue does tip over a real, palpable truth.

FREDERICA: What *are* you interested in?

EDWARD: I told you: blood and shit.

FREDERICA: Something passive.

EDWARD: The specimens I see are very active indeed.

FREDERICA: You should have married someone like Robin.

EDWARD: Like looking down a volcano sometimes. I think I *have* said I think your sister's quite a nice girl but a trifle more dull with it than I'd have thought necessary.

FREDERICA: Or Evangeline.

EDWARD: I thought we –

FREDERICA: Oh yes, you don't like intellectual women.

EDWARD: It's the truth.

FREDERICA: So you keep saying.

EDWARD: No. So you keep asking. Like most men –

FREDERICA: Of your background, yes –

EDWARD: I'm dim and dismal enough to find them intimidating.

FREDERICA: Intimidating? She's pathetic.

EDWARD: Not specially attractive I'd have thought, but pathetic no, no more than the rest of us. She's got a thumping success of a career, which is what she says all the time is the only really important thing.

FREDERICA: You mean it isn't?

EDWARD: To her it is, so she always tells me whenever I talk to her. I can't believe it's just a common . . . or a gambit or whatever. Being a man, as you say, I've never had to define myself about a career. Just a plain old blood and shit man who does it because it's the one skill he's managed to more or less master and the one he can pay the bills with in any sort of comfort . . .

FREDERICA: I think you're taken in by her.

EDWARD: I've always been prone to being taken in, as easily as a pussy cat's laundry.

FREDERICA: Now you're straining.

EDWARD: She's certainly no more pathetic than Robin.

FREDERICA: What do you mean?

EDWARD: You know quite well what I mean. You've said it often enough yourself.

FREDERICA: She's *my* sister.

EDWARD: Running off with the old Brigadier.

FREDERICA: I thought you said you liked him?

EDWARD: I do. I certainly don't hold him in the contempt you do.

FREDERICA: He's too old and doddery by half.

EDWARD: He'll outlast *her*.

FREDERICA: While the money holds out.

EDWARD: But then contempt comes easily to you.

FREDERICA: I keep most of it for myself.

EDWARD: Then try spreading the load or turning down the
pressure or something.

FREDERICA: I happen to like high standards, starting with
number one.

EDWARD: Perhaps you should have a go at observing them,
whatever they are. Like try charity for a bit. Give *that* a whirl.

FREDERICA: Don't start giving me St. Paul. That's the prig's
first.

EDWARD: You think you *don't* sound priggish?

FREDERICA: The woman was made for the man, not the man
for the woman or whatever it is.

EDWARD: If only he'd pop in on one of his journeys now –

FREDERICA: He'd be made welcome. I'm sure. Visiting
fireman.

EDWARD: Well, he *did* say better to marry than to burn. Perhaps
he meant it the other way round. Bad translation. Sort of
Hebraic inversion . . . Anyway, I think the Brigadier's
quite happy.

FREDERICA: So he should be.

EDWARD: Why should he be? Because he's a nice simple old
stick and he's happy pottering around all day building his
little walls and grottoes and making his dreadful old wine
for a bob a gallon?

FREDERICA: And drinking it . . . He'll not divorce that wife.

EDWARD: It doesn't seem as if he's able to.

FREDERICA: Doesn't want to.

EDWARD: And he's got his children . . .

FREDERICA: Oh, don't. He's so sentimental about them.
They're both six feet five and about thirty and doing better
than the old man. I can't understand how he ever held
down while he was in the Army.

EDWARD: The Army's never been short on either sentiment or
incompetence. And quite rightly. Anyway, Robin's not

exactly a chicken, and even if she is, she's not my idea of the prize of the battery.

FREDERICA: You accept her hospitality.

EDWARD: I do. And the fact that I'm not enjoying it too well is no fault of hers.

FREDERICA: You mean it's mine?

EDWARD: No, it isn't, Frederica. It's mine. We can't be –

FREDERICA: Responsible for others.

EDWARD: Well, I believe it.

FREDERICA: So you always say.

EDWARD: Yes. As I always say. It's my responsibility if I am tired, unspontaneous or pretty insubstantial . . .

FREDERICA: You're sounding pleased again.

EDWARD: Or *seeming* pleased with myself, which I only wish were sometimes true even.

FREDERICA: Come.

EDWARD: If I am unhappy, it is my own responsibility.

FREDERICA: *Are* you?

EDWARD: Responsible?

FREDERICA: Unhappy?

EDWARD: Fair to Middling to occasional Full Speed Ahead.

FREDERICA: Thanks.

EDWARD: I thank myself.

FREDERICA: You should. Be generous.

EDWARD: I try to be.

FREDERICA: To yourself?

EDWARD: I try not to give myself *too* hard a time . . .

FREDERICA: It's the others.

EDWARD: Others what?

FREDERICA: Give you a hard time?

EDWARD: No. That would be a delusion.

FREDERICA: You're not being very clear.

EDWARD: That's because I'm not what I appear to be.

FREDERICA: And what are you?

EDWARD: A middle-aged blood and shit man trying to mop up a bit of sunshine and eat, drink and swim too much, at least not in that order . . .

FREDERICA: I wouldn't like you to test *my* blood.

EDWARD: Well I've sampled enough of the other.

FREDERICA: Shit, you mean. Ah!

EDWARD: I'm sure your blood is just as lively . . . Well, here's to the Brigadier *and* his wife.

FREDERICA: You wouldn't say that if they were out there.

EDWARD: I see no reason to be ungrateful or unkind.

FREDERICA: What *is* your reason then?

EDWARD: And to his children, all six foot five of 'em. Perhaps they'll jolly him along when he's tired of it all.

FREDERICA: Of Robin?

EDWARD: No. Just tired. She's past that, anyway.

FREDERICA: You mean *he* is.

EDWARD: I'd say he was quite a good old rattler. Gets his oats twice a day like an old horse on his holidays.

FREDERICA: If he can get it up, more likely. Anyway, why should she want to have a child by him even if he could?

EDWARD: Or *she* could.

FREDERICA: And what makes you think she couldn't?

EDWARD: Well, she hasn't and she *was* married before for twenty years or whatever.

FREDERICA: So?

EDWARD: So.

FREDERICA: People are capable of making a clear decision about these things.

EDWARD: Like us.

FREDERICA: Like me is what you meant.

EDWARD: Whatever I meant, it turned out you were quite right. And if I ever thought different, I can see how wrong I was . . .

FREDERICA: Ho much do you really hate me?

EDWARD: I don't know the answer to that one.

FREDERICA: Why not? You're an intelligent man.

EDWARD: You're an intelligent woman.

FREDERICA: You don't think so.

EDWARD: So you say. And as your father would say, I think that is really an opinion posing as a question.

FREDERICA: You disapprove of his going on the telly all the time, don't you?

EDWARD: And *you* certainly can't reply to a question that expresses its own hatred –

FREDERICA: Don't *you*?

EDWARD: I don't disapprove any more than I do of the Brigadier and his wine-making, as long as I don't have to drink it too much.

FREDERICA: You don't though. And how can you compare the Brigadier with my father?

EDWARD: I wasn't and you know it . . .

FREDERICA: What is it that's so fascinating in the newspaper?

EDWARD: The Brigadier is retired and not particularly distinguished even though he's my host and I like him and your father is a busy working writer and very distinguished indeed. All of which is quite different and a waste of my breath and your ears, except they don't function too well.

FREDERICA: They function all right.

EDWARD: It's because I respect what he's done.

FREDERICA: Ah, past tense.

EDWARD: And will quite inevitably do.

FREDERICA: I thought you didn't go much on literature.

EDWARD: I don't. There's enough trouble . . .

FREDERICA: As it is.

EDWARD: Exactly. But looking up occasionally from my smears and slides, I do think someone who is as distinguished and been such a figure, yes, been, is, will still be, continue to be, in nearly all our lives or Western Europe's or at least a few schools and universities and weekly periodicals and newspapers, shouldn't have to clown about doing interviews and literary quiz games and being a fireside character or sage or whatever he is to people, which I've no idea what that is and don't care and neither will they for different reasons and in five minutes either before a new series or after the next programme even. Even . . .

FREDERICA: I don't understand that sentence.

EDWARD: Nor me. But there was some bacteria jumping about in there if you can be bothered and we neither of us can . . .

FREDERICA: You were saying?

EDWARD: I just hope he gets paid all he can get and gets some innocent pleasure out of it, which he's entitled to without censorious philistines like me over-reacting to . . . As for this paper, I quite agree with you that it's pretty deadly –

FREDERICA: Do you think you're getting your sense of humour back again?

EDWARD: As usual . . . I never lost it. It was taken from me by force.

FREDERICA: By me?

EDWARD: No. By the mysterious, satanic little creatures that even sober English ladies, Colonels' ladies, residents and missionaries' ladies used to occasionally spot after day-long tennis parties in the dusk of forgotten . . . colonial days.

FREDERICA: No. Not forgotten.

EDWARD: No, remembered in white and pink Georgian buildings . . . and the reef piloted through by Nelson himself, and the harbour where the American tourists throw their litter and cartons and beer cans and coke, on the way to the gift shops with their tour guides, and 'hello folks', the package smiles and surliness and black feeling all round, all, all of a dimness . . .

FREDERICA: This place really has got you down.

EDWARD: No it hasn't. And the reason I read the paper is because the Brigadier goes into town and gets it specially for me every morning.

FREDERICA: That's his excuse.

EDWARD: He can't afford it.

FREDERICA: You mean Robin can't.

EDWARD: And I know that he'll want to talk about it page by page from the Home news to the leader and letters, to the racing at Catterick and the obituaries and Court Circular.

FREDERICA: Fascinating.

EDWARD: Not at all fascinating. But probably as much or as more as he gets from Robin . . .

FREDERICA: Why do you have to knock my sisters?

EDWARD: I don't. As you know. You know better than I do.

FREDERICA: Come on.

EDWARD: What?

FREDERICA: Please.

EDWARD: Please come on? Come on what?

FREDERICA: Be friends.

EDWARD: We *are* friends.

FREDERICA: Married – friends.

EDWARD: Yes. Married – friends . . .

FREDERICA: You are having a good time, aren't you?

EDWARD: Yes. Are you?

FREDERICA: Sure. Can I have some of your drink?

EDWARD: I'll call Leroi.

FREDERICA: No. I'll have a sip of yours.

EDWARD: I'll get another. Leroi!

FREDERICA: What have I done now?

EDWARD: Leroi! Come on, you sullen, charmless, unbeautiful,
black bastard.

FREDERICA: Don't get one for *me*.

(LEROI *ambles in.*)

EDWARD: Are you sure? Well, I will, anyway. Another one
please, Leroi.

(LEROI *leaves into the cool of the house.*)

Sorry to be a bother!

FREDERICA: I wonder what it was like then, when Nelson or
Hood or poor old Admiral Byng used to drop in.

EDWARD: Rather pleasant after being aboard those ships I
should think.

FREDERICA: Would you like to go back?

EDWARD: Where?

FREDERICA: Home.

EDWARD: What for?

FREDERICA: You're restless.

EDWARD: One thing I'm not ever is restless, at home or abroad
. . . He said, trying to sound as pleased with himself as
possible.

FREDERICA: We're all right, aren't we?

EDWARD: Fine. All right . . .

FREDERICA: You don't sound sure.

EDWARD: Neither do you. But I take your word for it . . .

FREDERICA: Do you?

EDWARD: I *did* just say so . . .

FREDERICA: Do you think Robin and the Brigadier *will* have any children?

EDWARD: If they can and want to. Why don't you ask her?

FREDERICA: I don't like to.

EDWARD: Would you like *me* to?

FREDERICA: No. It's too personal.

EDWARD: Indeed.

FREDERICA: Private.

(LEROI *comes in and they watch him go through the slow business of putting the drink on the table. He goes.*)

Why do you get cross when I ask questions?

EDWARD: I don't. Only when you expect answers.

FREDERICA: Friends?

(*She puts out her hand to him.*)

EDWARD: Friends.

FREDERICA: I *did* put out my hand.

EDWARD: Yes. I know. *First.*

FREDERICA: Don't say anything . . . I try to be detached.

EDWARD: Why not? If it makes you feel more real?

FREDERICA: Real. What's *that*, for God's sake?

EDWARD: You can produce effects in *real* people. Including me, even. As if you *were* them. Or me.

FREDERICA: I'm afraid I don't understand that. And I shouldn't think you can.

EDWARD: No. Sometimes I don't feel I can understand a word of anything anyone says to me. As if they were as unclear as I am . . .

FREDERICA: Too abstract for me.

EDWARD: If you're wayward.

FREDERICA: *Way*ward?

EDWARD: Oh, or impossible or just dotty enough, you escape every, any coherence or intent that might be in the way . . .

FREDERICA: What'll we do today? Swim before lunch?

EDWARD: Don't think *I* will.

FREDERICA: Do you good.

EDWARD: I know. I've put on weight.

FREDERICA: You have.

EDWARD: Robin's cooking.

FREDERICA: Well I think *I'll* go.

EDWARD: I'll come down with you . . .

FREDERICA: Are you sure you wouldn't rather go home?

EDWARD: Sure.

FREDERICA: You wouldn't like to get back to your work?

EDWARD: No. I don't find work so irresistible.

FREDERICA: That's because you're lucky. You know it's there, waiting for you.

EDWARD: There are equally attractive alternatives to work.

FREDERICA: Like?

EDWARD: Idleness, for one. You can always make a choice.

FREDERICA: Not all of us. It's *behind* us.

EDWARD: Can we leave that one alone for a bit.

FREDERICA: Of course . . . I'll get changed. I can't bear abstractions. Sort of labour-saving devices.

EDWARD: *That* sounds like an abstraction.

FREDERICA: Does it? Well, I'll go for the concrete any time.

EDWARD: That can be just as evasive. Don't ask me what I mean.

FREDERICA: I wasn't going to. I've given all that up . . .

EDWARD: Just as well.

FREDERICA: Um?

EDWARD: I think I'll have a quick dip after all.

(*Enter* MARY, FREDERICA's *youngest sister. Her husband,* ROBERT *with her. Both about mid-thirty.*)

FREDERICA: Where have you been?

MARY: Just for a walk, keeping away from the tourists from the cruise ship.

FREDERICA: Not another lot!

MARY: I think thése are only here for the day. We went along the beach.

EDWARD: Oh, you hardly ever see them there. They don't like the idea of walking.

FREDERICA: Don't think they *can*, you mean.

ROBERT: Few little Nips popping away with cameras and an odd Kraut or two, bellowing at their Fraus.

EDWARD: Didn't you notice the little fleet of old cartons and coke bottles coming round this way? You can see it from here even. Regular armada out there.

ROBERT: Also, we thought we'd nip off early so that we didn't have to say goodbye to the Brigadier's mama.

FREDERICA: She has gone, I hope?

MARY: Unless the plane's crashed.

FREDERICA: As long as she's *on* it, that's fine.

MARY: Robin went with them, to see her off. And the Brigadier's getting the papers and a few other things.

FREDERICA: We stayed in bed till we thought she'd gone . . .

EDWARD: Well, the Brigadier seems quite fond of her.

FREDERICA: He doesn't have to put up with her like the rest of us. He's too busy with his vines or in his workshop making some object. Anyway, I don't think you should call him 'Brigadier'.

EDWARD: Well, he is, isn't he?

FREDERICA: I suppose he is, though I've got my doubts about it. But people don't call you 'doctor'. Besides you're the only one who calls him it to his face.

EDWARD: Why not?

FREDERICA: Because it sounds as if you're sending him up.

EDWARD: I don't mean to.

FREDERICA: Maybe.

MARY: I think you're all a bit mean about his mother. She's not that bad. And she *is* quite old.

FREDERICA: That is no mitigation any more than youth. She's a crabbed old rat bag. If I'd have known she'd be here I don't suppose I'd have come. Damn it, one of the reasons we came out here was to get away from having to have Edward's mother another Christmas.

MARY: *And* see Robin and everyone.

FREDERICA: Sure. But I tell you, I'd have got on the nearest dog-sled to the South Pole to get away from one more Christmas with that old gangster. Complaining, and wailing and scheming, impossible to please. Like having an incontinent, superannuated Mafia in your sitting room all day. Even Edward can't stand her, though he never tells her to her face and he really – and he really – hates her more than I do.

ROBERT: Men's mums *are* usually worse.

FREDERICA: The Christmas before I nearly went into the London Clinic afterwards for the rest of the year. Actually, I'll say this, which isn't much, for the Brigadier's mama – she's got a bit more class than Edward's, even if she does pretend she's not deaf. At least, she doesn't look as if she's had the curse every day for the past sixty-five years.

ROBERT: She's got chronic menstruation,
Never laughs, never smiles,
Mine's a dismal occupation,
Cracking ice for Grandma's piles.

EDWARD: Oh, *I* remember that.

FREDERICA: Men –

EDWARD: What's the verse after that?

ROBERT: Even now the baby's started,
Having epileptic fits;
Every time it coughs it farts,
Every time it farts it shits.

FREDERICA: If it's grubby-minded, *they'll* remember it.

EDWARD: That's it:
Yet we are not broken-hearted,
Neither are we up the spout.

FREDERICA: Or schoolboy enough.

ROBERT: Auntie Rachel has just farted,
Blown her arsehole inside out.

EDWARD: Or – innocent enough.

MARY: Who needs men?

FREDERICA: I think – mostly – other men.

MARY: Perhaps we should do without 'em altogether.

EDWARD: I hope you all shall.

MARY: Be careful.

FREDERICA: Yes. You're all likely to be taken up on it any moment.

EDWARD: We have looked upwards at the heavens and seen the signs brooding over us, and taken . . . due note.

FREDERICA: Good. (*To* MARY.) Coming for a swim?

MARY: Oh. I don't know really. I've got an odd sore on my thigh. It doesn't seem to heal.

FREDERICA: Nothing does here. Come on.

ROBERT: I think she's a bit self-conscious about it.

FREDERICA: In front of her sister and her husband – come on. Even the salt water in this sea must have *some* salty old natural antiseptic in it somewhere.

ROBERT: Do you mind if I have a drink first?

FREDERICA: If you don't mind waiting for Flash Leroi, the geni of the island.

ROBERT: Oh yes. (*Calls.*) LEROI!

FREDERICA: You'll have to do better than that. He'll just pretend he's not heard.

ROBERT: Leroi!

EDWARD: Leroi!

FREDERICA: Either he'll have heard it or we'll be trampled under a turtle stampede.

EDWARD: (*To* MARY) Would you like me to look at that sore place for you?

MARY: No, thanks. I've bought some stuff at the chemist and old Harry's given me something.

FREDERICA: Harry's got more medicines than Edward ever has.

EDWARD: Mostly local herbs and stuff but they're probably more effective than anything you'll buy. He's full of local folk-lore and benevolent witchcraft.

FREDERICA: Harry must be the only American to stay here longer than a week.

EDWARD: Maybe *they're* right.

FREDERICA: Maybe.

MARY: He must be the oldest – I was going to say European – well, resident.

FREDERICA: I think that palm goes to Lamb. He was clattering his golden typewriter out there just after the war.

ROBERT: *Our* war, you mean?

FREDERICA: Yes. Ours.

MARY: That makes Robin and the Brigadier practically newcomers.

EDWARD: Until the next wave. It's what I think they call 'ripe for development'.

FREDERICA: Nothing heals, everything goes rotten or mildewed. Slimy. It's like a great green bombed garden . . .

ROBERT: Look at those birds.

FREDERICA: Don't *you* start.

ROBERT: What are they, tern?

FREDERICA: We've named them 'the duffers'.

MARY: Why?

FREDERICA: Mr and Mrs Duffer. Because they're so helpless. Helpless and hopeless. They managed to bang out some eggs, half of which I think they broke themselves. They half built a nest, then it blew down. And when they finished one finally they can hardly remember where they put it.

EDWARD: I find that quite likeable.

FREDERICA: I don't know which of them is worse, him or her. Both hopeless.

EDWARD: Tending your own garden's not a bad resort, even if it *is* the last one *and* bombed at that . . .

FREDERICA: Well, if no one's coming, I think I'll have my dip before Robin and the Brigadier come back to tell me I mustn't spoil the lunch.

MARY: I'd come but Alastair's coming and he'll get cross if my hair's all full of salt and greasy.

FREDERICA: Is he coming to crimp your hair?

MARY: Yes. He's doing it this afternoon.

FREDERICA: Would you ask him to do mine? I've nothing to do.

MARY: Right.

EDWARD: I'll come and watch you.

FREDERICA: Just as you like . . .

(EDWARD *follows her off.*)

MARY: Did I say anything?

ROBERT: She's *your* sister.

MARY: I don't know what any of them are thinking. I never have done. Robin or Evangie neither.

ROBERT: Nor does Edward.

MARY: You *are* enjoying yourself?

ROBERT: The fare was expensive. But otherwise it's cheap. And the company's good.

MARY: Who?

ROBERT: *You*, dozey . . . The one thing about Frederica. She's adroit. She can even make Edward feel he's created a situation when it's all hers. We're all relatively innocent.

MARY: Do you think anyone's enjoying it?

ROBERT: Me.

MARY: And Robin and the Brigadier?

ROBERT: They have to. They've chosen to live here.

MARY: Yes. Odd to think of them actually *living* here.

ROBERT: Improvising. Getting things done. Plumbing, a new bathroom and shower, or extra guest room . . .

MARY: Yes, but swimming and sunshine.

ROBERT: Every day.

MARY: No taxes.

ROBERT: Hardly.

MARY: It seemed as if we were all on holiday again at first . . . Leroi never came.

ROBERT: I think one day we'll call and he'll not be there. And someone, Robin and the Brigadier anyhow, will be on their own.

MARY: I think I know what you mean . . .

ROBERT: Still, as you say, for the meantime, there's still tennis and water-skiing. The Club, long drinks. Golf course.

MARY: And Americans. Do you think they'll stay?

ROBERT: The Americans? Oh, build more hotels I dare say.

MARY: No, Frederica and Edward?

ROBERT: Don't know. They're rich enough to cut holidays short. Remember, with her, it's all or nothing, and as you can't get all, not really anywhere . . .

(*Enter* ROBIN *and the* BRIGADIER.)

ROBIN: Hullo. Where's everyone gone to?

ROBERT: Your dad's gone for a walk and to buy a new hat against the sun. And Fred and Ted have gone for a dip. At least, *she* has.

ROBIN: What about the others?

MARY: Well, Alastair should be here soon. And I expect Daddy won't be long.

BRIGADIER: Isn't Lamb coming?

MARY: I expect he'll pick up Alastair in his car.

ROBIN: Only the Brigadier's making one of his soufflés and he's already had too much at the airport *and* the Club while I was shopping.

BRIGADIER: I didn't.

ROBERT: Did the old lady get off all right then?

ROBIN: Usual delays.

BRIGADIER: Only thing left over from the *ancien régime* and that's red tape and it grows like flowers in this climate.

ROBIN: Examined her passport, money, search for firearms. Everything. She'd even managed to convince herself she'd had a good time before she got there. And then . . .

BRIGADIER: Better see what Leroi's up to. I can get the salad going, at least, and the wine.

ROBIN: I told *him* to do all that.

BRIGADIER: I know. Drinks all charged? Good.
(*He goes out.*)

ROBIN: And there's always Harry. He'll drop in any old time.

MARY: Can I help?

ROBIN: No. You're here to relax. After all, we *live* here. . . . Do you think they're having a good time?

MARY: Frederica?

ROBIN: Yes.

ROBERT: Enormous . . . You know what people are like.

ROBIN: That's the trouble. I don't. I just gave up, years ago. Even my sisters, no, mostly my sisters, except perhaps Mary here. And they've given *me* up too.

MARY: Well, you do live what's called 'out of the way'.

ROBIN: I know. But that's why we came here in the first place. Evangie's working on her book I suppose?

MARY: Somewhere.

ROBIN: She never seems to let up. I said to her: come for a 'holiday'.

MARY: You know Evangie. Work is everything.

ROBIN: Not if it's never play as well. Worrying about the reviews –

ROBERT: Which hardly anyone reads anyway.

ROBIN: Worrying about the next thing she's going to do.

ROBERT: And the one after that. And after *that*. No one owes *that* to posterity. What does it do for you?

ROBIN: I think Christopher may be right about the past after all.

MARY: What do you mean?

ROBIN: Looking over his shoulder all the time, living off the things Daddy's done, rather than what he's doing himself now.

ROBERT: Well, the future owes no one a living. After all, it's done nothing for you . . .

ROBIN: Still, it's a strange thing, giving yourself up to the reputation of an old man. And an old man so demanding . . . and self-protective. It isn't that the old thing is some *giant*.

MARY: We must not be the judges of that. He's not half bad . . .

ROBERT: Even if he's only half good, one shouldn't be on trial by one's daughters. It would make parlour King Lears out of a lot of us.

ROBIN: Perhaps having children of your own puts one in a different position to your own father, and that's why Frederica and I are more critical of him.

MARY: I may be just less critical . . . But Evangie worships him.

ROBERT: That might be because she feels in blood competition.

ROBIN: As a writer too.

MARY: *His* achievement.

ROBIN: An example.

ROBERT: Of excellence. Or, as you say, *nudging* it.

ROBIN: Christopher feels that obviously. Robert, as someone said, if you've no world of your own, it's rather pleasant to regret the passing of someone else's.

MARY: I think Evangie's a bit keen on him.

ROBIN: Is she really? I'd have thought he wasn't successful enough, too much of a disused hulk. Anyway, I can't see Christopher turning his head forward to an affair with someone like Evangie.

MARY: Or marriage?

ROBIN: Least of all. He's left that behind him. Just so much discarded wreckage and messy debris. Like bits of old cars dumped in the woods.

MARY: I can't think he can feel as bleak as all that, otherwise he couldn't be so cheerful at devoting all his time to Daddy and nannying him like he does.

ROBERT: I don't know. It might be a case of fatigue. Shaky structure. Apologetic for what one is, afraid of what we may become.

MARY: You make him sound such a mediocrity.

ROBERT: I don't think he is. He may want too much, and unlike Evangie, he's given up. People do sometimes choose mediocrity.

MARY: But can you really *choose* it?

ROBERT: I don't see why not. It's a way out of feeling isolated. Like a horse's twitch, you apply pain to the nose – to divert it from the knife cutting into it from behind. Or wherever it may be . . .

ROBIN: I think if he's got eyes for anyone, it's Frederica.

ROBERT: Not much joy there, I'd have thought.

ROBIN: No. She and Edward are at least matched.

ROBERT: That would be swapping one twitch for another. She'd eat him before breakfast.

ROBIN: I don't know about that. But it would certainly be hurtful all round. Still, I've watched him with her. He's certainly fascinated by all those straight, masculine gestures of hers and what he thinks is openness.

ROBERT: Instead of a disguise?

ROBIN: Yes.

MARY: Do you imagine Edward's noticed?

ROBIN: Probably. But she knows there's not much pain she can cause there. Besides, I don't think she has much regard for Chris. Though, that might not matter of course.

ROBERT: Could be the opposite.

ROBIN: And, he may be, even he, well, getting a bit tired of coping with the old man . . . I say, we do observe one another and speculate and chatter on about the others.

ROBERT: Perhaps it's being sisters. All four of you. Even to an outsider, there's something fascinating to watch in it. An inner circle of lives. One's almost tempted to try each one in turn.

MARY: Not any more, I hope.

ROBERT: I'm too near the circle.

ROBIN: Yes. And sharing the same parents. But all different.

MARY: And living different lives, having husbands and lovers or not, or children or not.

ROBERT: In-laws.

ROBIN: Don't. At least I know mine's safely on the plane for another twelve months anyway. Sometimes I don't give the Brigadier her letters to him. It often kills the morning. He sits out in his old shed, brooding and smoking and then drinks too much of his own wine for lunch and has to lie down for the rest of the day. What's going on today, anyway?

MARY: Well, Robert, I expect, will do nothing again. Alastair's coming to do my hair.

ROBIN: Ah, yes. I hope he doesn't bring anyone. Oh, well, doesn't matter. You all seem to like him.

MARY: He's thoughtful and attentive. And kind. He amuses Daddy. And the Brigadier likes him. And *he's* keen on Frederica. She's beautiful and she makes *him* laugh.

ROBIN: And she's got hair he calls 'good stuff'. Not like my mop.

ROBERT: Everyone *does* like him. He gives you a feeling he's just about to do or say something brave. Instead of just camp.

MARY: You're right about Daddy.

ROBERT: Oh yes, he's always saying to me 'When's that nice little queer boy coming round?'

ROBIN: Yes, he's always asking me the same things about people he's going to meet. 'Will I like him?' then 'Is he a bugger or a Jew?'

(*Enter* CHRISTOPHER *and* EVANGIE.)

CHRISTOPHER: You're talking about Wyatt. Behind my back.

ROBIN: Why not? We *have* known him quite a long time.

CHRISTOPHER: Sure. Longer than I have. Before I'd *heard* of him.

EVANGIE: He's said that as long as I remember. 'Will I like him?' And then 'Do you think he'll like *me*?'

CHRISTOPHER: I've been asleep. Apart from a phone call. Then Evangie's typewriter woke me –

EVANGIE: Sorry.

CHRISTOPHER: I should have been up. I made her come out for some sea air. Where's the old boy?

ROBIN: Up first thing. Gone for his walk. And a new hat. I said I'd throw the old one away.

EVANGIE: I think he inherited it from George Moore or somebody.

CHRISTOPHER: Yeats, I think.

EVANGIE: Oh. Sorry.

CHRISTOPHER: Don't. It's not very important.

EVANGIE: It is – to him.

CHRISTOPHER: Not necessarily.

ROBIN: Alastair's coming for lunch. Do you want your hair done?

EVANGIE: Oh, yes.

ROBIN: What's Wyatt up to after lunch?

CHRISTOPHER: I've arranged an interview for him. With the island newspaper, whatever it is . . .

MARY: He'll hate that.

ROBIN: No he won't. He'll make us and Christopher *think* he does. Or try to.

EVANGIE: And why not?

ROBERT: Why not?

CHRISTOPHER: Indeed.

ROBERT: You can't make people like Wyatt do things he doesn't really want to do. Even Christopher. It's a mistake one's inclined to make.

(*Enter* WYATT. *He is about seventy, flushed and hot from his walk.*)

WYATT: What's that? What are you saying? You can't be talking about me. Gosh, I'm in a soak from all this sun! What a *day* it is! Think of all those people freezing in the Home Counties, hoping the rails and points won't ice up again! Ice and floods to *come*, I dare say. And everybody'll be *so* astonished. As usual. I *have* had a time. Spoke to such a nice lot of people. Charming lot in the shops, and I went to that smashing little market. Got a splendid new hat. Do you like it?

ROBIN: Quite an improvement.

WYATT: Couldn't bear to part with the old one. Poor old thing. They put it in this parcel for me, all done up. Can't remember who gave it me.

EVANGIE: George Moore.

WYATT: No, it wasn't him.

CHRISTOPHER: Yeats.

WYATT: No. Someone . . . I say, you *do* look in the pink, all of you. How nice. You're such a good sight to come back to. I'm quite tired. Been walking since breakfast. Old Leroi can be quite good, you know. I know you don't go on him much but lovely poached eggs he got. Asked him what he thought about the English, and do you know what he said: 'I'm glad they've gone, sir, but an English millionaire is still worth more than an American millionaire.'

ROBERT: Depends on how many millions.

ROBIN: He means we're better tippers.

WYATT: Went all round the bay. Quite empty. Not an American in sight. Not even old Harry.

ROBIN: He's not exactly a tourist.

WYATT: No. Sweet old thing. Had a good squiz at all the coral. Remarkable. Real Captain Cook, Darwin sort of thing. Saw Nelson's little place. If ever it was, anyway, all jolly nice. What's for lunch?

ROBIN: Salad and soufflé. And some fish. The Brigadier's laid it all on today.

WYATT: Good old Brigadier. Officer material all right. I often think of him in the war and all that. All I ever did was fill in forms for supplies in Delhi most of the time. What have you all been doing?

ROBIN: Chatting, seeing off mothers . . .

WYATT: She go off all right?

ROBIN: Yes, but it seemed like touch and go for a while. When it took off I had a large brandy.

WYATT: Oh, dear, she's not all that much older than me. I hope you don't have to have large brandies after seeing me off.

ROBIN: Don't be silly, Papa. You know you're welcome as long as you like.

MARY: The thing is you're too restless to stay anywhere too long.

EVANGIE: Besides, you do, at least, seem to enjoy everything – while it lasts, anyway.

ROBERT: Instead of looking like a professional spare prick at a wedding.

WYATT: Oh, that *is* good!

MARY: Robert! Really . . .

WYATT: Oh, dear, do I seem easily bored? I don't think I am. No, I just like to waddle off in all directions. While I'm still able to. She seemed quite a sprightly old trout. Of course, I suppose we had odd common points of interest, people we both knew. That's one of the things about age, you find less and less people who remember the things you do. Of course, the Brigadier's father was in the Colonial Service, like your grandfather, so there was all that. Then there was the war. She remembered that.

ROBERT: Yours or ours?

WYATT: Mine, I suppose, though I don't remember much of it. I remember yours, as you call it, all the ration books and being snubbed and kept waiting at the Food Office.

ROBIN: Don't!

EVANGIE: Most of the people I meet don't even remember *that*. Or they've forgotten.

MARY: Or they think you mean Korea or even Vietnam.

WYATT: Only things I remember well are the list of names of old boys killed or wounded being read out by the Housemaster in chapel. That and being chased by a horde of women, very middle-class sort of women, half way across Southsea because I wasn't in uniform. Jolly thankful I was too. Too feeble to be a conchie and too much of a funk to face all that mud and bullying and limbs blown off. Oh, no. Of course, I was only about fourteen but 'tall for my age', as they said then. 'Outgrowing my strength'.

School was bad enough, at least I suppose it wasn't *quite* as bad. Do you know, I was asking the Brigadier the other day why this house was called 'Mesopotamia'? Apparently, his father was there in 1917 or whenever it was. Always thought if I'd had to go, or be dragged off, I'd rather have gone there. Except I'd have been stung by a wasp and died like poor little R. Brooke. Funny end for a poet, I mean *genuinely* funny. I think I'd prefer to be stung to death rather than to wake up in some agonizing ward with half of me shot away and the rest in torment. Don't you?

ROBERT: Right. What school *did* you go to?

WYATT: Marlborough. That was *my* Western Front. Perhaps it wasn't so bad, though all the ones I've spoken to who were there then who say they were happy are the most awful types. Overweening little swots or thumping great Prussian sons of Great Albion. All become florid M.P.s or sarky-tongued bullies at the Bar; clammy old bishops and archbishops or those huge surgeons who tower over you in green and rubber wellies and call their patients 'the meat'. Of course I was the only one who didn't go to Eton. My father went, so did all my elder brothers.

CHRISTOPHER: Why was that?

WYATT: For one thing I was a skinny, runtish thing, although I was tall and none of my brothers' clothes ever fitted me. Because, of course, being the last, I wore their cast-off jackets and even trousers. Always had a patch on sleeves just below the elbows, so I always felt cold and had chilblains. Anyway, Father decided I needed 'toughening up' at a really tough school. *Actually* it was because he'd already sent five sons to Eton and the year I left my prep school, the roof of the house had to be completely renewed and the old boy said he couldn't afford the fees at Eton, even with reductions. So: that's how I got to Marlborough. Though I believe it's quite a jolly place nowadays, pop music and even girls, girls! What it *could* have been like! Do you know what the cure for chilblains was then? Soaking your feet and hands in your own pee. *Most* unpleasant – you ponged all over the classroom and weren't even warm when you dunked yourself.

ROBIN: Well, *I'd* better rescue the Brigadier from Leroi. I hope Frederica isn't too late for lunch. The old chap gets awfully upset if his cooking is spoiled.

MARY: Start without them.

ROBIN: No. He likes everyone to sit down.

WYATT: Quite right. We'll wait for her. I say, the old boy's jolly clever with his cooking, isn't he? Must be nice for you, old thing. I could never cook an *egg*, not even at Oxford, where everybody seemed to.

ROBIN: Well, it's better than relying on *my* cooking and anything's better than Leroi. You'll get lunch about tea time.

CHRISTOPHER: Shall I go and look for Frederica?

ROBIN: No, she'll come in her own time. Edward's with her, anyway. He'll hurry her somehow.

CHRISTOPHER: Pretty exhausting – hurrying people up. Like picking up a child's clothes for him.

MARY: *You* should know . . .

EVANGIE: I think when you love someone you should do so, knowing that one day you will hate them.

WYATT: I say, *what* an interesting remark!

EVANGIE: I've seen it happen too often –

MARY: To others?

EVANGIE: Most of us.

WYATT: Do you know, I haven't thought of it? I suppose I must be a thundering old nuisance. Am I, Christopher?

CHRISTOPHER: You're scrupulous about the things that matter.

WYATT: No, Evangie's right as usual.

EVANGIE: I wish I *were* 'right as usual'.

CHRISTOPHER: Do you? I don't. But I don't expect it. Certainly not of myself.

WYATT: No. I *am* disorganized. I forget things, leave things about, crash in everywhere, like some maddening old toddler. I *must* watch it. Otherwise, you'll *all* need large brandies when you see the back of me . . . Your mother was a bit like that and I never realized it till she was dead. I must have enjoyed a few brandies since that funeral. Awful thing to say, but I think that was almost the most enjoyable day of my life. When those ropes slid down into that grave, I had to lower my head right down so that no one could see my face . . . I must be very unfeeling indeed, I mean not to feel anything but, no not relief, merriment, that's the word for it, merriment at my own wife's funeral! Even good old Cranmer's words didn't affect me. Well, of course, none of you really remember her. Except Robin, I suppose?

ROBIN: Not much. Try and hurry them up.

(*She goes out.*)

WYATT: Is that nice little queer boy coming?

MARY: Yes. He's crimping the entire family.

WYATT: Oh, good. I do like him. I didn't know whatsit, crimping, was such an interesting business. Like being in the mess or common room. Wish he'd do *mine*. He's got a splendid head of hair.

MARY: It's a wig.

WYATT: Good heavens – a wig! Is it really?

MARY: Yes, *really*, Daddy.

WYATT: Perhaps he'd get *me* one. How do you *know* it is?

MARY: Some of us do notice these things.

WYATT: Did *you* know?

EVANGIE: Yes.

WYATT: Robert?

ROBERT: Yes, but he told me too. First time we met he said 'You know I'm just an uptight little bald Scots queen under this red rug. They all send me up and call me either the Virgin Queen or Mary, Queen of Scots! It used to upset me but now I'm not bothered.'

WYATT: Did he say that? Poor little devil! I suppose he must really be bothered, in fact.

EVANGIE: It's not only hairdressing that's cut-throat in his line.

WYATT: Yes, I see what you mean. Gosh, I'm so glad I didn't mention it to him. It would have seemed most unkind. I wish I noticed things like *you* all do.

MARY: I think you do, really, Daddy. You don't miss the tricks.

WYATT: Devious, you mean? Yes. I see you do. That's not a

nice trait either. Pretending not to notice, when all the time you do.

EVANGIE: We forgive you.

MARY: Like your calling Robin 'old thing'.

WYATT: But I call everyone 'old thing'. Why, oh, even Leroi.

MARY: Exactly, it makes her feel old.

WYATT: It's just that she *is* the oldest of you all.

MARY: And inferior and played out.

WYATT: I honestly didn't mean to . . .

MARY: Whether you did or didn't, it still sounds disparaging and unkind. To her, anyway.

WYATT: Oh dear, I am sorry. You make me feel quite awful.

MARY: Like you never call Frederica 'old thing' or me even. Or call her Fred, Fred and Ted, like some do, because you know she hates it. She gets 'lovely long legs and hair like your mother . . .'

WYATT: Do I do that? Oh, dear. Poor old Robin. There I go again! It's just that I think of you all differently, different parts of my life. Robin, well, the eldest, first born then, you the young, pretty one with your own babies, and Evangie, the intellectual one.

EVANGIE: Thanks. I know what a pejorative 'intellectual' is to you.

WYATT: Not at all. I'm just frightened of people who are cleverer than me. They are even worse than the physical bullies at school. You could always *despise* them, even when they were making you cry.

EVANGIE: Men don't want 'intellectual' daughters any more than they do wives.

WYATT: Oh, my dear, I seem to have hurt you all. I never meant to . . .

EVANGIE: Not Frederica. She was the only one who couldn't care.

WYATT: It's just that a lot of things I don't understand, and I suppose I've stepped over them or discarded them like my boots on the floor. I never even knew what 'growing out of your strength' meant when it was said to me as a boy. Though I said it to Evangie, I know. Oh, dear . . . This hat's not as good as the old one. I feel quite hot. I'd better go into the shade, I think . . .

MARY: Alastair's probably coming with Lamb.

WYATT: Lamb? What's that?

MARY: The writer.

EVANGIE: Is he? Gosh, how good.

WYATT: Not a *writer*? Oh, Lord, I hate meeting writers.

EVANGIE: But why?

WYATT: They *know* about you usually. They can trip you up if they've a mind to. If they're better than me, I get all yellowy and envious, and if they're worse it just depresses me. For them. And then again, if they're bad, they perform themselves so *well* and amuse everyone. And if they're really good, they don't bother to perform at all, quite rightly, all lordly. Oh dear, Lamb is it? But he's frightfully successful, isn't he, invented tax havens and things and writes best sellers?

CHRISTOPHER: I shouldn't worry about all that. Anyway, he's quite shy.

WYATT: Is he a bugger?

CHRISTOPHER: Almost certainly.

EVANGIE: But not necessarily literally.

MARY: And not Jewish.

WYATT: Is that why he's coming with little Alastair?

EVANGIE: Possibly. Alastair would tell you if you ask him.

WYATT: Oh no. How awful. I wonder if he takes his wig off in bed. Lamb . . . Lamb. I remember him. We got frightfully drunk together in some club somewhere years ago. Savile or somewhere like that. But he's frightfully impressive. Rather good too, they tell me. I remember he asked me why I pretended to be an ageing schoolboy all the time and I was so embarrassed I didn't go out for a month afterwards. Then he said to me 'How queer are you?' And I was so nonplussed because we didn't talk about that much at that time. So, like an awful coward, because I was pretty sure he *was*, I said a bit too airily, 'Oh, about forty-five per cent.' And he said 'Are you? How interesting, I'm ninety-five. You see, I don't trust women.' And I said something foolish and gauche. Like 'Oh, but all your best friends must have been women.'

ROBERT: What did *he* say?

WYATT: 'Oh *exactly*', or something of the sort. I was so confused by him. Do you think he'll remember?

EVANGIE: Might do.

WYATT: Oh, dear. He must have thought me the most unbearable little prig. I do hope he doesn't. I mean he's really *famous*, isn't he?

CHRISTOPHER: Not in the way *you* are, and he'll know it.

WYATT: You know, I thought of him then as being lots older than me, but, if anything, I suppose he's even a bit younger. He wasn't at Marlborough, I do remember. Eton or Winchester, much grander altogether.

CHRISTOPHER: Don't worry. He'll be more worried than you are. Anyway, you've got this interview this afternoon.

WYATT: What interview?

CHRISTOPHER: With the island newspaper.

WYATT: Oh no, I say, can't we cancel it?

CHRISTOPHER: He sounds quite a nice young man.

WYATT: Can't put him off? Oh, he'll expect me to be clever and say witty things instead of just being an old duffer who happens to be a writer.

EVANGIE: I think you'll manage.

MARY: Just say all the things you usually say. They won't have heard them out here.

WYATT: What a good wheeze! After all, they all ask the same questions, like have you moved further to the Right; should writers be seen on television; are they any longer relevant to the global village, wherever that is; or just plain do you use a pen or a typewriter? Is he a native? An islander?

CHRISTOPHER: Well, he – she's not English.

WYATT: Then she should be all right I'd think.

CHRISTOPHER: As Mary says, it doesn't matter, anyway.

ROBERT: If it doesn't matter, why does he need to do it?

WYATT: Look a bit childish I suppose. And you know how sensitive they can be in these little places. Especially ex-colonies or whatever they're called.

EVANGIE: Independent states.

WYATT: That's right.

(*Enter* ALASTAIR *with* JED. *Both in their early twenties, but* JED *with shoulder-length black hair. Behind them is* LAMB, *expensively dressed and with a club tie.*)

ALASTAIR: Don't talk to me about independent states. This place is just Tel Aviv, U.S.A. in Atlantic. Have you seen that lot come in this morning on that boat? My dear, they've been in all morning in their mickey mouse glasses and Florida Blue dilly-dilly hairdo's. As if I'd touch the one of them. Complaining and carrying on, they didn't like Fiji, they liked Australia better. *Australia*! All those beaches, none of which they'd dare go near, but India was worse, and, as for *Europe*, that was worse, even the culture they didn't see much of. Or *think* much of, anyway. Talk about your Young Geriatrics Tours, Inc. 'Can you tell me the way to the Gift Shop, young man? Oh, because we've lost our tour guide.' I wish we'd lose *them*!

WYATT: Oh, Alastair! How nice it is to see you! You *are* a jolly old thing. *Do* tell us about the Americans.

ALASTAIR: Don't ask – oh, well I'm bound to bore you about it, anyway. They just make me *mad*. *You* know. Oh, I don't think you know Mr Lamb, any of you?

WYATT: My dear Lamb, how nice, what a pleasure to see you here. Do you remember? I was just saying – we met once and got awfully drunk and sorry for ourselves at the Savile – or was it the Travellers?

LAMB: Somewhere like that.

WYATT: This is my daughter, Evangie and my youngest, Mary. That's her old man, Robert. Seems a bit surly when you first talk to him but he's North Country, East Riding I think, *and* a schoolteacher so it's not all his fault and he's a cracking good sort underneath it all, aren't you, old thing?

ROBERT: A little cracker.

WYATT: Then there's Frederica, my other daughter and her husband, Eddie. But they're down at the beach. She's rather beautiful, but I'm not supposed to say it and *you* certainly mustn't. She's a frightful flirt, even with me and I know she doesn't care for me over much. Evangie, she's awfully brainy and *writes*. She'll probably trap you in a corner, so I should watch it. Mary's the youngest and prettiest and quite the least trouble of any of them, enjoys everything, doesn't carp, well not much, does as she's told and smiles and has lots of lovely little kiddies, which the others don't and who can blame them if they're as selfish as me? I never bothered with *my* children. Some people would say I was selfish and maybe it's so but I've always been fascinated by myself long after everyone else was bored to death with me.

ALASTAIR: Stop it! How can you *do* it in this weather?

WYATT: Who else is there? Oh, old Harry. He's not here yet but we think he'll turn up sometime. He's an American but not like the others at all.

LAMB: I know.

WYATT: Well, of course, you must know him better than any of us.

ALASTAIR: This is Jed. He's a student. He's just on his way.

WYATT: How do you do, Jed. Where are you on your way to?

JED: Wherever . . .

WYATT: Yes. I know what you mean. When Alastair says you are a student, are you an eternal student like, say, Trefimov?

ALASTAIR: He's an eternal student, you can take it from me. Shall we get ourselves a drink inside? I'll have a word with Robin to let her know we're here. Is she with Leroi and the Brigadier? Oh, she'll be wanting help then.

(*The three of them,* ALASTAIR, JED *and* LAMB, *go in.*)

WYATT: Was I all right?

CHRISTOPHER: Fine. He was nervous. I think I'll go and see if I can find Frederica and Edward.

MARY: I shouldn't worry. They'll come if they want.

CHRISTOPHER: I'll just have a look. All right, Wyatt?

WYATT: Fine, dear boy, fine. Oh, I say, I forgot to introduce you.

CHRISTOPHER: It doesn't matter.

(*He goes off.*)

WYATT: Do you think I hurt his feelings?

EVANGIE: No.

WYATT: I do hope not. He's such a dear boy.

MARY: Let's go in. I'm hungry.

ROBERT: Me too.

EVANGIE: Right.

(*They rise.*)

WYATT: I feel a bit tired. Anyway, I think I'll wait for
Christopher and Frederica.

EVANGIE: Just as you like.

WYATT: Won't be a jiffy . . .

(*They go off. He closes his eyes for a few moments. Then opens
them as* HARRY, *an enormous figure in late middle age, comes
in.*)

Harry, my dear boy. We were talking of you.

HARRY: Yes? Americans, I suppose?

(*He lowers his great frame into a chair.*)

Ah! That's better.

WYATT: Not like *you*, Harry. Not like you. You're *special*.

HARRY: That's what we're here for, Wyatt. That's what we're
here for.

WYATT: Are you all right? You look awfully tired.

HARRY: I'm OK. You know. You get, just tired, and in this
climate . . .

WYATT: Yes. I know what you mean, old thing. I wonder where
Frederica's got to . . . I miss the cold and the damp and
the colours that change all the winter and then . . . I miss it
. . . I wish I didn't . . .

HARRY: Well, guess I'd better make myself known to Robin and
the Brigadier and warn 'em I'm here. (*He rises.*) You
coming?

WYATT: Later, dear boy. I think I'll wait a little longer.

HARRY: OK. You'll miss the Brigadier's *plat de maison*.

(*He goes into the house.*)

(WYATT *closes his eyes against the sun.*)

ACT TWO

SCENE ONE

After lunch. The same scene. Resting in the shade are WYATT,
ROBERT, CHRISTOPHER, LAMB *and* EVANGIE. *Only* FREDERICA
is standing, looking across the bay.

WYATT: (*Presently*) I *thought* this new hat was a mistake.

FREDERICA: Sit in the shade, you old silly.

WYATT: Oh, *aren't I?* (*He moves his chair.*) Gosh, it's a scorcher!

FREDERICA: There's a great breeze if you stand up here.

WYATT: Couldn't stand anywhere after all that lunch the
Brigadier got for us. I say, he *is* hot stuff in that
department, isn't he? But he *was* quite a soldier.

FREDERICA: I suppose it usually is.

WYATT: What?

FREDERICA: Quite a scorcher. Here.

WYATT: Oh.

LAMB: There's a cool season. It rains and there's mist and the
mildew sprouts for a few weeks. But it never lasts long.

WYATT: (*Re-settled*) Oh yes, that's more like it.

ROBERT: It'll be cold at home.

WYATT: Perishing. Nice though.

FREDERICA: What are you thinking about?

WYATT: Me?

FREDERICA: Anyone. Don't go to sleep. Robert, keep awake.

ROBERT: Sorry. I was trying *not* to think about the new term
starting next week. Breath on the grey playground, frozen
lavatories and Irish stew and sweating middens of cabbage.

WYATT: My dear boy! Don't! How awful for you.

FREDERICA: They're only children.

ROBERT: We're all children once.

FREDERICA: What a pious remark. We may be, but some are
more so than others. And leave it behind more quickly.

ROBERT: I'm sorry I sounded pious.

FREDERICA: Now you're piqued.

WYATT: I didn't think so at all.

LAMB: No. It's like saying: what's 1950 got to do with 1980?

FREDERICA: Well, *what*?

LAMB: We'll be the same people.

FREDERICA: Will we? What were *you* thinking?

LAMB: What I usually think of after lunch here. Walking down Bond Street in mid-afternoon with a nice evening to look forward to at Covent Garden or somewhere and time for tea at the Ritz and money to buy myself a present or, even better, someone else as well.

FREDERICA: Daddy?

WYATT: Blackfriars Station and George Moore.

FREDERICA: You're making it up.

WYATT: No, I'm not. I was thinking of the beastly cold like Robert. Of waiting for trains and then looking up at the front of Blackfriars Station and seeing it inscribed in the stone: Broadstairs; Dresden; Cheltenham; and *St. Petersburg*. So I asked the booking clerk for a cheap return to St. Petersburg.

ROBERT: What did he say?

WYATT: 'I'm afraid you'll have to go to Victoria.'

LAMB: When was this?

WYATT: Nineteen sixty-one. What was the other thing?

ROBERT: George Moore.

WYATT: Nothing. I did meet him a couple of times when I was a young man. Ebury Street, I think, he lived. Anyway, he always looked dreadfully ill at ease in company, especially mixed company, keeping his hands in his pockets all the time. And one day someone asked him why and he said: 'Well you see, whenever I stand up I'm afraid my underpants will fall down and it's a very uncomfortable feeling in company. Especially mixed company.' And so, whoever it was, said: 'But George, do you not have those little tabs inside to put your braces through?' And Moore replied: 'Oh – *those*. Do you know I've always been wondering what those were for!'

FREDERICA: I know why you like that story.

ROBERT: Why? I'd not heard it.

FREDERICA: Because he likes writers being made out to be divine simpletons or holy innocents, and himself most of all.

WYATT: Unholy. I think we're a dismal bunch, on the whole, to meet, anyway. Don't you think so?

LAMB: The *performers* are the worst.

WYATT: That's true enough! Indeed. When I think . . . I was dreading meeting *you*. What a relief it's turned out. He's a modest old thing, don't you think?

LAMB: I'm not proud of living out in the sunshine if you mean that?

WYATT: Certainly not. Where people choose to live is their own business.

ROBERT: Listen . . .

FREDERICA: Not those bloody birds?

ROBERT: The surf.

FREDERICA: What about it?

ROBERT: I can't get used to the sound of it.

FREDERICA: I can. That's the trouble.

WYATT: Not like Cornwall.

ROBERT: Or Pembroke.

FREDERICA: Or Northumberland. Or Brighton. Do *shut up*, both of you! You're being like those people who are never bored again and we know what a deadly lot those are.

LAMB: It makes quite a fair old row –

FREDERICA: In the wet season.

ROBERT: Robin's never bored.

FREDERICA: No. She never was.

ROBERT: Neither's the Brigadier.

WYATT: No. Not him.

ROBERT: Cooking.

FREDERICA: Washing up.

ROBERT: Digging, watching his vines and waterfalls and rock gardens.

FREDERICA: Smoking his pipe. I wish men wouldn't smoke pipes.

WYATT: Oh, don't you like it? You used to say you liked the smell of mine.

FREDERICA: I did. I do. It's just *some* men. The way they *do* it.
Putting you in your place . . .
ROBERT: Watching, observing, feeding the lizards –
WYATT: Oh, birds. Birds of boredom. What does that make me
think of?
FREDERICA: Trafalgar Square . . . How strange you all seem
sometimes.
LAMB: We are. And not. And you?
FREDERICA: I don't feel that. No. Not at all.
WYATT: Tedious flight of tern,
How I wonder what you'd earn.
ROBERT: Did you make that up?
FREDERICA: What else?
WYATT: If you fumbled in the sky for words
Would you still just bore like birds? . . .
ROBERT: Good.
WYATT: No . . . Chatter. Frederica is right as usual. Birds
chatter and *that* is their mortal flaw. Chatter sins against
language and when we sin against the word, we sin against
God. Gosh, I *am* pompous.
FREDERICA: I wasn't going to say it.
WYATT: Must be the Brigadier's cuddly, loving little grape.
Where's your old man got to?
FREDERICA: He's out there on the beach talking to Jed.
LAMB: Oh, *does* he talk?
ROBERT: I think *there is* someone who could sin against
language if he could bring himself to it.
WYATT: Do you, really? Seemed a quiet little chap to me. I tried
talking to him but he never said a word.
FREDERICA: Why should he? He despises us.
WYATT: Oh, do you think he does? Yes. Of course. You're
right. Oh, dear . . . Perhaps I said the wrong thing . . . I
only asked him about himself.
FREDERICA: He doesn't want your interest. Or anyone's.
WYATT: I thought dear little Alastair was his chum.
FREDERICA: He despises him too.
WYATT: What a shame. Perhaps I should try again?
FREDERICA: Don't. Anyway, you know you've no intention.

You dislike him as much as the rest of us. No. More. He
frightens you more.

WYATT: I wonder if I should have a sleep and then a walk. Or a
walk and *then* a sleep. What do you think?

FREDERICA: Either. On the other hand: both.

ROBERT: The first. Except chatter a bit.

WYATT: Oh. Shall I? I'll annoy old Fred there.

FREDERICA: Would that stop you? I wonder if you can get lung
cancer from smoking pot?

ROBERT: Ask Jed.

FREDERICA: I will. There's something about that boy . . .

ROBERT: What?

FREDERICA: I don't know. But he shouldn't *be* here.

LAMB: Well, he is. And plenty more.

FREDERICA: I shan't be sorry to leave this place.

WYATT: Well, don't let old Robin and the Brigadier know.

FREDERICA: Oh, I know. They've taken such pains to give us a
good time.

ROBERT: And they live here.

FREDERICA: I'm sorry. I know. And so do you. (*To* LAMB.)

LAMB: That's all right, my dear. I see everyone think it. The
ones who come to visit, I mean. Friends. They sit in the
sun, and are waited on and bathe and chat, barefoot on the
white evening sand, watching the sea and thinking . . .

ROBERT: That they're glad not to be you.

LAMB: Not to be rich enough to be an exile, browned and
attended on by sun and by the regular wind and service.
But back to cold, uncertain tides and striving pavements.
And the marriage of anxieties . . . domestic . . . oh . . .
extremes . . .

FREDERICA: Where were you born?

LAMB: Me? Kuala Lumpur. Natch.

FREDERICA: Yes. But it doesn't – warm you – as it should do.
No. It leaves you open to all the chills when you come back
. . . over the other side.

LAMB: You?

FREDERICA: Kandy. Ceylon . . . Robin too.

LAMB: You?

EVANGIE: Singapore.

ROBERT: As they used to say, 'their father had a bike'.

WYATT: What's that?

EVANGIE: Grandpa was in 'the Service'.

WYATT: Papa? Oh, I'll say he was.

ROBERT: Where were *you* born?

WYATT: Srinigar. Kashmir. Shalimar. Bit like the Thames near Henley. Lots of lush and vegetables and Weybridge-type curry and pink blancmange in little elephant moulds. Oh, the old boy wanted *me* to go in it, of course. All I did was sire four daughters at his various postings. Trying to be *A Writer*. But you *can* write and give Some Service as well. Give some service. Well, I never did. Just his non-paying guest. With a wife and four thumping daughters. Well – *he* gave service. Old thing . . .

LAMB: And your husband?

FREDERICA: Rangoon.

WYATT: What about you, old thing?

ROBERT: Hastings Royal Infirmary.

WYATT: Hastings Royal Infirmary! What about the Brigadier? Where do you suppose *he* was born?

FREDERICA: Mesopotamia.

WYATT: Mesopotamia. Of *course*.

ROBERT: That's why the house is named.

WYATT: To: Mesopotamia. You can see him . . . setting out. Or someone . . .

FREDERICA: I wish Edward would stop talking to that boy. Man . . .

WYATT: Who? Little Alastair?

FREDERICA: No. Not little Alastair. Jed.

ROBERT: Perhaps it's his scientific curiosity: 'the young mind'.

FREDERICA: No. The young, whatever they are, bore him even more than I do.

WYATT: My darling Fred, he adores you.

FREDERICA: Maybe. But he's not a pathologist for nothing.

ROBERT: Examining blood.

FREDERICA: All day.

EVANGIE: Frederica's right.

WYATT: Of course. She always is.

EVANGIE: About being born. Away from home.

FREDERICA: Home?

EVANGIE: Whatever . . .

WYATT: Out of all . . . hearts . . .

EVANGIE: Do you remember Grandfather's study?

WYATT: What? The boy's?

FREDERICA: I'll say.

WYATT: All my life . . .

EVANGIE: The joss sticks and Burmese guns. Saddle oil . . .

FREDERICA: Even the books smelt of curry powder. The Casino Palace, Port Said.

EVANGIE: Back numbers of the *Times of Natal*. A Zulu grammar.

FREDERICA: Manuals in Urdu.

EVANGIE: Rawhide shields and dried python skins and brass iguanas. And the photographs.

FREDERICA: Brown. Brown to yellow.

WYATT: The Casino Palace!

EVANGIE: The Groups.

WYATT: What did the old boy say? I know – 'The Royal Navy always travels first class'.

EVANGIE: Probyn's Horse, the Peshewar Vale Hunt, tennis parties.

WYATT: Signed photograph of Lord Minto.

EVANGIE: Tent pegging. 'Robin: aged one year'. A cricket match on the parade ground; amateur theatricals.

FREDERICA: Mummy as Lydia Languish in *The Rivals*.

WYATT: Daddy on the prompt book.

EVANGIE: Field batteries, elephant batteries! I never understood them going into torches . . . The Newcastle Mounted Rifles.

FREDERICA: Inspected by Grandfather. Men *do* inspect.

ROBERT: England Inspects . . .

EVANGIE: Frederica on Grandmother's pony.

FREDERICA: In a white party frock.

EVANGIE: A timetable of the South India Railway, the oars of Jesus College; *In China with the British* – two vols. 'Setting sail aboard the *Rawalpindi*'.

WYATT: Old *Pindi* – torpedoed first month of the war.

EVANGIE: Taking arsenic instead of baking powder. Talk in the mess. The club.

FREDERICA: In the club. Mummy four times. Lizards on the ceiling above the mosquito net, sweat, the mail. Knick-knacks. Junk and boa constrictors . . .

WYATT: I'm surprised you remember so much. *I* don't. You were all such *children* . . .

FREDERICA: Ah – home to England.

WYATT: *I* don't. At least I don't think so. Do I? Yes. I suppose so. I took it for granted then. Busy being a 'writer'. God, Lamb, why do we do it?

LAMB: For the money. And being treated well, or better than you *should* be by any rights . . .

FREDERICA: The sky is *so* clear . . . the trees seem even darker than they are . . . What was it like before?

LAMB: Before? Oh, not so very different I suppose. The Governor General's house is still there though he's called something else now; Royalty of some sort came out. New flag went up. The police band played the dreadful National Anthem, all deliciously out of tune; you couldn't believe it, the comedy and pain of it. I think someone actually recorded it as a collector's item. Some relief, I suppose. A bit of apprehension, but not over much. The climate was the same, the people were the same, we were the same. Except . . . You see. . . . There was despair in a lot of hearts. Even in those who . . . who . . . oh, who . . .

WYATT: Yes. I can see all that. Can't you? The lady-in-waiting; the umbrellas; the marquee.

LAMB: It was comic then. And it's comic *now*. If anyone could ever think of it or remember it. But it was full of pain. *And* some quite good people. Thing about pain. It changes as *you* change. But it doesn't go, does it? *Does* it? Or am I mad as I often think I am when I'm alone, or begging Robin and the Brigadier's pardon? . . .

WYATT: You're not mad, old thing . . .

LAMB: Wish you weren't all going.

WYATT: Still a bit of time.

LAMB: There's me and Robin. The Brigadier. Alastair chatting
up the tourists in his crimping parlour. Going on his crying
jags, threatening us all with his too many sleeping pills,
falling in love with young Americans he despises and who
despise him. Looking to an Old Etonian queen like me,
who's respectable only because he's rich and famous.
Turning to Jed, who hates him slightly less than the rest of
us . . .

WYATT: Oh dear . . .

LAMB: Mortified by the sunlight on his wig join.

FREDERICA: That could have been a song once. When you
think of it. 'Sunlight On My Wig Join'.

LAMB: I'm sorry.

FREDERICA: No.

LAMB: It's just that we shall miss you. But I shouldn't have
really said so.

FREDERICA: Why not? You *thought* it.

LAMB: Do *you* say everything you think?

FREDERICA: No. People think I do. Sometimes *I* think I do.

LAMB: Robin will miss you.

ROBERT: Sisters are strange things.

FREDERICA: We all travesty ourselves. It seems unavoidable.
Totally . . .

WYATT: (*Reading paper*) Good God!

LAMB: What?

WYATT: Do you know what we're missing on B.B.C.! At this
almost very moment? Robert, *you* read it. You've got good,
young eyes.

ROBERT: (*Reads*) 'Europe Since 1945. The fifth of twelve
programmes on economic and social change in Western
and Eastern Europe since the end of the Second World
War. Next: New Structures in Society . . .'

LAMB: Oh, no . . .

ROBERT: 'To what extent have such factors as economic growth
increased educational opportunity, and welfare of post-
European societies both east and west, towards a single
type of industrial society? . . .'

FREDERICA: Help!

ROBERT: 'By the Professor of Social and Industrial Studies at the Sorbonne. *Worker Participation Control:* A discussion of different forms of worker power in industrial management, from participation French style, through West German co-operation to Yugoslavia's worker-control. Thursday: Managing the economy Number Seven. Prospects for an Incomes Policy. How to contain rising prices is something that has baffled one government after another . . .'

WYATT: Baffled!

FREDERICA: Stop!

LAMB: Oh, yes. Please.

ROBERT: 'Does the present exercise in regulating prices and incomes offer any real chance of a break-through?'

FREDERICA: Can't wait! Let's go home *now*.

ROBERT: '*People in Towns*.' Urban Sociology. A course. The existence of social problems in our towns has produced its equal and opposite reaction – the social work movement.

FREDERICA: Even the birds look good after that.

ROBERT: 'The Lecturer for Social Work Training . . .'

WYATT: Social Work Training?

ROBERT: 'Talks about –'

WYATT: What does the Old Thing talk about?

ROBERT: 'About social workers and about the work of the Seebohm Committee, of which he was a member . . .'

FREDERICA: Poor soul.

ROBERT: 'Further publications relating to this series include: *Second Year Russian.* Eight shillings. *Starting German.* Books One and Two, price four shillings each. *Europe Since 1945. Study Notes*, five shillings. *Study Notes II*, seven shillings. *People in Towns* will cost you eighteen shillings. *Manet* (colour slides) two pounds; *Renaissance Exploration*, eleven shillings; *Helping Your Neighbour*, three shillings and *Problems of Learning, Study Notes*, three shillings.'

WYATT: My goodness! What you're missing, old thing!

ROBERT: Mustn't be patronizing now.

FREDERICA: Why not? I'm always being patronizing.

ROBERT: That's because you're more clever and assured than most people.

FREDERICA: Oh no, I'm not. Evangie's the clever one.

EVANGIE: I'm not. Still a lot of people do . . . No, I won't say it.

LAMB: Why not?

EVANGIE: Because it sounds priggish and what people think I am.

LAMB: Which is?

EVANGIE: A rather voracious intellectual.

WYATT: Oh, come!

EVANGIE: It's true. Isn't it?

FREDERICA: Yes.

EVANGIE: True – or what people think?

FREDERICA: Both I should think. Don't ask me. They're all cleverer than I am . . .

WYATT: I rather like '*Helping Your Neighbour*' *Study Notes*.

EVANGIE: No. I'm sure you're right.

FREDERICA: You said it.

EVANGIE: And you agreed.

FREDERICA: Shouldn't I?

EVANGIE: Yes. I think you should. It's hard on me but probably harder for you.

FREDERICA: It's not hard at all.

EVANGIE: Then it should be. Even if it is your sister . . . I'm off to the beach I think. Daddy?

WYATT: Think I'll stay in the shade a bit, old thing. I'm so *feeble*. We'll have a walk before dinner, right?

EVANGIE: Right.

(*She goes. Pause.*)

FREDERICA: You all think I'm a shit, don't you?

LAMB: *I* don't think so. Not me, anyway. But then I *am*. You're a clown. With all the privileges and penalties. You say what is obvious but not necessarily true, or the whole truth, at least. But that's something else and in the meantime there's the performing dog act of partiality.

FREDERICA: Thanks.

LAMB: Don't thank me. Everyone is grateful to you.

FREDERICA: Meaning?

LAMB: Please don't pick a fight with me, my dear. I like and admire you though, of course, don't know you or ever will.

I may not, and I don't wish to, be able to hurt you. But this
I do know: that nothing you could say or do would ever
hurt me. Which is *my* misfortune.

FREDERICA: That was a bit glib, even for you, wasn't it?

LAMB: Not really. I tried a little more with you but it didn't
come off. Quite clearly . . . I was thinking the other day
about moon landings . . .

WYATT: God, the sun does BURN, doesn't it?

FREDERICA: The birds *sing*.

ROBERT: The surf – what? Pounds I suppose.

WYATT: Why are we all so cruel to one another?

FREDERICA: *You're* not.

WYATT: Yes. I am.

FREDERICA: Yes. You are.

ROBERT: Frankly.

FREDERICA: Frankly. But no one thinks you're a shit. They
think you're loveable.

LAMB: Don't be intemperate. You lose your style.

FREDERICA: I don't know what intemperate means, or what you
mean by it and I'm too proud to find out, do you mind?
And, as for style, I haven't.

LAMB: I don't know you any more than I know your father but
he has some concern for himself, as we all have. You
mustn't grudge that.

FREDERICA: Why not?

LAMB: Because I feel it.

FREDERICA: There! That's all.

LAMB: Of course, you're right.

WYATT: She always is.

LAMB: No more than that.

WYATT: Always was. Evangie *seemed* the clever one. But she's
not, poor old thing. Oh dear, I must stop saying that.

ROBERT: What?

WYATT: Old thing.

FREDERICA: Quite. You should.

WYATT: I know.

FREDERICA: It isn't half as cute as everyone thinks or thinks
they think.

WYATT: Yes. Pretty nauseating really. Well: I am.

FREDERICA: Don't sound pleased about it.

WYATT: I'm not. Actually. I don't quite know how to make it ring true. Or. Indeed . . . anything. I think moon landings must be pretty morose, don't you, I mean as we're being morose and we are, at least I am . . . (*To* CHRISTOPHER.) You're very quiet, old thing.

CHRISTOPHER: Am I?

FREDERICA: Yes. Exhausted.

CHRISTOPHER: No. Tired. It's a tiring island.

FREDERICA: It is. So are we.

WYATT: Should we get him a doctor?

FREDERICA: Is that a real question?

CHRISTOPHER: I'm all right. I was just wondering if I should go for a swim or walk or something with Evangie.

WYATT: Too hot . . . Phew!

FREDERICA: She's all right.

CHRISTOPHER: Is she though?

FREDERICA: She's thinking about writing a piece about this place. Or some book. Or some insight she's fishing around for.

CHRISTOPHER: If it's well enough done and for the right reasons.

LAMB: I never know what the right reasons are.

FREDERICA: Oh, for *its* sake. And your's. Or neither – Who knows?

LAMB: Clearly, *you* don't.

ROBERT: Who would you send to the moon?

FREDERICA: Oh, the usual. Me, I expect.

WYATT: Yes, who *would* we?

FREDERICA: I wonder why people have children. Do they *want* you? What do you think, Robert?

(*At this stage* ROBIN, *the* BRIGADIER, ALASTAIR, JED *and* HARRY *come out on to the porch and join the company.*)

(*To* ROBERT.) That man's dying.

ROBERT: Who?

FREDERICA: Harry. The hulking American.

WYATT: There you are, old things. I say, we did have a good lunch. Brigadier, you're a genius. We were just talking about moon landings and who we'd send up there.

ROBIN: Customs officers.

WYATT: Naturally.

LAMB: Women journalists.

WYATT: Good.

ALASTAIR: American tourists.

FREDERICA: But not Harry.

ALASTAIR: Harry's not exactly a tourist. He dropped in with
Nelson. Anyone who goes on cruises. Do you know who
we've got in today? The American Folk Dance Society.
Eight hundred of them?

BRIGADIER: All local officials.

ROBIN: The High Commissioner.

ALASTAIR: The High Commissioner's wife.

FREDERICA: People who give poetry readings.

WYATT: Oh, I say, yes.

(*They all settle into their chairs and relax in the shade.*)

I was just thinking about what the girls were saying.

BRIGADIER: What were they saying?

WYATT: Don't think you were here, old thing. About the old
boy, Papa. The way he'd talk about the Black Noons and
sage and the gazelle and the bustard and all those camel-
mounted soldiers, shuffling along in a freezing night with
the animals gurgling and moaning and the men in their
Section messes . . . and singing . . .

FREDERICA: We'll all be home soon.

ROBERT: Except for Robin and the Brigadier.

WYATT: Well, it's their home. And old Lamb's of course.

ALASTAIR: And mine, God help me. Why I should be crimping
in a place like this I'll never know.

ROBERT: (*To* JED) What about you?

JED: Any place is home for me. So who cares?

(LEROI *enters with* MRS JAMES.)

LEROI: Mrs James is here to see Mr Gillman.

WYATT: (*Shouting off*) Christopher! (*To* MRS JAMES.) How nice
of you to come and see me.

MRS JAMES: Not at all. It's quite an honour. I was told you
wouldn't give interviews.

(CHRISTOPHER *appears*.)

WYATT: This is Mrs James, Christopher. She's come to have a chat.

FREDERICA: Do you want us to all go?

WYATT: Not at all. I shan't feel half as self-conscious if I've got my chums around me.

CHRISTOPHER: Do sit down, Mrs James. Thank you, Leroi.

WYATT: How very nice to meet you.

MRS JAMES: I hope it will be.

CHRISTOPHER: Shall we start off right away? Or can I get you a drink or something?

MRS JAMES: No, thank you.

CHRISTOPHER: Only he gets a little fatigued in this heat.

MRS JAMES: So do we all. I shan't take much of your time. If you've no objection, I'll just turn on this little tape-recorder. I hope it works all right.

CHRISTOPHER: They all say that.

MRS JAMES: Do they? Well, I'll try and get it working. Could you just say a few words for level?

WYATT: Who, me?

MRS JAMES: It is you I've come to interview.

WYATT: Right. What about politics? Well, I'm just an old radical who detests progress. But then nobody hates it more. Don't you think, Mrs James?

MRS JAMES: You're the one being interviewed. I'll just play that back.

(*She does so*.)

MRS JAMES: That's fine.

WYATT: Well, where shall we begin?

MRS JAMES: Wherever you like.

CHRISTOPHER: You're the one conducting the interview.

WYATT: I don't really know why you should want to talk to me at all. I've got no interesting views or opinions about anything. Never have done. I don't believe in much, never have done, never been inspired by anything. I'm simply over-talkative, vain, corpulent, and a bit of a played-out hulk, as I think most of the world knows and I'm surprised the news hasn't even reached this delightful little island of yours.

MRS JAMES: Isn't it a bit early to start being patronizing?

WYATT: I am never patronizing. I am in no position to be so. And never have been.

MRS JAMES: How do you feel at the moment? How do you feel at the moment?

WYATT: Just about the same as usual. Except hotter. Always weary, ineffably bored, always in some sort of vague pain and always with a bit of unsatisfying hatred burning away in the old inside like a heartburn or indigestion.

MRS JAMES: I can see we may not get very far.

WYATT: Does it matter?

MRS JAMES: Not to you. I've simply been sent to do a job. Well, let's take an easy one first: what do you think of your fellow writers?

WYATT: Fellow writers! What a dreadful expression!

MRS JAMES: I'm sorry, I couldn't think of anything else to describe the people who practise the same profession.

WYATT: I try not to think of my fellow writers. If they're better than I am, I am disturbed. If they're worse, which is unusual, I simply feel sorry.

MRS JAMES: What do you think about the state of English literature at the moment?

WYATT: Nothing at all.

MRS JAMES: Would you say that you strike postures with people whom you regard as provincials?

WYATT: Very likely, I'm afraid. But not in your case. You're quite clearly very sophisticated. I mean, you wouldn't have much trouble getting the edge on me. You can never win an interview if you are being interviewed.

MRS JAMES: I'm not trying to win anything. I'm simply trying to arrive at some sort of approximation of the truth.

WYATT: Do you think there is such a thing?

MRS JAMES: I don't think you should ask me facile questions, even if you are a famous man and paying us a visit.

WYATT: I'm not paying you a visit. I am visiting my daughter and her husband. And staying with my other daughters and friends.

MRS JAMES: Do you think we should give up this interview?

WYATT: I think that onus is entirely upon you.

MRS JAMES: Quite right. What do you think of as being Utopia?

WYATT: A place without pain, passion or nobility. Where there is no hatred, boredom or imperfection.

MRS JAMES: What do you think of man?

WYATT: As a defect, striving for excellence.

MRS JAMES: Do you really think that?

WYATT: No, but presumably you want me to say something, however dull. However, I do think that there is a disastrously false, and very modern, idea that you can be absolutely honest.

MRS JAMES: How do you feel about your present work?

WYATT: At the moment I don't really have any present work to speak of.

MRS JAMES: But has any of it been an advance?

WYATT: The idea of advance is only something that is nurtured by uncreative people and critics.

MRS JAMES: You are well known for being over-sensitive to criticism.

WYATT: Am I? I simply dislike it like a dog dislikes fleas.

MRS JAMES: Didn't Doctor Johnson say that?

WYATT: Probably, but I should have thought the old boy would have put it a bit better, don't you?

MRS JAMES: Do you deliberately adopt a public pose?

WYATT: Yes.

MRS JAMES: Why?

WYATT: Because it makes life slightly more tolerable. The same applies to private life.

MRS JAMES: Then why do you consent to be interviewed?

WYATT: I need the money.

MRS JAMES: But we can't afford to pay you.

WYATT: I'm afraid Christopher didn't tell me that.

MRS JAMES: What do you think about religion today?

WYATT: I think about religion if I think about it at all as it was in any time in human history. I think about it as the exercise of law as applied by each man to himself, even if that law be anarchy, negation or despair. If you're really interested, and it's pretty clear that you can't be interested in a pontificating old English buffer like me, that I also believe in what St. Augustine called 'the harsh necessity of sin'. It's a ponderous phrase but probably no worse than 'make love not war' and of course, I've always been very keen on the King James Bible and the English genius to boot, which it is being booted very swiftly, oh and good old Cranmer's Book of Common Prayer. It's like the Bible, it combines profundity without complexity.

MRS JAMES: What do you think about protest movements?

WYATT: Protest is easy. But grief must be lived. As dear old Yeats said, dear old thing, be *secret* and *exult*. Secret . . .

MRS JAMES: Would you say that you are a neurotic?

WYATT: On the whole, yes, all neurotics are bullies. But then so are most interviewers.

MRS JAMES: Going back again to one of your favourite topics, critics . . .

WYATT: One of yours too, so it seems.

MRS JAMES: What would you say was the function of critics, if any?

WYATT: Critics are sacrosanct. You must make it clear to your readers that they are simply and obviously more important than poets or writers. That's why you should always get in with them. You see, what we chaps do may be all right in its little way but what really counts is the fact that if it weren't for the existence of critics, we shouldn't be around at all or would just be on the dole or running chicken farms. Never make cheap jokes about critics. You've got to remember this: the critic is above criticism because he has the good sense never to do anything. He's up there helping us poor little guys to understand what the hell we're doing, which is a jolly helpful thing, you must agree. And if he stops you from writing at all then he's done the best job possible. After all, who wants to read or listen to what some poor old writer has pumped out of his diseased heart when he can read a balanced and reasoned judgement about life, love and literature from an aloof and informed commentator.

MRS JAMES: Now that you have reached a certain stage in life, what, in fact, do you think about things like being in love?

WYATT: I think: thank God I don't have to be in love any more.

MRS JAMES: What do you think you are?

WYATT: I think I'm probably what my daughter Frederica says she is, just a lot of hot shit, if you'll pardon the expression, blood, vanity and a certain prowess.

MRS JAMES: There is a rumour that you have given up writing altogether.

WYATT: Heard that did you? Hear that, Christopher? God, that was the rumour I tried to spread about myself.

MRS JAMES: In these changing times, do you still believe that words in themselves have any meaning, value or validity?

WYATT: I still cling pathetically to the old bardic belief that 'words alone are certain good'.

MRS JAMES: Do you still live in London for any reason?

WYATT: Same reason as dear old Yeats again. Lived in Dublin. Great hatred. Little room.

MRS JAMES: Do you see art as going in any particular direction now?

WYATT: I can hardly see the table in front of me. All art is simply criticism now. Posturing as art, self-evaluating, categorizing, constitutional, branded, hectoring and elbowing everyone out of the way.

MRS JAMES: What do you think about friendship?

WYATT: A lost art. You should be able to discuss your friend's colds or toothaches as if they were railway disasters. As long as you both know they're not.

MRS JAMES: Now, to a difficult question, as I know you have not been here long. What are your feelings about the island and the people you've met?

WYATT: All the good things I've seen of the island seem to be legacies of the British, the Spanish and the Dutch, particularly in the buildings and what's left of any proper dispensation of the law. As for the people, they seem to me to be a very unappealing mixture of hysteria and lethargy, brutality and sentimentality.

MRS JAMES: Would you like me to turn this thing off?

WYATT: Not for my sake. I'm past protection. Aren't I, Christopher?

MRS JAMES: Women have figured a great deal in your life.

WYATT: That sounds like a criticism veiled as a question.

MRS JAMES: What would you say your feelings are about women nowadays?

WYATT: I have very little to do with women nowadays. As you can see, I've never been particularly attractive and if you want to ask that sort of question, and you clearly do, I'm pretty well past it anyway. The trouble with women is that I've always made a cardinal mistake: of treating them as friends and equals which they patently are not. Women only really love bullies.

MRS JAMES: Don't you think that's a sweeping statement?

WYATT: Yes.

MRS JAMES: What do you think about the class situation in England?

WYATT: I'm very fond of it. It provides a great deal of entertainment, fun and speculation for people who have nothing better to do. Like many of the upper class, I've liked the sound of broken glass.

MRS JAMES: What about God?

WYATT: I say, we are getting down to it, aren't we? Are you sure you won't have a drink? I've always had a bit of a leaning towards him. I think perhaps people nowadays, people make the mistake of thinking of God as some sort of competitive family concern. You know, who might be pushed out of the market by a bit of smart operation.

MRS JAMES: You seem to keep referring to boredom. Is it an obsession with you?

WYATT: No, I'm a bit too keen on myself. But I think everyone should have a daily ration of it.

MRS JAMES: Going back to literature –

WYATT: Oh, is it still there?

MRS JAMES: Do you believe in the New Testament idea of the Gift of Tongues?

WYATT: Yes I do. Mine was just a rather flabby, flailing thing. Everyone said I was rhetorical rather than recondite. And I think they were right.

MRS JAMES: How would you describe yourself politically?

WYATT: I wouldn't attempt to. For one thing it isn't interesting enough. I believe in work but not in work to keep out all this desolation we live in. I believe in charity and I don't mean in the American sense, which is having buddies so that you can get on. I don't think I really believe in going on strike, even when some poor devil's in the right. My father believed that. Do you know one thing I'm really ashamed of? I drove a bus in the general strike. I thought I was such a dashing fellow.

MRS JAMES: Everyone always thinks of you as a very English writer –

WYATT: Oh, do they really?

MRS JAMES: You know perfectly well. Do you think that there is still something special about being English rather than some other nationality?

WYATT: I don't know. I always think that there's something like a certain form of, say, cloud formation, called the English imagination. And if ever there was a critic's phrase, I think that's probably one.

MRS JAMES: Do you think of yourself as an artist?

WYATT: Everyone nowadays is apparently an artist.

MRS JAMES: But do you believe it?

WYATT: No. I believe in special gifts. Just as I believe some people are better than others.

MRS JAMES: Do you believe in the family?

WYATT: I don't believe in its continuance, if that's what you mean. I do think it had its pleasures while it lasted and I was fortunate enough to have enjoyed and suffered them. I had a father whom I loved and now I have daughters whom I love, no doubt largely selfishly. But I wouldn't call it a write-off either for them or me. Or indeed their mother. Like the passing of empires and pride of tongue.

MRS JAMES: Do you think that the relation between the sexes is healthier now than when you were a young man?

WYATT: Yes. But less pleasurable and less enduring. But that is not a question to ask an old man.

MRS JAMES: What do you think of young people?

WYATT: I try not to. But then I've always preferred the instinct of friendship to that of the herd.

MRS JAMES: What do you think of as real sin?

WYATT: The incapacity for proper despair. About talking about loss of faith as if it were some briefcase you've left behind you on the tube.

MRS JAMES: What do you look on as virtue then?

WYATT: True innocence.

MRS JAMES: Lastly, Mr Gillman, what do you dread most at this stage of your life?

WYATT: Not death. But ludicrous death. And I also feel it in the air.

(*Long pause. Enter* TWO AMERICAN TOURISTS. *They are* MR *and* MRS DEKKER.)

FREDERICA: Yes?

MRS DEKKER: Oh, we were just looking for the gift shop.

FREDERICA: Well, I'm afraid this isn't the gift shop.

MRS DEKKER: Oh, dear, I'm so sorry. It's just that my husband and I, Mr Dekker here, wanted to buy a few things to take back home. We've bought something from every place we've been.

FREDERICA: I think the place you're looking for is just down the road.

MRS DEKKER: Oh dear, I'm so sorry. This must be a private home.

FREDERICA: That was what my sister hoped.

MRS DEKKER: Only you see Mr Dekker and I are on this cruise and they told us the gift shop was just down the road.

FREDERICA: Well, it is. But I'm afraid we've nothing to sell.

MRS DEKKER: We're with the Folk Song and Dance Society of America.

ALASTAIR: How nice for you. You all have such lovely hair.

MRS DEKKER: Do you live here? You actually live here?

FREDERICA: My sister and her husband live here and so do two of these gentlemen. The rest of us are what is known as 'passing through'.

MR DEKKER: Having intruded upon you in this way, may I ask you a small favour?

BRIGADIER: Certainly.

MR DEKKER: May we take a photograph of your beautiful home?

BRIGADIER: By all means. Garden as well if you like.

MR DEKKER: And could we take a picture of you all as well?

FREDERICA: Why not go the whole hog?

MRS DEKKER: My husband, Mr Dekker, just loves to take mementos.

FREDERICA: Yes, they are nice, aren't they?

(*They all pose quickly while* MR DEKKER *takes his photographs.*)

MRS DEKKER: Well, thank you all so much. It was a real pleasure meeting you all.

FREDERICA: Likewise, Mrs Dekker.

(MR *and* MRS DEKKER *wave farewell and go out.*)

(*Pause.*)

HARRY: (*To* FREDERICA) You didn't have to be like that, you know. They're harmless.

FREDERICA: You think so?

HARRY: I know so.

FREDERICA: Why do you really live here? Is it really just because you want to bring water down from the mountains to a lot of people who aren't that bothered anyway?

WYATT: I thought they were a nice couple of old dears.

FREDERICA: No, you didn't. You pretend that you did. Like you've pretended to so much else always.

ROBIN: Frederica – leave Father alone.

FREDERICA: Why should I? (*To* WYATT.) The trouble with you is that you've always been allowed to get away with it. Yes, I mean, get away with it. Like some of us can't. You get away with it all. Bad manners. Laziness. Cowardice. Lateness. Hurtful indiscretion. And we're all supposed to be stunned by the humour and eccentricity of it.

(*Pause.*)

WYATT: I *am* a clown . . . People laugh at me in the street when they see me. But, as you say, it's my own fault.

(WYATT *gets to his feet.*)

Think I need a bit of a walk after that lunch with the Brigadier.

(*They all watch him go off in the direction of the beach.*)
(*Curtain.*)

SCENE TWO

The same evening, as before. The air seems still and there is a strange
noise of resentful-sounding music in the distance. Dogs howl.
FREDERICA *picks up a cushion dropped by* LEROI. *She goes for a*
cigarette and, having got it, turns and almost bumps into
CHRISTOPHER.

FREDERICA: Edward's talked to that boy down on that beach
nearly all day long. Why can't *he* shut him up! Or Robin!
She's supposed to be such a hostess. Any of you. You.
You're Wyatt's Great Protector . . . Aren't you? But, no,
you all let the boy just go on and on – and Daddy
pretending to be deaf . . . all the while. Don't bother to
answer . . .

CHRISTOPHER: I won't. Even if I could.
(*She offers him a cigarette.*)
Strange sound . . .

FREDERICA: What?

CHRISTOPHER: The music.

FREDERICA: Not very attractive. I suppose they think it has a
simple, brooding native charm and vitality. Which is about
the last thing any of them have got. Anyway, they never
stop playing it.

CHRISTOPHER: Tourists like it, I suppose.

FREDERICA: They would . . . Why did you leave your wife and
give up everything for the old man? It can't be much fun.
Or is it?

CHRISTOPHER: You do ask direct questions, don't you?

FREDERICA: Only when I think I might get a direct answer.
Rather charmless really.

CHRISTOPHER: Well . . .

FREDERICA: No. You needn't tell me if you don't want. Or
fictionalize just to please me.

CHRISTOPHER: I want to please you.

209

FREDERICA: Please *me*? Why?

CHRISTOPHER: Because, well, I've simply got a thing, this thing about you. For you.

FREDERICA: Why?

CHRISTOPHER: Oh, lots of reasons. You're in pain a lot of the time.

FREDERICA: I don't need a nurse, thanks. Anyway, you've got the old man and he needs ten blooming nursemaids and God knows what.

CHRISTOPHER: No. I didn't fancy my chances.

FREDERICA: Right. There's no future in me. Not for anyone. One day it'll be just . . . *out* . . . Tell me about your wife.

CHRISTOPHER: She just, didn't fancy me, that's all.

FREDERICA: Perhaps you weren't very fanciable.

CHRISTOPHER: Indeed. So I left her the house, most of the money . . . and the child . . . I minded that . . .

FREDERICA: The child?

CHRISTOPHER: Yes.

FREDERICA: I wonder if you really did. Or was it the house and the money? Is the old boy a fair exchange?

CHRISTOPHER: I think so . . . I admire him.

FREDERICA: Do you?

CHRISTOPHER: Do you think I'm bent?

FREDERICA: No. Just a bit potty. Like most of us . . .

CHRISTOPHER: There was another woman who didn't fancy me either. So I just gave up.

FREDERICA: Faint of heart.

CHRISTOPHER: Quite.

FREDERICA: You're quite attractive.

CHRISTOPHER: Not very . . . You know that boy Jed. He reminds me of a young S.S. man I killed in the war. Unarmed prisoner. A G.I. tried to stop me so I shot him too.

FREDERICA: Now, that's *not* attractive.

CHRISTOPHER: No . . . Not a bit . . .

FREDERICA: Did you get away with it?

CHRISTOPHER: Oh, yes. It's amazing what you can.

FREDERICA: Don't we all know? . . . Why does he pretend to be deaf and in front of Jed?

(Pause.)

(The rest of the company come in from the dining-room. They all look uneasy, particularly ALASTAIR, *who is hysterical.)*

ALASTAIR: *(To everyone)* I told him to go! I told him to go! But he won't! He just won't! Oh God!

*(*ALASTAIR *sits down and weeps silently.)*

Just another of my crying jags . . .

*(*JED *looks down at* ALASTAIR *contemptuously and then turns to address everyone else.)*

JED: You all, you all bastards . . . I sit here listening to you. Having your fancy dinner and your wine from France and England. You know what I think of you? What *we* think of you? What we think of you? Fuck all your *shit* – that's what we think. One person, not like any one of you here, even if he's the God-damnest cretin, I'd make him God, yes, man, rather than you. You hear? Hear me. Listen to me if you can hear anything but the sound of your own selves and present. I'm not interested in your arguments, not that they are, of your so-called memories and all that pathetic shit. The only thing that matters, man is blood, man. Blood . . . You know what that means? No, no, you surely as too hell don't. No, no when you pigs, you pigs go, it ain't going to be no fucking fourth of July. All I see, and I laugh when I see it, man, I laugh, is you pigs barbecued, barbecued in your own shit. *We're*, yes, we're going to take over and don't you begin to forget it. Man, I feel real sorry for you lot. No, I don't . . . You got it coming. And you *have soon.* Think of the theatre of the mind, baby, old moulding babies, except you won't. We count and we *do*, not like you, we *really*, really do . . . Why, we fall about laughing at you people, not people, you're not people, you pigs. We are people. *We* are. But not you. You don't understand and why should you because, believe me, babies, old failing babies, words, yes I mean words, even what I'm saying to you now, is going to be the first to go. Go, baby. Go. You can't even make love. Do you understand one word, those old words you love so much, what I mean? No. And you won't. If it ain't written down, you don't believe it . . . There's only one word left and you know what that is. It's fuck, man. Fuck . . . That's the last of the English for you babies. Or maybe shit. Because that's what we're going to do on you. Shit. That's what you'll all go down in. One blissful, God-like shit. *You* think we're mother-fucking, stinking, yelling, shouting shits. Well that's what we are, babies. And there's nothing, not nothing you or anyone else can do about it. Jesus is sort of shit. But you're not even *shit*. We think, we fuck and we shit and that's what we do and you're on the great gasping end of it. Because you're pigs. Just take one little look at yourselves. You're pigs, babies. Pigs. And we're gonna shit you out of this world, babies. Right out of this mother-fucking world. You know what? I just had an idea. Like that old prick writer there. Colonialism is the fornication of the twentieth century. You can't be young . . . So all you'd better do, all you *will* do, is die, die, baby. And pretty soon. Just real soon. Like tomorrow. Or even tonight.

(*There is a short pause.*)

CHRISTOPHER: I remember killing someone like you. Only he was blond.

JED: Yes? Well, just remember it. Because you may not remember it much longer.

(*Pause.*)

WYATT: I was never a *young* man. I think I always felt old. I was always wrinkled somehow. More than I am now. Well, nearly. Now I am sort of old. No, old. But something always kept telling me I was young. Very young. But, of course, I never was. Something started without me. Too slow. Never got off the old ground. Never got off the ground. Wasn't sure about the ground at all. Never capable of inspecting it. Or, anyway, closely. Not closely . . . Not closely . . . I think I ought to go to bed.

(*As* WYATT *rises to go, several armed islanders appear out of the darkness. He looks at them with their firearms pointing at the group and turns to run away. They shoot him down.*)

(*Pause.*)

EDWARD: There's an old English saying. Don't suppose you'd
know it . . .
JED: So? What is it?
EDWARD: My God – they've shot the fox . . .
(*Curtain.*)

TIME PRESENT

'A time to embrace and a time to refrain from embracing. A time to get and a time to lose: a time to keep, and a time to cast away.'

ECCLESIASTES

CHARACTERS

EDITH
PAULINE
CONSTANCE
PAMELA
MURRAY
EDWARD
BERNARD
ABIGAIL

ACT ONE

CONSTANCE's *flat in Pimlico. For the present she is sharing it with* PAMELA. *There is some evidence that it is lived in by two people with different temperaments and interests. On the whole, the impression is rather severe, more a working area than a place to lounge around. The influence of* CONSTANCE *is in the Scandinavian furniture and abstracts. There is also the evidence of her profession of M.P. There is a prominent, large Swedish desk covered with still more books, newspapers, reports, galley proofs and a typewriter with paper in it. A glass table with a large selection of drinks, a record player, a television set. Records on the floor (*PAMELA's untidiness*). A couple of modish, uncomfortable steel and leather chairs. Two doors leading to bedrooms. A partitioned kitchen full of jars for exotic herbs, chopping boards, wine racks, business-like knives, strings of garlic and so on. In the less severe part of the room there are Japanese lampshades, a day-bed and a pile of expensive looking clothes wrapped in plastic covers, clearly just back from the cleaners. On one wall on this side is an old poster. It says simply '*NEW THEATRE, HULL. GIDEON ORME – MACBETH – WITH FULL LONDON CAST *etc'. On the table is a rather faded production photograph of an ageing but powerful-looking actor in Shakespearian costume. It is late at night and when the curtain rises* EDITH, PAMELA's *mother, is sitting on one of the uncomfortable chairs with a cup of tea and reading a copy of Hansard. She is in her late fifties, and looks tired but alert. The doorbell rings. She goes to it and calls out firmly before opening.*

EDITH: Who is it?

VOICE: Mummy? It's Pauline.

(*She admits* PAULINE, *her youngest daughter, who is about eighteen and pretty.*)

EDITH: I thought Pamela gave you a spare key.

PAULINE: She wouldn't.

EDITH: Wouldn't?

PAULINE: No.

EDITH: Well, why not? She gives them round to all sorts of peculiar people.

PAULINE: Don't know. Thinks I'm going to have a rave up while she and Connie are out I expect. Any news?

EDITH: I rang about twenty minutes ago. Pamela's been with him since eight o'clock. She said he was a bit quieter. Whatever that means. He always seems to chatter whenever she's there. She lets him go on and on then gets more exhausted than ever. By the time I get there, he complains all the time about how tired he is and can't sleep. Why am I so tired, Edith? I haven't done any work for years. Not since I was at the Shaftesbury. He even got that wrong last night. That was long before the war. He complained all the time just before *I* left. Are you sure you want to come? It's not much fun, darling. You know, sitting up all night in a hospital room.

PAULINE: No, I'll come.

EDITH: Want some tea before we go?

PAULINE: No thanks.

EDITH: I've got a flask for us. That night sister, not the other one, she's not very concerned for your comfort.

PAULINE: Glad I'm not a patient. I've never been ill in bed. It must be a bit odd.

EDITH: Yes, you have. You've had measles and tonsillitis. And very badly.

PAULINE: Yes, but I don't remember that. I mean being ill, like a, like an experience, lying there. Wondering what they're going to do to you if you're going to get up. So he complains?

EDITH: Nurses, the doctors, the food, the bed, oh everything.

PAULINE: He never says anything to me much. Oh, he looked at me a long time Tuesday night and then just asked me if I took drugs.

EDITH: Oh, he asks me silly questions.

PAULINE: He said would I get some for him. What'd he ask you?

EDITH: Oh, nothing. I think he often doesn't know what year it is. He thinks he's still on the stage or that we're still married. You really needn't come you know.

PAULINE: I know.

EDITH: Pamela's *his* daughter. He's made that *very* clear. And besides it's different with him and her.

PAULINE: Hello, reading the old Hansard?

EDITH: Yes.

PAULINE: Daddy?

EDITH: No, Constance.

PAULINE: Ah. Any good?

EDITH: I should think so. Not exactly my subject. 'New Humber and Fisheries Development Act'. Second reading.

PAULINE: I should think not.

EDITH: One of the brightest of the last batch. So Daddy says. Perhaps we should ask her to dinner one evening. When all this is over.

PAULINE: Odd fish for Pamela to shack up with.

EDITH: How do you mean?

PAULINE: Oh, I don't know but I suppose she's frightfully intellectual and an M.P. and all that. And – well, I mean, Pamela's an actress.

EDITH: She's not exactly unintelligent, darling. Even if she does get her life in a bit of a mess. And I think Constance has been kind to her and after that last affair bust up and all.

PAULINE: What? Oh, Alec. But that was for years. Like marriage. Worse.

EDITH: And I think she genuinely admires Pamela. As an actress. And *she* says Constance is the only person who's really encouraged her in her work. Which is true. I used to take an interest. But I had two younger children. And your father's impossible to get to a theatre.

PAULINE: Didn't the old man encourage her?

EDITH: Well, with her own father it was complicated of course. I could never make out what he really wanted for Pamela, being such a famous actor. But then when I said she ought to get a good degree and a profession, he wasn't too keen on that either. Still, she might have spent fifteen years or so, like I did, training her mind to end up washing nappies and getting up coal.

PAULINE: Did you mind much?

EDITH: Of course I minded. Well, I had three children. But of

course, I minded. One always minds waste. And the worst
waste I can think of is training a woman to the top of her
potential and then just off-loading her into marriage when
she's probably at her most useful. Probably at the height of
her powers.

PAULINE: Well, you can't say Pam's done that.

EDITH: No, but then she's an actress. I meant someone like,
well, like Constance is a good example.

PAULINE: Do you think she'll end up first woman Prime
Minister?

EDITH: She's got a very good chance of being a Cabinet
Minister. Well, so Daddy says, and she's always in the
papers. Still, Pamela hasn't done too badly. Having a
famous father may not have always helped her. It's hard to
tell. They either expect too much of you or compare you
unfavourably. She should have done better.

PAULINE: Perhaps they don't write the parts. I mean Pamela's a
bit special too, isn't she?

EDITH: How do you mean?

PAULINE: Well, she's not a raving beauty exactly but she's not
ugly but you don't quite know what to *do* with her. I
suppose it doesn't matter these days. But she's been at it a
long time. I mean years.

EDITH: I wonder if she'll want some tea.

PAULINE: I mean I remember coming up to London to see her
play Titania *years* ago. I was a little kid. I'd just started
school.

EDITH: I don't remember.

PAULINE: She wasn't very good.

EDITH: If you were so young, you wouldn't have known. I
thought she was excellent. And a beautiful costume.

PAULINE: You just said you didn't remember.

EDITH: Well, I do now. I'm tired. It's these long waiting
sessions with Gideon. And that place is so freezing.

PAULINE: Would you like me to go for you tonight? I don't mind.

EDITH: That's very sweet of you, darling. But I think it has to
be me. Me or Pamela. I think it's all right for you and
Andrew to help out in the daytime.

PAULINE: I don't think he likes me all that much.

EDITH: I don't know if he really wants anyone with him. He's certainly not particularly pleased to see me. He usually just grunts when I go in or makes me do something for him. Make him comfortable or change his pillows. Or sometimes he just looks away as if he's not seen me . . . Pamela, I suppose. He must want her with him. But he's harsh with her too sometimes, I've heard him.

PAULINE: He's jolly old.

EDITH: He's only seventy-two for heaven's sake, Pauline.

PAULINE: Well, if you don't think that's old –

EDITH: Well, I'm fifty-eight. I suppose you think I'm half in the grave.

PAULINE: No. But the old boy really seems different somehow. Different scene altogether. What else did he ask about?

EDITH: Gideon? Oh, oh, he rambled. I think he thought I was some actor-manager he used to know. Kept talking about seeing the returns, and the week – and then he asked, well, if Daddy, and I still made love to each other.

PAULINE: What did you say?

EDITH: Asked me in front of the nurse. Anyway, he didn't really want to know.

PAULINE: No?

EDITH: He was never a jealous man. Sexually, I mean. They said that's why he was no good as Othello. He simply couldn't understand. I'd say he was pretty free of all jealousy. But then he's rather a simple man in many ways.

PAULINE: And do you?

EDITH: What?

PAULINE: What he asked you. You know, Daddy?

EDITH: Good heavens, Pauline, I've told you, I'm not a zombie just because I'm not *your* age any longer.

PAULINE: Sorry.

(CONSTANCE *lets herself in. She is in her early thirties. Bulging briefcase.*)

EDITH: Hello, Constance. I'm sorry we're still here.

CONSTANCE: Please. You're welcome. Did you get yourself anything? Hello, Pauline.

PAULINE: Hi.

EDITH: All I wanted, thanks. I usually have something in the waiting room – just a sandwich or something – and either Andrew or Pauline go in with him for a few minutes. Just to give me a break. But it's very good of them. Hospital rooms aren't places for young people to hang about.

CONSTANCE: There are worse places.

EDITH: But it's such a help being able to come over here and put my feet up while Pamela's taking over. Otherwise it takes me an age to get home.

CONSTANCE: How is he?

EDITH: All right. I spoke to Pamela about half an hour ago. She should be back now.

CONSTANCE: Who'll be there in the meantime?

EDITH: Andrew. It'll only be for ten minutes.

CONSTANCE: Isn't there a night nurse?

EDITH: Yes, but she's not there all the time. I mean they can't be of course. And he panics if he's left alone. Especially if he nods off and there's no one there when he wakes up.

CONSTANCE: It must be frightening, especially at this time of night.

EDITH: He won't trust anyone, I'm afraid. He's convinced he's going to be alone.

CONSTANCE: Not even Pamela?

EDITH: Yes. I suppose he *does* trust her?

CONSTANCE: And no improvement?

EDITH: There's always hope I suppose.

CONSTANCE: I wish that were true.

EDITH: One has to carry on on that basis. You look tired yourself.

CONSTANCE: Looked like being an all night sitting for an awful moment.

PAULINE: Did you speak to Daddy?

CONSTANCE: We had a coffee together. He said he'd pick up Andrew from the hospital.

EDITH: We'd better go. He'll be tired too. Where's Pamela got to!

CONSTANCE: Perhaps I'd better get some scrambled eggs or something. How did she sound?

EDITH: Um?

CONSTANCE: On the phone.

EDITH: Oh, all right. Not very communicative. Old men can be very wearing indeed. Especially in these circumstances. I know what he's like with me. But with Pamela it's even worse. (*Pause.*) I don't think he's really afraid.

CONSTANCE: No?

EDITH: No.

CONSTANCE: Isn't everyone?

EDITH: I don't think so.

CONSTANCE: Especially when you're in full possession of all your faculties. It isn't as if he's drugged stupid.

PAULINE: He wishes he was.

CONSTANCE: Pamela tells me he talks endlessly. And makes jokes.

EDITH: He doesn't know who I am half the time. I know it. He's *very* difficult to understand.

CONSTANCE: Really? He sounded rather coherent from what Pamela said to me.

EDITH: Well, I don't know about that. I only know what I see.

CONSTANCE: He is, he is dying isn't he?

EDITH: I suppose so.

CONSTANCE: Does anyone know?

EDITH: You know what they're like. They're not interested. Especially if you're what they call 'the relatives'. They make it pretty clear what a nuisance you are – just the fact that you exist.

CONSTANCE: Can *I* do anything at all?

EDITH: I don't think so, thank you, Constance. My husband's as well placed as –

CONSTANCE: I know. Of course. But, well, you know what I feel for Pamela, and I hate to feel there's so little I can do to help her.

EDITH: You're her friend. That's enough. She needs friends. Without her father. Well, she'll find it harder still (*Pause.*) *We're* not friends. She and I, I mean. Well, certainly not like Pauline and Andrew and I are friends. In an odd way, we three seem to be more like the same generation. We understand each other. Perhaps it's just the old problem of remarrying and having more children. Something happens. It's different with the other child. It must be. However intelligent you try to be. I think that's true isn't it, Pauline? Or am I deceiving myself? Pamela seems in the middle somewhere.

PAULINE: No. That's right I guess.

CONSTANCE: Can I ask you?

EDITH: Well?

CONSTANCE: About Sir Gideon. What are your feelings about him?

EDITH: Gideon hasn't been my husband for over twenty years.

CONSTANCE: It seems strange when you put it like that.

EDITH: It's the fact. We went separate ways long ago. Not that our ways were ever joined particularly. He was a lot older than me, you see.

CONSTANCE: Yes.

EDITH: And he was also famous long before I met him, I never even saw him play very much I suppose . . . I had a degree in English and French and . . . oh, well, all long past history. Where do you suppose she's got to? We'll go, I think.

CONSTANCE: She probably walked.

(*Enter* PAMELA. *She is in her early thirties too.*)

PAMELA: Hello. Hello, Edith. I walked.

EDITH: Are you all right, darling?

PAMELA: Oh, all right.

CONSTANCE: Sure? Something to eat? I'm getting some. Scrambled eggs?

(*She shakes her head.*)

Tea?

PAMELA: No, thanks. I'll have a glass of champagne.

CONSTANCE: (*To others*) Are you sure you won't have something. You've got a long night.

EDITH: We must be going.

(*But she doesn't move. The attention of all of them is on*

PAMELA, *as if she had brought danger or ill fortune with her.*
She waits. Sees her clothes.)

PAMELA: Ah, the old plunder's back from the cleaners. At last.
What's left of it.

EDITH: How is he?

PAMELA: Chatty.

EDITH: Still?

PAMELA: Don't worry. Andrew's boring him to death quite
literally. About being turned on and dropping out and all.

EDITH: I don't know what I'd have done without Andrew in
that place.

PAMELA: Constance, would you open it? I'm too exhausted.
That bog faced night nurse hadn't put any in the fridge.
You have some, Mother. It'll get you through.

EDITH: No. Thank you. We must go.

(*Pause.*)

PAMELA: Rested?

EDITH: Not much.

PAMELA: You should take a pill. I do. Don't look so glum. I tell
you, he'll have quietened down by the time you get there.

EDITH: He'll wake. He always does. How is he *really*?

PAMELA: How do I know? Sometimes I think he'll live forever.
He'll last tonight. Why pretend?

(CONSTANCE *pours champagne.*)

PAMELA: That's what I want. That's what he wanted, poor
darling. Constance?

CONSTANCE: No, I'm making tea.

PAMELA: Oh, go on. For my sake if not yours.

CONSTANCE: All right then, I will.

PAMELA: Mother?

(EDITH *hesitates.*)

Andrew's all right. He's having a bedside happening all to
himself. Papa's pretending to be asleep. He might even
drop off with the effort. I won't offer you any, Pauline. She
doesn't approve of alcohol, do you? Haven't got any
L.S.D. to offer you.

PAULINE: Thanks, Pamela. I think I will have a glass.

PAMELA: Oh, good. Unless Constance has got some pot

upstairs. Didn't your lover leave his tin behind the last time? There! Nothing vulgar. Just good trusty old Moet. Her lover drinks nothing but Dom Perignon. Very vulgar. Oh, that's better. (*To* CONSTANCE.) Did you vote or divide or whatever? (*She nods.*) Don't tell me – you won. What were the figures?

CONSTANCE: 245–129.

PAMELA: Surprise. Like playing for matches really isn't it? (*To* PAULINE.) I suppose that hippie outside belongs to you?

EDITH: Who?

PAMELA: Does he have a name or is he a group? It was a bit difficult to tell if he was one or several.

PAULINE: You know perfectly well.

EDITH: Did you bring Dave, darling?

PAULINE: He doesn't mind waiting.

EDITH: You should have brought him up.

PAMELA: No, she was quite right.

PAULINE: He's O.K., Mummy. He said he'd come with us.

EDITH: You know Pamela.

PAMELA: Well enough. Anyway, Constance has just had her nice carpet cleaned.

PAULINE: So what are you supposed to be proving?

PAMELA: I'm just enjoying my first drink of the evening.

PAULINE: Just bitchy and you know it.

PAMELA: You see, you really don't know me. But no loss. For either of us.

EDITH: Are you sure you haven't had a drink?

PAMELA: I told you.

EDITH: You do seem – a bit exhilarated.

PAMELA: I walked through the side streets. No Andrew.

EDITH: I shouldn't stay up, Pamela.

PAMELA: *You've* never been an actor. One needs to wind down.

PAULINE: Have you been performing then?

PAMELA: No, but my papa has. You don't think someone will tow Dave away if you leave him?

PAULINE: Oh, you're a drag –

PAMELA: Looks pretty high to me.

EDITH: What's the matter with him?

PAMELA: He's on what your children call a trip, Mama. Having unmemorable visions in a psychedelic, sort of holiday camp shirt and a raccoon coat in my doorway. Trip clothes, right, Pauline?

PAULINE: You just hate any sort of fun or anything.

PAMELA: Give him the trip home, will you, darling? And I don't think it's such fun taking Dave, Dave for an all night rave in hospital, so just get your skates on will you and get rid of him?

PAULINE: No. I'm not going to.

PAMELA: Don't look at your Mother. Do as *I* tell you. I'm bigger than you.

PAULINE: And he's bigger than you. So *you* get rid of him.

CONSTANCE: Shall I go down?

EDITH: It's not necessary. We're going.

PAMELA: Not with him you're not. My Father was always very particular about who visited him. Whether it was at home or at work. Getting into his dressing room was like going into Fort Knox. And I don't see why he should be invaded by Dave the Rave. Hippie Andrew's bad enough.

CONSTANCE: I'll speak to him.

PAMELA: No, you won't. He'll be back in the doorway tomorrow night if you chat him up. Pauline –

PAULINE: You kill me. You're a provincial.

PAMELA: Very likely. As your Mother will remember, I was born in India. It's where a lot of us come from. Just as you like then. I'll call the law.

PAULINE: Oh, come off it. (*To* EDITH.) I'll have a word with him.

EDITH: Well, do hurry then. Pamela may be right. Perhaps just the two of us.

PAMELA: Just send him back where you found him. Where was it? The Sidcup Rave Cave. Yes?

PAULINE: Get lost, draggy.

PAMELA: I'll get the law, if you don't move, darling.

EDITH: Oh, stop sniping at the girl, Pamela.

PAULINE: We just do fun things, so what's the matter with *you*, then?

EDITH: But do tell him, darling. Or else let me go on my own. Perhaps that's the best idea.

PAULINE: No, you can't stay up on your own.

PAMELA: Well?

EDITH: I don't think I even remember Dave.

PAMELA: Why should you? He's an American. You met him, Constance. He's been here before. He writes a regular column – when he's not too high – for the farthest out paper. The 'Village What'. Sorry, that's just what it's called. Don't you remember: thought London was on the way to being the leadingest place, round the clock city, oh and for freak-outs, cats, chicks, soul groups, and pushing things, like the senses as far as they will go.

CONSTANCE: Oh, that one.

PAMELA: Has a very bad skin.

PAULINE: So what about it? What's so wrong about a bad skin? Why should we change what we really are for you? What are *you*, anyway?

PAMELA: Just a gipsy, dear, that's all. And I don't think blackheads or spots are exactly an aesthetic, whatsit imperative.

PAULINE: All that's finished.

PAMELA: I forgot. He also plays the finger-cymbals. Seven thousand people came to hear him accompany his fellow poets at the Albert Hall.

PAULINE: You wouldn't know a clarinet if you saw one.

PAULINE: Where did seven thousand beautiful people come from, he said. Did he say that to you?

CONSTANCE: Repeatedly.

PAMELA: They were all hideously self-conscious and ugly, I'm afraid. Just like Dave.

PAULINE: You don't know it yet, Pamela, but you'll wake up to it, all your scene is really out, and it'll be out for good and you with it.

PAMELA: I think you're right.

PAULINE: Those draggy plays. Who wants them?

PAMELA: Who's arguing?

PAULINE: Oh – you're just camp.

PAMELA: So I've been told. Just like my father. I wish I could say the same for you. It's impossible to argue with someone wearing such cheap clothes. Take a glass of champagne down to Dave. He doesn't *need* to look quite so ugly, you know. I suppose he thinks *he's* beautiful, of course.

CONSTANCE: Do you want me to come with you?

PAMELA: Why not? You're party authority on education or about to be or something. You could, let's see, you could try to apply the problems of relating poetry, freak-outs, crazy slides, happenings, action painting and so on to the Comprehensive School. Or the Grammar School. Or trip clothes. She actually sells those things she's wearing. What's the name of the shop? Switched Off or Knocked Off or something. Oh, no, I forgot, that's finished now isn't it? The shoddy clothes scene. It's the bookshop, she sells books and records and dope I shouldn't wonder. 'Ecstatic' that's the name of that one. 'Ecstatic'. And there's an art gallery attached. Quite a scene, isn't it, Pauline. And then there's her pad in the evenings.

EDITH: She's helping me through a very difficult time, darling.

PAMELA: Is she? What time is that?

EDITH: What's the matter with you?

PAMELA: What difficult time?

EDITH: Gideon's illness, you stupid girl, what else?

PAMELA: You're doing all right. It's nearly over. Her pad, where she raves in the evening, whatever you might wonder that is, getting laid, I suppose, well, now and then, lying about mostly, getting high in her pad, which is just a bed-sitter full of unappealing modish junk and old laundry.

EDITH: I'll ring you at the usual time. Try and get some sleep. You've been too long in that little room.

CONSTANCE: Perhaps I could go. Tomorrow?

PAMELA: She could take over from you.

EDITH: That's not necessary. Poor Andrew – he'll be wondering. Goodnight, Constance. Do go to bed Pamela.

PAMELA: I'm not tired. Goodnight, Mama. I'll see you in the morning . . . you'll ring me?

EDITH: Yes, I've told you.

PAMELA: No, I don't mean leave it to Pauline or Andrew.
You'll get straight through yourself. You will?
(EDITH *nods.*)
Anyway, I don't think anything'll happen tonight.
Goodnight, Pauline.

PAULINE: Goodnight.

PAMELA: Wave to Dave for me.

EDITH: Why don't you take your own advice and have a pill?

PAMELA: I probably shall. Goodnight Mama.
(*Pause. They go out.* CONSTANCE *closes the door on them.*)
Thank God! They've gone! We must be *going*. Why didn't
she *go*? Instead of drinking champagne and going on about
it, being so busy looking tired and distressed. She's
Madam Distress Fund, my Mama. Calling her Mama is
better than Edith. Edith almost makes her sound dignified.

CONSTANCE: I suppose she hasn't had much sleep for quite a
while. None of you have.

PAMELA: They don't need it. My Mother's a bat, and, as for the
kids, they're only half conscious most of the day or night
so, as they'd say, who needs sleep. *I* need sleep. Lots of it.
I sleep my life away. Or I would if I could. Now *we* can
talk. Have some more. How are *you*?

CONSTANCE: I'm all right. I've been worried about you.

PAMELA: At least she didn't call you Connie. I've got her out of
that. Do they call you Connie in the Party? I'll bet they do.

CONSTANCE: Some of them.

PAMELA: Does lover?

CONSTANCE: No. I thought it was test number one.

PAMELA: Yes. I should say, I should say it probably was. They
don't bring out the best in me. If there's a best nailed
down under somewhere. Not even you, not much.

CONSTANCE: Your worst can be pretty attractive.

PAMELA: I can't think that's true. I think you believe it though.

CONSTANCE: I don't want to sound like your Mother, sorry –
Mama, Edith or whatever you like, but I think you *should*
get some sleep.

PAMELA: Yes. In a minute.

CONSTANCE: I suppose they've dealt with Dave?

PAMELA: Oh, he's harmless.

CONSTANCE: How was it?

PAMELA: How was what?

CONSTANCE: Your Father?

PAMELA: Oh, all right.

CONSTANCE: Was he chatty?

PAMELA: Not very.

CONSTANCE: Darling, you're exhausted. Why don't you let me go first thing? Just at the beginning. You could have an extra couple of hours. Your Mother wouldn't mind.

PAMELA: Why should she? *He* might.

CONSTANCE: I see.

PAMELA: I told you. He's particular.

CONSTANCE: No. Well, I suppose I don't really know him.

PAMELA: He'll grumble at her a bit. If he's able.

CONSTANCE: You look afraid.

PAMELA: Do I? I'm not panicky, if that's what you mean.

CONSTANCE: No, I didn't . . .

PAMELA: I held his hand mostly. I brought him some caviare but he didn't want it . . . I just couldn't stay any longer. I knew I couldn't get rid of her once her turn came. He won't like it if it's tonight. She can make the 'arrangements' anyway. What do you do? Ring the place in Ken. High Street. Well, she'll enjoy all that. Great organiser, Mama. Great, sloppy minded organiser. She'll be telling young Pauline that I'm over tired and strained. What she means is venomous and evil tongued and selfish.

CONSTANCE: Well, you're not. So do shut up.

PAMELA: Oh I *am* selfish. I won't give money to take full page ads about Vietnam or organise them like Mama. I certainly wouldn't give money. I'm too mean. Too mean and too poor. Just because I share a bath and an inside lavatory doesn't mean I'm not poor. Well, does it? I'm even unemployed. Oh, you think it's funny, but I am, I'm unemployed. My Father will leave nothing but debts, as Mama will tell you. He's left me what's left of his wine cellar, all his junk that nobody wants and he asked, yes he asked me last night, to leave all his empty champagne bottles to the Inland Revenue. Don't think he's got many of those even. I'll send mine for him. The kitchen's full.

CONSTANCE: I got the dustmen to take them away.

PAMELA: Well, please don't. They're for Father's Area Inspector. I promised him. Oh, I think about Vietnam. Not as much as you do. But I'm not giving my money away. Thank you. And then I think of myself. Don't you?

CONSTANCE: Yes. Pamela –

PAMELA: What? More?

CONSTANCE: Let me, let me try and help.

PAMELA: Help?

CONSTANCE: Yes.

PAMELA: What had you in mind?

CONSTANCE: You believe in friendship, don't you?

PAMELA: Yes.

CONSTANCE: Well. Let me do something. Was tonight bad?

PAMELA: Worse than yesterday. Oh, the same. The same. Could you close that window? I know you like fresh air, but this is ridiculous.

CONSTANCE: Sorry, I think your Mother –

PAMELA: Oh, of course. Yes, I believe in friendship, I believe in friendship, I believe in love. Just because I don't know how to doesn't mean I don't. I don't or can't. I wish she wouldn't call him Gideon. Oh, I suppose he doesn't mind. I do though. No, it's right for her to call him Gideon.

CONSTANCE: Isn't that what she always called him?

PAMELA: Yes. Well, it's his Christian name. Or one of his Christian names. His names are a bit of a mess, really. Well, his Father was a bit dotty and called him Tristram. Tristram, Gideon. Yes, well, you see, sort those out if you're a lovely, struggling boy. And Papa thought of Gideon and the Midianites, being brought up on the bible and not much else, and liking earrings, I think it was the earrings did it. He gave all his wives and mistresses and girls, gave them all earrings. He gave me some. What do I mean *some*? Have you seen my jewel-case? Oh, you must see it. He was very good at women's jewellery. Well, what was I saying? Oh, Gideon. Then, then there was his name, his professional name. Prosser, Tristram Prosser, the old boy must have been out of his mind, well, I think he was a bit. He didn't want the old boy's name because he didn't want to, to use the name even if it was a rotten one, *and* Welsh one, mark. Because the old boy, *his* Father was a big deal in the provinces. I mean he was so big in the provinces he'd never come to London. Never came to London in his life. Wasn't good enough for him. Conceited old devil. So, anyway, Papa, when he started out of regard for his Mother's agony in producing him – called himself Orme. Passed the Square one day, small but dignified he thought, that's it: Gideon Orme. Of course, he was mad. But whoever knows about names? Gideon Orme. Good God. I mean you couldn't get on the epilogue with a name like that now. But then, well . . . But people tried to talk him out of it. I think it was trying to get away from the Welsh and his Father and he got somehow stuck with the Orme. He'd a Jewish grandmother. Always said that was the best part of him. I doubt it but it might have helped. But he used to say, I mean he never wanted *anyone* to know about the *Prosser*, he'd say when the woodnotes go really wild, my dear, it's just that keening old Welsh self-regard. *Do* tell me. When I let it out. Pamela, if you ever hear me put the PEW into PURE, call out something and something English and derisive or something because then I'm being bad. And if I'm being bad, I'll go on because no one will notice. They'll think it's just me. So everyone called him Orme. I never called him anything else. Not after Mama left. She *always* called him Gideon. But in the profession he was just Orme. The Welsh are like the Irish, he'd say they're too immodest to be really good actors. I don't want to be mistaken for one of these. Not that they'd know the difference. Except the Irish are a bit worse. Well, they invented the stage Irishman and blamed it on the English like everything else just to cover up. Dear Orme. He should be rescued from Andrew by now. He doesn't know how to abuse Andrew.

CONSTANCE: Haven't you told him?

PAMELA: He knows his ground with Edith. But with Andrew, he just doesn't know what he's about. You haven't met Andy, well, he's got none of Pauline's instinct to please, which is at least something, though not much. Mama thinks he's saint-like, and he probably is, except he's earth bound, he's saint-like, he's an opportunist, indulged, enclosed and supported by your colleague, his Father. What's *he* like?

CONSTANCE: I should say he's pretty able. Persuasive . . . quite attractive in some ways.

PAMELA: No, not him. Oh, then Daddy's brother saint character. Too good for politics. That's his badge.

CONSTANCE: Well –

PAMELA: He's too good to be true. That's why Mummy fell for him. He's not tough enough. For politics. And he's not good enough. Now, you're nearly tough enough but probably too good.

CONSTANCE: Thank you.

PAMELA: No, Andrew. Well, he started off as a wine snob.

CONSTANCE: Are you sure you won't?

PAMELA: Yes thanks.

CONSTANCE: I wish you'd talk to me.

PAMELA: What do you mean? I never stop talking to you. Why don't you tell me to shut up. I can go to bed, as you say.

CONSTANCE: No. Let's stay up a bit longer. I could do with an unwind myself.

PAMELA: What was *your* day like?

CONSTANCE: Busy. Bit end of term atmosphere.

PAMELA: Bit like a girls' school isn't it?

CONSTANCE: More like a boys' school where a few day-girls are tolerated.

PAMELA: I shouldn't have said you were ever tolerated. The place needs a bit of pash and glamour. You looked frightfully sexy in that pink dress, in the paper, you know meeting that delegation thing.

CONSTANCE: I don't think my constituents were too enthusiastic about it. They probably thought I didn't look serious enough.

PAMELA: You looked as if the entire Cabinet was lining up for you. They should be grateful you don't look like that woman – what is she, in the Treasury – the one with the teeth?

CONSTANCE: I wouldn't mind being as bright as she is.

PAMELA: I wouldn't mind if she were as pretty as you.

CONSTANCE: I don't think you should judge by externals so much.

PAMELA: I've just a superficial manner, often saying serious things. Which is the other way round to people like her. Just because she's got a double first in P.P.E. or I.T.V., there's no reason why she shouldn't get her teeth fixed. That's arrogance and self-deception. Perhaps that's why she's a big wheel in the Party.

CONSTANCE: I think she's a nice woman, really, shy and, yes, well a bit serious, but a first rate mind.

PAMELA: Um. Well, you know her. I find it hard to believe she's really wise to inflict those green teeth on people. Sort of autumnal teeth, aren't they? That should make her shy but she's not. I think someone must have told her once she looked like a tiger and she's been flashing them at you behind that crimped up seaweed she thinks is a serious politician's hair-do ever since. Is it a wig?

CONSTANCE: No. Poor woman. We can't all look like film stars.

PAMELA: Well, perhaps she should, poor dear. How can you be really intelligent and be satisfied with that? It's obviously all a great production number. Even if she does feel she's got unfair competition with the men.

CONSTANCE: It isn't easy, Pamela. It's easier in your line.

PAMELA: Nonsense. Why do you have to strive? Besides, I don't look like a film star.

CONSTANCE: Yes, you do.

PAMELA: Yes, which one? It sure ain't Garbo. How old is she?

CONSTANCE: Garbo?

PAMELA: No, your lady.

CONSTANCE: Oh, thirty-seven, eight.

PAMELA: Well, she looks eighty-eight of course. Thirty-eight! You must be joking. Perhaps she should have the jabs, or a face job, or the lot. Perhaps she has already. Constance!

CONSTANCE: What?

PAMELA: Well – poor woman! Think! No wonder she's so solemn. Why, she's got tits like old ski-socks filled with sand. And a pre-form bra *no* one could make a wedge in. Is she married?

CONSTANCE: Oh, to some academic, I think.

PAMELA: Marriage must be pretty academic, too. Just as well.

CONSTANCE: I don't think you'd mind her so much if you met her. She's quite harmless.

PAMELA: You *can't* bring her back here – can you? To one of your parties? I know these brainy girls, they get terribly girlish and all frilly when you're not expecting it. They turn up at things like your Annual Conference Ball looking like Americans in cashmere sweaters with sequins on. And rhinestone spectacles. She's not harmless, she's not harmless at all. She's spending my money, and I haven't got any, you sit up there all hours of the night debating about how to spend my money. How to get hold of my money. What have you been doing with my money today? Give me those things, whatsit, Order Paper thing. What's this? Humber and Anglia Fisheries and Redevelopment Act. (*Pause.*) And you won? Why don't you introduce the Lady Politicians' Teeth Filling Development Act? What's this?

CONSTANCE: Something I'm working on during the recess. Can I have it back, please? It's not interesting.

PAMELA: Then why are you working on it? 'Striding into the Seventies with Labour!' You're really joking!

CONSTANCE: Please, Pamela. (*Pause.*)

PAMELA: Bit like school isn't it? Please can I have my satchel back? And then they throw it over the hedge for you. (*She gives it back.*) Striding into the seventies. I haven't got used to hobbling about in the sixties yet. Give us a chance.

CONSTANCE: Time is in short supply in the present.

PAMELA: Then we should keep it in its place. Whenever we can. Just because we can't win.

CONSTANCE: It's very easy to poke at people who are trying to cope realistically with the future. And glib.

PAMELA: But what about the meantime? We've got to get through that, haven't we? I don't know about striding off anywhere. I seem to be stuck here for the moment . . . that's not being glib. We have to wait up . . . not be able to get to sleep . . . it's strange how easily men seem to get off to sleep . . . always before you . . . off . . . and you wake up tired . . . but not in the seventies . . . Tomorrow . . . that's early this morning, *this* morning . . .

CONSTANCE: Why are you so scornful to me?

PAMELA: I'm not.

CONSTANCE: It's as if you hate what I do, what I am, everything about me. I know a lot of it seems funny and wasted effort but a lot of effort *is* funny and wasted.

PAMELA: I don't mind effort. I'm not so keen on strain.

CONSTANCE: You make me feel very shabby and inept and all thumbs sometimes.

PAMELA: *I* do! But, Constance, I don't . . . I don't know anything I'm ever talking about except for odd things. I'm almost totally ignorant, you know that.

CONSTANCE: No, you're not. You're very perceptive.

PAMELA: I'm not perceptive. I'm just full of bias. *And* I'm uneducated. I went to about twenty expensive schools and I never learnt anything in any of them. Except to play tennis.

CONSTANCE: You know how I admire you and what you do.

PAMELA: But I've never done anything very memorable. How can you?

CONSTANCE: I know you have formidable qualities . . .

PAMELA: Even if they haven't been exploited yet?

CONSTANCE: I respect and admire you for what you are.

PAMELA: I respect and admire you.

CONSTANCE: I don't think so. I wish you did.

PAMELA: It shouldn't matter to you.

CONSTANCE: Well, it does. Your good opinion is important to

239

me. More so than most of the people I deal with. I know we inhabit different worlds, but they're not really so different always. And, also, I thought that we were, were very much alike you and I.

PAMELA: Yes. I always did too.

CONSTANCE: I couldn't believe it when you agreed to come and stay here.

PAMELA: Well: both left behind by our chaps. It gave us something to talk about in the long unconnubial nights.

CONSTANCE: I don't think it was as simple as that.

PAMELA: It wasn't so different moving out of my house. I didn't have much affection for it.

CONSTANCE: You wouldn't rather move back?

PAMELA: No. Are you suggesting it?

CONSTANCE: You know I'd like you to stay. But only if you want to. If I bore or irritate you –

PAMELA: Of course you don't, you idiot. We get on rather well, I think. You sounded like a wife then.

CONSTANCE: Did I? Sorry. It's just that I didn't want you to feel obliged to stay. You helped me over a difficult patch.

PAMELA: So did you. If I go back there, I only keep finding bits of his things in cupboards and drawers. Each time I think I have thrown everything out or sent it back to him, there's a belt or a tie or an old cheque book. I suppose I ought to let it. I just can't bring myself to all the bother of it.

CONSTANCE: I could find someone for you. It's not difficult to arrange. We always seemed to like the same things and react similarly. Most women just seem to make me impatient.

PAMELA: You prefer men. That's because you're such a gossip.

CONSTANCE: Really – I hate it.

PAMELA: Well, men are great on it.

CONSTANCE: But you know what I mean?

PAMELA: Yes. You like crowds too. So do men mostly. The sort you know.

CONSTANCE: What sort is that?

PAMELA: Oh, clever. Successful.

CONSTANCE: Do you know any unsuccessful men?

PAMELA: Well – not many maybe. But I know some pretty stupid ones. Oh, darling, please don't look so upset. I'm only chattering and going on about that poor lady's rotten teeth. Everyone makes jokes about M.P.'s., they're like honeymoon nights and mothers-in-law. Don't hold that against me. I admire what you do tremendously. Just because I haven't got the ability to do it myself.

CONSTANCE: You don't mean that.

PAMELA: But I do, my darling. It's like everyone thinks actors have got no brains and live in some world walled up from the realities everyone else is immersed in. Something . . .

CONSTANCE: Your voice sounds quite different sometimes. I suppose it's when you don't believe in the lines you're reading.

PAMELA: How can I convince you?

CONSTANCE: You have.

PAMELA: Oh, for God's sake. Have some humour.

CONSTANCE: Please don't be angry. I'm sorry.

PAMELA: Sorry for what? Sticking up for yourself?

CONSTANCE: O.K. Let's not talk about it.

PAMELA: Well, why not talk about it? I've obviously upset you.

CONSTANCE: You didn't mean to.

PAMELA: Perhaps I did . . . I don't know. Maybe we should talk about it.

CONSTANCE: Have some more of this. I'm glad you liked the pink outfit. It was horribly expensive.

PAMELA: I could see. And don't change the subject. I don't think I'm the only one who knows about clothes. I wish you wouldn't buy cheap clothes.

CONSTANCE: Thanks.

PAMELA: Oh, hell, you know what I mean.

CONSTANCE: You just said it – I buy cheap clothes.

PAMELA: Well, it's all right for kids like Pauline.

CONSTANCE: She's young, you mean.

PAMELA: Yes, if you like. Who cares if she wears badly finished day to day rubbish, and if her skirts are up around her fat little thighs by her crutch.

CONSTANCE: We don't all have long legs like you.

PAMELA: But I wear them down to here.

CONSTANCE: Well? You have style.

PAMELA: So do you.

CONSTANCE: You don't think so.

PAMELA: How do you know? What I think? Nobody knows. I certainly don't at all.

CONSTANCE: Don't let's quarrel.

PAMELA: I thought we were having a parliamentary style debate on skirt length. Anyway, public opinion is on your side. They're not going below the knee for fifty years. I read it last night. (*Pause.*) Perhaps we aren't very alike after all, you and I?

CONSTANCE: Because we argue about skirt lengths?

PAMELA: I've thought about it lately. Orme was asking me about you tonight and I suppose it occurred to me then. I don't really think we are.

CONSTANCE: Probably.

PAMELA: You should be pleased. Not sad.

CONSTANCE: Perhaps I've always wanted to be someone like you. To have long legs, and style. Instead of just making efforts. But I suppose what's saddening is that you make it sound all like a rejection.

PAMELA: What?

CONSTANCE: Your attitude to me.

PAMELA: You make me sound like a selection committee that's turned you down.

CONSTANCE: I think you have.

PAMELA: Well, don't lose any sleep over it. I've turned down better people than you. (*Pause.*) I didn't mean that in the way it came out.

CONSTANCE: It probably came out purely enough. It seemed like it.

PAMELA: Why don't you make me shut up, go home. No, well go to bed, stop being a bitch.

CONSTANCE: I've told you: I like *you* as you are.

PAMELA: Well, you must be a pretty small club.

CONSTANCE: I really have made your teeth grate. I can see it.

PAMELA: You look so damned fragile sometimes. Someone

should take you in his arms. Why doesn't that priggish, self-righteous husband come back and give you a cuddle or something. And own up he's been sleeping around himself for years and years!

CONSTANCE: He's got rigid standards. Besides, that's not what I need.

PAMELA: Oh, come off it, Constance, that's what we all need – love and friendship and a hot cuddle. And they really *are* on short supply.

CONSTANCE: It's very clear what your true opinion of me is. It's like the way some men look at one. Patting you on the head if you show signs of being bright, and picking you up and putting you down in *their* way –

PAMELA: Listen. You're far more likely to be bored by what you think of as my green room banter.

CONSTANCE: No. I think you're a very serious person. And I pay you the respect due to a serious person and what they do.

PAMELA: And what they do! That's it. You get this thing because you think I don't respect what you do. What you do, what you do, what you do, what's it matter? I don't care what anyone thinks.

CONSTANCE: I think you're lucky. At least you appear to. I'm afraid I *am* different.

PAMELA: My opinion about you or anything isn't worth – what – any more than that great booby of a tinker bell, Abigail! Abigail: just because she's made a movie and someone's talked about the mystery behind her eyes, she's just myopic which enables her to be more self-absorbed than ever and look as if she's acting when she's just staring at wrinkles on your forehead.

CONSTANCE: Thank heavens! Oh – come, there's more to her than that.

PAMELA: I'll tell you just what there is. And this I do know about. She moons about on street corners in a French movie, looks listless and beautiful in her own big, beady way while you hear a Mozart requiem in the background. She plays with herself, gets the giggles while she's doing it and they say she's a cross between Garbo and Buster Keaton. Abigail – who's never seen a joke in her life when it was chalked on a blackboard for her, who was the only person in the entire world who didn't know the truth about her Daddy until she found him tucked up with a Greek cabin steward and the family's pet bulldog! And that was before she got engaged to the biggest poove in the business. She was *23*. And *20* already when she stood up to her nanny and told her she *would* go on dressing up as Castro if she wanted to. I hope her movies are big in Cuba. They should be. They ask *her*, that blow-torch Mary Pickford what she thinks about the Russian and Chinese doctrinal conflict, and actually print what she says out of the hairy mystery behind her eyes.

CONSTANCE: That's better. You've stopped being cross with me.

PAMELA: Yes, I'm cross. What do you think she knows about it. She belongs to Disneyland. So do I. She doesn't even understand what's going on *there*. Except she knows she wants fat, sympathetic parts because she's dim enough to enjoy them and making sweeping, spurious gestures all over the place while she'll trample on a pussy cat or the char's baby to death while the world wonders how anyone can be so young, gifted, touching, and spirited and full of simple sorrow for the world's unloved and unwanted, while she herself is the most loveable and wanted of all starry creatures.

CONSTANCE: Hasn't she got a dress rehearsal for her play?

PAMELA: Yes. And she'll probably ring me if it's over and ask after dearest Orme. Not wondering whether or not I'm asleep. I know – I'm not. I'm talking about her. Give me some more of that. And silly actresses who don't know what they're talking about, and people like you bothering to listen to them.

CONSTANCE: Well, you're not Abigail.

PAMELA: No, I'm not. But if I were, I'd be what I'm not – a whopping, enduring, ironclad, guaranteed star!

CONSTANCE: I think I'd better open another one. After Abigail.

PAMELA: Yes. If she rings, *you* talk to her. As for – are you all right now?

CONSTANCE: Fine. We both are. We *are* rather alike.

PAMELA: Maybe. Do you miss your child very much?

CONSTANCE: Yes.

PAMELA: How often do you see him?

CONSTANCE: About twice a week.

PAMELA: Do you mind *him* having custody. And all that meeting in the zoo and stuff?

CONSTANCE: I don't often enjoy it much.

PAMELA: What is he – four? I wouldn't mind having a son. Except I couldn't possibly look after it.

CONSTANCE: Of course you could. I think you'd be a lot of fun for a child.

PAMELA: Do you? I think I'd be easily bored. You have extraordinary belief in my abilities.

CONSTANCE: I don't think so. It's a little like feeling freshly looted each time.

PAMELA: Somebody loses. Somebody's guilty, somebody else comes through. When you win your constituency, the other poor candidate loses.

CONSTANCE: That's politics. He's a Tory.

PAMELA: So am I. I don't see why you should get on at my expense.

CONSTANCE: That's just an affectation.

PAMELA: No, it's not. I mean a real one. Not the sort you sit and make faces at. I couldn't afford a child in a property-owning democracy. I'd have to have loads of nannies. It could sit in the dressing-room sometimes – if I was working. But I'd have to be always working to pay for the nannies, and that wouldn't work at all.

CONSTANCE: You could get married.

PAMELA: What for?

CONSTANCE: It works for some people.

PAMELA: Tories like me are not 'some people', Constance.

CONSTANCE: Some things do work you know.

PAMELA: You sound like Edith.

CONSTANCE: Thanks. I know what you think of her.

PAMELA: If I had a son, I wouldn't have a clue what I'd want him to be. I don't mean like an engine driver or something futile like an astronaut or a star export manager. I mean would he prefer champagne to drugs. I mean, I *wonder* about your child. Will he get stoned . . .

CONSTANCE: I believe the statistics suggest it's more likely than he's going to a university.

PAMELA: Oh, he'll go to university. If you've got 'A' levels, we're after *you*! And even if you've only got 'O' levels, we're *still* interested. Fancy. Lower streams of the poor little devils, upper levels of the bigger fish. I'd be in no stream at all. All those school inspectors and examiners and seducers from industry hanging about like men in raincoats, offering prospects and excitement and increments. How awful. If a man comes up to you, darling, however friendly he might be, talking about your 'A' levels, don't, repeat don't, talk to him. He's after *you*, he wants to make a University Challenger out of you. Don't talk to them, they're sick. Yes, but Mummy's known it for a long time. Get back home before the park gates close or he'll take out his careers section in the Daily Telegraph and show it to you. Come home and you can have crumpets and champagne for tea with Mummy. Did you know that's the perfect device for testing whether your gynaecologist is any good or not? Do we drink champagne at bearing down time? Or do we not?

CONSTANCE: I wish I'd known.

PAMELA: My dear, first thing to ask. No, I don't really feel like you. I know, I don't, for instance, feel that most things I do must be an improvement on what I did before. So much improvement – like sex. I don't know. It's hard to tell, isn't it?

CONSTANCE: I think one knows pretty well. Well, at our stage of the game.

PAMELA: Yes. Perhaps you do have a more accurate notion. You and Murray make it pretty big don't you?

CONSTANCE: Very.

PAMELA: Yes. I can see you do know.

CONSTANCE: I think you don't believe I know any more than you know.

PAMELA: Do stop reproaching me. With my late gentleman, it was pretty good I should say. *He* said it was. I suppose he was being truthful – as he saw it. However he saw it. Sometimes it was amusing. Or, of course, lonely. Or sometimes something not very much at all. That's not been your experience either much has it? Edith's always supposed to be great in the hay. Don't like to think about it. Least of all with Orme. *He* never spoke about it to me. But she's always telling me her ratty little details. She's not exactly fastidious. Now Orme. You could eat your dinner off his taste in anything. Constance: what's your other name?

CONSTANCE: Sophia. Female wisdom.

PAMELA: Oh my God, they lumbered you, didn't they? I'm not telling you mine. My Mother was really being pretentious. Pamela's bad enough. And *don't* tell me you like it. If you do, I'll tell you you don't have any style after all. (*Pause.*) Suppose it's trying to be honest to say you're not sure. (*At desk.*) 'Going into Europe'. Sounds like getting into the Pudding Club. Public spending, the price we have to pay, private sectors, incentive and exports, both – guess – both sides of industry, productivity, exploiting our resources to the full, readjustment. I suppose they're like words you're supposed to believe in, like your Catechism, I believe in God the Father, the Holy Catholic Church, forgive us our trade gaps.

CONSTANCE: I'm sorry, Pamela, I wish you wouldn't rummage around my desk. It's arranged very carefully.

PAMELA: So I see. I don't see, I mean I don't *see* economics at all. I mean I see astrology. Fine. But, well, ever since I have been born there's been an economic crisis. We went off something called the gold standard I think when I was born, there's been no confidence in sterling, crashes, devaluing, loans, and all the star gazing and at the end of it people are better off, better fed, better housed than ever and if you never look at these forecasts, it makes no difference.

CONSTANCE: I think that's one of your simplifications, to put it mildly.

PAMELA: Would you? Say that would you? I'd say it was one of my commonplace revealed truths. However, you're the one who knows.

CONSTANCE: Oh, do stop saying that.

PAMELA: I don't think I've said it before. Did any letters come for me this morning?

CONSTANCE: No. I don't think so. Oh, a card from a gallery, I think. Any for me?

PAMELA: Don't know why I asked. No one ever writes to me. Except for some occasional sun-questing queen who sends me a card from wherever the wog rumbo is thickest at the moment.

CONSTANCE: Was there any afternoon post, I asked you?

PAMELA: No, I don't think so. Some bills maybe.

CONSTANCE: Are you sure?

PAMELA: No. Why should you be in such a tizz about a few letters? Slow down.

CONSTANCE: I don't want to slow down if you mean come to a sort of standstill –

PAMELA: Implying?

CONSTANCE: It may seem inconsequential to you, but it *is* my work.

PAMELA: Not expecting a love letter. I thought Murray always rang.

CONSTANCE: No. He'll ring soon. I expect he's at a party.

PAMELA: Orme used to write beautiful letters. In superb handwriting, of course. He'd write to me regularly if he was on tour or in America. With little drawings, drawings of himself and what his mood was and what his performance looked like. He drew quite well. But he hasn't written to me for years. Not since he gave up work.

CONSTANCE: Why do people give up? I think I under-rate it.

PAMELA: I don't. I'm miserable when I'm not working, which is about half the time. You know what I'm like.

CONSTANCE: Well, then?

PAMELA: I think: excessive effort is vulgar.

CONSTANCE: Thanks again. Is that part of your high Toryism? It's a little shopsoiled. That kind of romancing and posturing I mean.

PAMELA: I think there's a certain grace in detachment.

CONSTANCE: You sound like an old-style lady journalist.

PAMELA: I thought you said saying 'lady' anything was condescending? That men did it to belittle women they saw as rivals.

CONSTANCE: You never sound particularly detached. Your onslaught on poor Abigail, for instance. Sounded just vicious to me.

PAMELA: Ah, Constance, like so many people you don't understand the content of tone of voice. You're like an American, you have no ear. All voices are the same to you. It's only what is said that seems significant. Old Orme *had* to give up. What was there left for him? He'd done everything. He said I can't dodder on as Lear again. It needs a younger man. Anyway, nobody liked it before when I did it. Lost twenty thousand pounds. Said I was too young and didn't care for the verse. You know how they say it as if you ill-treated children. Now they'd say I was too old. Mind you, I'd still be better than anyone else.

CONSTANCE: Must be great to have that degree of surety.

PAMELA: He just knew himself. And the others. He didn't want to be liked particularly.

CONSTANCE: Lucky.

PAMELA: Essential if you're any good at all. He was cool. Pauline and Dave think they're cool. But you can't be cool if your sense of self and, well, ridicule is as numb as *theirs*.

CONSTANCE: Seems to me you're doing what you accuse me of – theorizing.

PAMELA: True. Didn't somebody say 'Addison in print was not Addison in person'?

CONSTANCE: So? Miss Ignorant.

PAMELA: I think you *should* pay more attention to tones of voice. They are very concrete. You have plenty of them.

CONSTANCE: You mean I dissemble?

PAMELA: I mean you are many things to different people.

CONSTANCE: A trimmer?

PAMELA: In the House, to your constituency, in the papers, on the telephone, in bed; I don't know about that, but you're determined not to be caught out. You're determined. You've read the books the others have, the reports, the things in the air at the moment, the present codes and ciphers. It all has to be broken down. The information has to be kept flowing. Or you'll feel cut off, left behind. You keep trying.

CONSTANCE: What should I do then?

PAMELA: What your fears and desires tell you together, I imagine. As you say, it's all stuff you enjoy. I tried writing love letters to someone. For quite a long time. Then I found my handwriting was getting like his. I don't know what I can go on saying. I love you. I need you. I want you. I ache for you. I need you beside me and in my bed. Don't let's part like this again. It's more than I can bear. It's never been like this in my life before. I never thought it could be. (*Pause.*) I tried writing erotica to him. But I couldn't bring myself to send it ever. I'd write it down, pages of it. I'd like to. I want you to . . . I dreamt that . . . Then made up a dream. But it was too explicit. And then it seemed impersonal. Puritanism, I expect you'd say.

CONSTANCE: It's a pity you couldn't have gone with Murray to the party. He was frightfully sorry you couldn't go.

PAMELA: Was he? What did he think I'd do? Look in on my way from the hospital?

CONSTANCE: No, of course not. I think he just finds you very attractive. And it sounded as if there might be some interesting people there.

PAMELA: I've been meeting interesting people for years. I just wish people would stop trying to fix you up. So and so would like to meet you. Just scalps. I'm thirty four . . . twenty six years old, and I don't need to go to parties and meet interesting people. I can make out for myself even if the terrain *is* all married men, pooves and tarted up heteros head over heels about themselves.

CONSTANCE: Like your friend Edward?

PAMELA: He's not my friend or my lover or anything. He just comes in and talks to me. I suppose even he gets bored with his dollies and scrubbers. Not with himself, mind, but he can't believe that there's someone who doesn't think he's the greatest knock-out a woman ever laid eyes on.

CONSTANCE: He's intrigued by you.

PAMELA: Well, he shouldn't be telling you then. It's unfair and unkind. What's the matter with him?

CONSTANCE: He doesn't. I've watched him look at you. And sometimes I know he's thinking of you.

PAMELA: He hardly knows me.

CONSTANCE: He knows you through me.

PAMELA: That's scarcely the same.

CONSTANCE: It's quite potent.

(*Phone rings.*)

I'll take it.

PAMELA: Why are you always so sure it must be for you? It's probably some man sniffing around. The moment you've been detached, they're on the doorstep seeing what the chances are.

Especially for you – married women on the shelf. Wanting to be taken down and given a bit of what they need.

CONSTANCE: It's probably Murray.

PAMELA: If it's Lady Tinker-Bell Abigail, I'm in bed.

CONSTANCE: (*Phone.*) Hello . . . Oh yes, just a minute . . . It's Andrew.

PAMELA: Hello . . . Yes. I *am* in bed. You've woken me up . . . Well, your Mama may send him to sleep . . . What time? . . . No, all right . . . Well, I'll just have to manage, won't I? Yes, I know you have to work . . . What *are* you doing? Good God. Oh well – what's all that noise? I see . . . Night.

CONSTANCE: Nothing wrong?

PAMELA: Oh, he wants to leave the hospital earlier to get to work.

CONSTANCE: We shouldn't bicker. Please forgive me. I know what it must be like for you.

PAMELA: We're not quarrelling are we?

CONSTANCE: Well, I think we're a bit out of kilter.

PAMELA: Do you know where he is? Andrew? He's just left Orme and gone to that party. I suppose he's one of the interesting people. What's the betting Edward isn't there too? He told me to tell you your gentleman's just leaving.

CONSTANCE: I didn't know he knew Murray.

PAMELA: Well, they know each other now. Lucky Murray. I wonder what other celebrities he's met.

CONSTANCE: It sounded rather more a literary-political sort of do.

PAMELA: Oh, I think Andrew's got literary connections of a kind.

CONSTANCE: What's he do?

PAMELA: At present? Seems he's a waiter in one of the fag amateur restaurants in Brompton Road. Dressed as a lion tamer, I think.

CONSTANCE: Perhaps we should go? Murray adores those sort of places.

PAMELA: Not if you're hungry.

CONSTANCE: Do they let girls in the place? Or just tamper with their food?

PAMELA: The food doesn't go to much tampering. He's a poet. I think he cuts out bits of old copies of the Illustrated London News and American comics and pastes them together. Yes, they get published. He used to paint a little in the same fashion. He'd glue bits of his levis on to strips of glass and top them up with different coloured paints and plaster. He told me this evening he wants his Dad to put him into publishing. Perhaps that's why he went to Murray's party. He's very keen on a lot of American plays, sort of about leaving nude girls in plastic bags at railway stations. Non verbal, you understand, no old words, just the maximum in participation. I don't know whether the old boy will stump up. Perhaps Murray could help him.

CONSTANCE: Why should he?

PAMELA: I don't know. A lot of people find him 'interesting'. Some weekends he runs old movies backwards on the ceiling in an old Bethesda chapel in Holland Park.

(*Door bell.* CONSTANCE *rushes to it.* MURRAY *is there.*
Thirtyish.)

CONSTANCE: Darling!

MURRAY: Get my message?

CONSTANCE: Yes. Come in.

MURRAY: Am I too late?

CONSTANCE: No. We're just having some champagne.

PAMELA: Have some.

MURRAY: Thanks. How are you, Pamela?

PAMELA: Not bad.

CONSTANCE: She's exhausted, poor darling. Make her go to
bed. I can't.

MURRAY: You look remarkable for it.

CONSTANCE: (*To* PAMELA) See?

PAMELA: See what?

MURRAY: How's your Father?

PAMELA: Oh. The same. As far as I know.

MURRAY: I'm sorry. I just met your brother.

PAMELA: Please – *step*-brother.

CONSTANCE: Sit down, darling. Doesn't he look smashing?

PAMELA: Ravishing. How was the party?

MURRAY: Not bad. Heard one or two interesting things. What
does your step-brother do?

PAMELA: Now? He's a part-time pouve's waiter.

MURRAY: He told me he was going into publishing.

PAMELA: I expect he will. He started off as a wine snob, going
to vineyards and reporting on growth and so on. It was for
this City firm and he used to dress like an old Etonian
then. Before that he was at one of Mama's pet schools and
wore levis and wax in his ears like pearl earrings. Same at
the university.

MURRAY: Which one?

PAMELA: Oh, I don't know, one of those new estates where all
the furniture looks to have come from Heals' January sales.
He became a probation officer for a bit. He'd a degree for
that kind of service. He wanted to do something
'meaningful' as my American gentleman used to say. He
got accused of having relations with a boy from an

approved school. Anyway, they thought he'd got the wrong meaning and I think he was bored and underpaid, so he did do Zen for a bit but I don't think he got paid for it. Then the Committee of 100. He's always been pretty violent so he enjoyed hitting his great head against brutal bobbies for a spell. Oh, and he went to Cuba. Same time as Lady Tinker-Bell the blow torch.

MURRAY: Lady Tinker-Bell?

CONSTANCE: She means Abigail.

MURRAY: Do I detect professional envy?

PAMELA: Professional boredom. He'd send me cards and pictures of Abigail in her Castro hat singing people's songs. But he got some Cuban girl in the pudding club and got knifed by a fellow revolutionary, so perhaps he wasn't bent after all. Anyway, he got slung out for bourgeois carryings-on.

MURRAY: You're not exaggerating of course?

PAMELA: Murray, I *never* exaggerate. You're like your Constance. No ear for inflection.

MURRAY: He seemed pretty lively to me.

PAMELA: Did he? Yes, I suppose he did. He'd been cooped up in quite the wrong scene all the evening. What's the matter? You think I'm frivolous?

MURRAY: I don't know you.

PAMELA: Constance says you do.

CONSTANCE: She's no more frivolous than I am.

PAMELA: No? I think Murray's one of those intellectuals who thinks all actors live in a narrow, insubstantial world, cut off from the rest of you. Well, kid yourself not. You're all of you in Show-Business now. Everybody. Of course, Orme was never in Show-Business. Books, politics, journalism, you're all banging the drum, all performers now. What are you busying yourself with these days?

MURRAY: Oh, usual stuff. Reviewing, articles, bits on the box.

CONSTANCE: He's written a play. I think it's quite extraordinary. Tell her about it.

MURRAY: If you'd like me to.

PAMELA: No. I can't bear people describing things like that to me. The people who do it well are usually no good anyway. They're just critics passing as writers.

CONSTANCE: Then you must read it. Really.

PAMELA: All right, Constance. But don't sell it to me.

(*Phone rings.*)

Yours, I suppose.

(CONSTANCE *has got to it.*)

CONSTANCE: Yes . . . Abigail?

PAMELA: I'm asleep. No thanks to her.

CONSTANCE: I made her go to bed. She's worn out, poor dear . . . Yes, nearly all day . . . No different I'm afraid.

PAMELA: As if she cares. Get rid of her.

CONSTANCE: Yes, I'll tell her . . .

PAMELA: No, don't.

CONSTANCE: How was your dress rehearsal? . . . How exciting for you . . .

PAMELA: I'll bet.

CONSTANCE: And now you go on tour first? Well, I hope it goes well . . .

PAMELA: Oh, it will. A bomb in Brighton. They should burn that joint down. They think it's 1950.

CONSTANCE: I'll give it to her . . .

PAMELA: Tell her to get her girdle washed.

CONSTANCE: Of course, we'll come . . .

PAMELA: No, she doesn't wear underwear, lovely.

CONSTANCE: Yes, we'll come round after. If you'd like us to . . .

PAMELA: Isn't there a touring date in Vietnam?

CONSTANCE: No, I was up, anyway . . . 'Bye . . .

PAMELA: Well done.

CONSTANCE: I could hardly be rude to her could I? I don't know her.

(*Door bell.*)

PAMELA: Oh, God, open house! I *will* go to bed.

MURRAY: I'm sorry –

PAMELA: No. Not you.

(CONSTANCE *goes to the door.* EDWARD *is there. Looks about twenty-eight.*)

PAMELA: What do you want?

CONSTANCE: Edward.

EDWARD: Sorry. I saw your light.

PAMELA: No, you didn't. You just rang. Why don't you knock up Abigail in the middle of the night. She likes pure, spontaneous gestures.

EDWARD: I just left her. I went to her dress rehearsal.

CONSTANCE: Come in then. Have a drink. You know Murray.

EDWARD: Hi.

MURRAY: How was it? The dress rehearsal.

EDWARD: Oh, O.K. I was in the bar in the middle act with some of the kids.

PAMELA: Fine.

EDWARD: I guess it was all right. I just think plays are a bit of a drag.

CONSTANCE: Didn't you do one last year?

EDWARD: Yeah. But six weeks was all I could take. And I had to fire the director and keep fighting to keep the author out and all that jazz.

PAMELA: That and never knowing his lines and getting drunk and not turning up twice a week.

EDWARD: We broke the house record.

PAMELA: You're a big star, darling. One epic in two and a half years and a nose job.

EDWARD: Am I in the way?

CONSTANCE: Not at all.

PAMELA: Would you mind?

CONSTANCE: We can't get Pamela to go to bed.

EDWARD: No. Well, it's early.

PAMELA: Why aren't you out hell-raising or whatever you do in the newspapers.

EDWARD: Things are pretty quiet. Don't know where everybody is.

PAMELA: London's full of interesting people, especially for you Edward. I don't know why you're called a hell raiser – it's only getting drunk all night – that and working at being louder and more Welsh than even you are – and you've got a very poor head. No dollies tonight?

EDWARD: Well, Sue's at home. But I thought I'd look around.
PAMELA: Sue won't take that so well. She likes to go out with you. She's like the old line about justice – not only must be done but must be seen to be done. Why don't you two go to bed?
CONSTANCE: What about you?
PAMELA: I'm coming. I'll put the lights out and get rid of Edward.
EDWARD: Any brandy in the house?
CONSTANCE: Sure. Murray? How about you?
MURRAY: All right. I'll take one to bed with me.
CONSTANCE: Please don't keep her up, Edward. She's flaked out.
EDWARD: Right. (*Helping himself.*)
MURRAY: Goodnight, Pamela; I hope your Father's better.
PAMELA: Thanks.
CONSTANCE: Don't forget. If you want *anything* tomorrow. I'm so sorry about tonight.
PAMELA: *I'm* sorry.
(CONSTANCE *embraces her.* MURRAY *watches.*)
CONSTANCE: Goodnight, Edward.
EDWARD: 'Night.
(MURRAY *and* CONSTANCE *go into the bedroom.*)
EDWARD: Big thing going?
PAMELA: I imagine so.
EDWARD: Things same at the hospital then?
PAMELA: Yes. Sorry to be rude, Edward. But you should know by now. You're thirty-four, even if you do say you're thirty-one.
EDWARD: How do you know?
PAMELA: I always know these things. I will go to bed in a minute so let yourself out when you've finished will you?
EDWARD: Sure.
PAMELA: Why don't you go back to your famous bachelor pad. Sue'll be in a state if she doesn't know where you are.
EDWARD: I'll let myself out.
PAMELA: You ring her and say you're on your way if you like. Shall I?

EDWARD: You know, Pam, I've always thought you were a very sexy kid.

PAMELA: You told me the other week for about five hours. Well, I'm rather disappointing I believe, and I'm twenty-six and I'm no kid.

EDWARD: You're not twenty-six but you've got a lot going. I never saw Orme in Macbeth. What was he like?

PAMELA: The best.

EDWARD: So they tell me. Bit before my time.

PAMELA: Too bored to bother, you mean.

(He picks up cuttings book.)

EDWARD: Here he is. Playing Arthur Bellenden. Of the 21st London Regiment. Act One. Nutley Towers. A Friday Evening. He looks quite something.

PAMELA: He was – he was ravishing.

EDWARD: Act II. The Conservatory, Nutley. Sunday Evening. Act III. The Marskby Drawing Room. Fitzroy Square. Monday Evening. What's it called?

PAMELA: 'The Call of Duty'.

EDWARD: Good Stuff. Orchestra under the direction of Mr Reginald Garston. What's this entracte?

PAMELA: Quite ravishing.

EDWARD: Shaftesbury Theatre, May 7th, 1922. Here's a good one. 'The Undecided Adventuress'. Wonder what she couldn't decide.

PAMELA: Mary or a life of sin. Great long thighs.

EDWARD: 'Master, you owe on the firm £7,000. If it's not deposited in the company's bank by midday on Monday, you shall have to face up to the dishonour. Your rank is nothing to me. I will brook no arguments, no entreaties. Not even for the sake of Effie.' Effie! 'You have brought disgrace enough on her already.' I'm sorry. I didn't mean anything.

PAMELA: Why not try Abigail again?

EDWARD: She's tired.

PAMELA: Tired. I'm sure she'd accommodate *you* if you persist.

EDWARD: She's not all that great at it, anyway.

(Phone rings.)

Don't worry. I'll go. Shall I take it?
(*She nods. He takes phone.*)
Yeah . . . Hang on . . . Pauline.
(PAMELA *goes.*)
PAMELA: What is it? I'm asleep. I'm asleep. I'm trying to stay
asleep . . . When? Why didn't you ring before . . . I could
have come then . . . No, I'll come down later . . . I've
taken a pill. Oh, Mother can make all the arrangements.
She'll enjoy all that . . . No, don't put her on . . . Hello
. . . No, well, I mistimed it didn't I? . . . Please don't get
hysterical *now*, it's bad timing . . . No, I can't . . . Get
Andrew . . . get Andrew to come down . . . Yes . . . Later.
(*She puts the phone down.*)
EDWARD: Pamela. I'm so sorry. I suppose you're not surprised.
Can I get you a drink?
PAMELA: There's one more bottle of champagne in the fridge.
(EDWARD *goes to get it. She looks at the open cuttings book,
while he opens the fresh bottle.*)
'A Weekend Gentleman'. He was a vile seducer in that.
'And your unborn child. You shall never see it, Gerald. I
shall see to it that it grows up in sweetness and ignorance,
far, far away from where your guilty hands can ever find
her'. Sounds like a paedophiliac or whatever.
EDWARD: What's that?
PAMELA: Someone who likes children. No, he wouldn't have
played that. He would have thought it most improper.
Besides, it would have made him giggle. He was a terrible
giggler. He must have been the other man. They didn't like
him to be a rotter. When he was, he was a frightful flop.
And he giggled too much. (*She raises her freshly filled
champagne glass.*) Oh, Orme . . . Orme . . . my darling . . .
EDWARD: Shall I stay a little?
PAMELA: If you like. We can finish this together.
(*Curtain.*)

ACT TWO

Same scene. Some weeks later. PAMELA *is in a nightdress and dressing gown. It is late afternoon. She is drinking a glass of champagne. In the room are* EDITH *and* PAULINE. EDITH *is rather formally dressed. Even* PAULINE *is slightly subdued.*

EDITH: I still think you should have come.

PAMELA: So you said.

EDITH: There were quite a lot of people there. After all, when you think he hadn't been on the stage for about ten years. And a whole generation have hardly even heard of him.

PAMELA: You sound as if you're surprised there was anyone there. After all, you're the one responsible for the thing happening. Orme would have hated the idea. I don't think he ever went to a memorial service in his life. He'd have laughed his head off at the idea, rows of his friends having to listen to Handel and Wesley and knighted actors reading the lesson. He'd have thought it very common.

EDITH: I don't think he'd have said that.

PAMELA: Well, it wasn't for me. It was for Orme.

EDITH: I saw Constance there.

PAMELA: Well, she likes a good blub. It's like singing the Red Flag to her.

EDITH: And that man in the opposition Front Bench. The one who's so hot on the arts. You always see him at Covent Garden.

PAMELA: Can't think. Tory poove I suppose.

EDITH: After all, he *was* knighted himself. He can't have been that aloof.

PAMELA: Mama: only because he knew you wanted it so much. Which is why he kept turning it down until after you'd broken up.

EDITH: I hope that's not true. It sounds very petty. And if it is true, it isn't kind to point it out.

PAMELA: Wit very often is petty, Mama, and, knowing him, I can't honestly believe it hadn't occurred to him. I told him it was petty myself. And rather common. However, he didn't make too many mistakes. And today's circus he can't be held responsible for. That's your fault.

EDITH: In that case, there may be a certain ironic justice in it.

PAMELA: You really didn't like him did you? How's the bookshop, Pauline?

PAULINE: Oh, I goofed over that. I went broke in two weeks. Don't know why. Business was fine. Management I guess. That's what Dave thinks.

EDITH: Have you been out, Pamela?

PAMELA: Out?

EDITH: Since the funeral. You never seem to answer the telephone.

PAMELA: I take sleeping pills during the day and turn off the telephone. Constance doesn't like it. I think she's terrified the Prime Minister will ring up and there's no one to take the message. She's getting an answering service.

EDITH: Very wise. I should think you must be losing offers, don't you?

PAMELA: Work? I shouldn't think so.

EDITH: I mean people will probably think of you at the moment.

PAMELA: People never think of me as Orme's daughter. There's too much space between us. Besides, you don't get offered work like compassionate leave. They leave you alone. They'd rather. It only reminds them. So what are you doing, Pauline? Changing your scene then?

PAULINE: Yes. Dave and I thought we'd try the sun for a bit.

PAMELA: Oh, yes, I've had offers of going to the sun. It's a little like when your chap has left you. They suddenly remember you and see if you're on top again.

PAULINE: Oh, Spain. Somewhere . . .

EDITH: But you'll need to work again soon, won't you? You haven't done anything for ages.

PAMELA: That's right.

EDITH: I mean you do know Gideon's left hardly anything except a few debts and mementoes, which he seems to have left mostly to you.

PAMELA: They're not worth much. He had a comfortable retirement.

EDITH: Don't you think you ought to be looking? Seriously?

PAMELA: Don't worry, Mama. I shan't come to you for anything.

EDITH: Isn't your agent, Bernard whatsaname doing anything for you?

PAMELA: If there's anything, he'll come and knock the door down and wake me up. I think the time comes when you no longer follow the sun. Orme and I used to go to the west coast of Scotland – at least we did a couple of years running. I'm rather bored with my useless golden body. It's had thousands lavished on it in air fares and sun oil and hundreds of broiler bikinis. I think I shall use a sunshade. I'm tired of juggling face down with my bra straps and all that. I think a sun tan is definitely vulgar. It's like dieting. *That's* vulgar. It's just uncollected effort.

PAULINE: You're lucky.

PAMELA: No, I'm fastidious, fortunately I don't like rich food. And I don't like getting drunk in a certain way. That's vulgar. You and Dave both diet, don't you? I'm not surprised. He's far too fat for a man of his age. What is he – twelve? He eats too much and drinks too much. You can't eat *and* drink. One or the other. Orme drank. Better for you. If you drink the right thing.

PAULINE: Dave doesn't drink.

PAMELA: Well, sitting around smoking pot in groups is vulgar. So are nervous breakdowns. Meretricious. I've had at least three. I lay in them like I used to water ski and play tennis. Like I made love at your age, with those acrobatic, expert wogs in Milan and Paris. Mind you, I always *used* people like ski-instructors. I promised them nothing and gave them nothing. Instructors. Like theatre directors. Only faggots and middle-aged women in books written by faggots have affairs with ski-instructors.

EDITH: But what are you going to do, Pamela?

PAMELA: I told you. I shall probably take my sunshade to the South of France for a week or two. It's warm and I can drink champagne and swim. I like to swim still. And I can usually avoid anyone I know. I'll wear a black armband. I've got a couple of nice new frocks that will go very well with it.

EDITH: You don't have any work, any aim, hardly any friends now, except for a few –

PAMELA: Homosexuals? Well, they've mostly given me up. I'm ultimately unrewarding to them. Which is just as well. Except for Bernard of course. If you're a woman or a moll, you do have to spend quite a lot of energy flattering them with your sympathy and admiration and performing like captured prize dogs for them. I think Bernard's different. But they do conform to their archetype. Like most sizeable pressure groups, I suppose, and not even poor liberal Constance can really escape the fact, beyond all her Parliamentary recommendations, that as a group they *are* uniformly bitchy, envious, self-seeking, fickle and usually without passion.

EDITH: You do generalize, Pamela.

PAMELA: Mama, if you've never had the discomfort of having what are commonly known as crabs – which I know you haven't – do listen to someone who has suffered from them constantly. Even Bernard agrees with me. In fact, I think he said it to me.

PAULINE: Is Constance going to marry that guy?

PAMELA: I expect so. Yes, I expect I shall have to change my scene. Constance is very accomplished. She can cook every sort of cooking, write books, give you an opinion on anything from Marxist criticism of the novel to Godard, she's even managed to get herself a child, an ex-husband and now a well thought-of lover.

EDITH: Perhaps you should try writing a book. You could do a biography of Gideon. Who could be better?

PAMELA: Not me. He wouldn't want it either.

EDITH: Or a novel. Look at the people you've met in the past ten years or so, not just in your own line.

PAMELA: You're like Constance.

EDITH: Well, she's right. You don't look at all well. Staying indoors, sleeping all day for weeks on end, living on champagne. Which you can't afford.

PAMELA: One of the several reasons I am getting out of here is that I fancy Constance is going to write a book with me in it. You should always beware of lady writers. They hover and dart about like preying fish in a tank. They've their eyes on you and little tape recorders whining away behind their ears by way of breathing apparatus. Then they swallow you up whole and spew you up later, dead and distorted. Nothing has happened to you in the mean-time except that they turn you into waste material. Because the trouble with lady writers is they've usually no digestive juices. They're often even surprised you're not pleased. There, I gobbled you up whole. Aren't I swift, don't I move, don't I watch. Like hell you do. You just can't deal with it decently once you've got it. That friend of yours – oh, Mildred – that one did it to *me* once.

EDITH: I didn't think she meant it was you.

PAMELA: She wasn't sure whether to be pleased when people recognised me, or to just pass it off as her own inventive craft.

EDITH: I can't remember.

PAMELA: She even described me physically – she's a mess herself of course. Then a quick run down on my character and finished up patronizing me for being less intellectually perceptive, and so ending up as a puppet – and I mean puppet – in her clever dickdyke thirty bobs worth, and not being similarly bright enough to write a book about her and the mess *she* is.

EDITH: You're not being fair to Mildred. She's got quite a reputation.

PAMELA: She has.

EDITH: You're unfair to everyone. Including yourself.

PAMELA: I hope so. Help. You've seen I'm still around, Mama, why don't you get back. Your old man must be worried about you.

EDITH: I'm concerned about you Pamela.

PAMELA: Well, don't be. We've managed quite well without each other for about twenty years.

EDITH: It's not been easy.

PAMELA: I couldn't have changed it.

EDITH: What's going to happen to you?

PAMELA: I shall go on as I have done for twenty nine years.

EDITH: As you say, you've never married or had children. Well, that's all right, there's no reason why you should if you don't feel the need to. At least people are beginning to realise a woman isn't a freak if she wants other things out of life. But there *are* other things, like work, yes and having affairs and even making love. You can't want to stop all that at your age. You're young and intelligent and healthy and attractive. And a lot of people like you. Constance adores you. She says lots of people do and you aren't always aware of it.

PAMELA: Constance sometimes has her ear to the ground of the wrong building.

EDITH: You seem to have no impulse about these things, or even ordinary things like whether to move or take a holiday, go out or sit in the sun. I know you're upset about Gideon but you'd been like this for a long time before.

PAMELA: I shall manage within my own, my own walls. I've no ambitions. I've told you: I love acting. I'm not so keen on rehearsals. I don't wish to be judged or categorized or watched. I don't want to be pronounced upon or do it for anyone.

EDITH: Will you go back to your house?

PAMELA: I suppose so. At least it's mine.

EDITH: Won't it seem strange without a man about the house.

PAMELA: Really! Edith. No, it won't seem strange at all. (*Phone rings.*) Answer it, will you? I'm out.

PAULINE: Hello . . . Just a minute, I'll see . . . It's your agent, Bernard. I thought you'd want to . . .

EDITH: We'd better go.

PAMELA: It's nothing you can't hear. (*On phone.*) Darling! How nice . . . Oh, I'm all right . . . Yes, really . . . Well, I've not been answering the phone . . . Well, I'm glad you didn't

. . . I couldn't afford to get the door fixed . . . Oh, you
went? . . . No . . . I know Orme wouldn't have gone for it
. . . What made you go? . . . Oh, well I'm glad you enjoyed
it . . . It seems to have been a success. I thought it was all
frightfully respectable. Who let you in, you great Jewish
queen? . . . Oh don't you start 'what's your scening' me,
baby! Well, you're a very mutton old hippy dressed up as
lamb! And how are things for you? What a love life you do
have . . . How do you find the time? No, I'm twenty nine
this week. Period of mourning has aged me for a bit. Till
next week . . . You must tell me all about it . . . Yes, all
the details . . . you know I must have them . . . I'll tell you
. . . what . . . nothing . . . only my stepmother . . . yes, and
my little stepsister . . . oh, years younger . . . can't you
hear her shaking her cannabis rattle?
(*Enter* MURRAY *front door. She motions him in.*)
All right, listen Bernie . . . you know that address book of
yours. The one with names of the gentlemen in it. Yes,
Ladies' Services. Can you give me a few numbers and
which names to mention when I ring? . . . No, of course
I'm not, darling. After all this time . . . Yes, for a little
friend . . . All right, ring me back. But don't leave it . . .
Yes, well it *is* urgent. It always is, isn't it . . . Oh, and I'm
changing my address. No, not scene, I'm going back to my
house . . . Yes, of course, I'm all right . . . Right . . . soon
now, mind . . . Hello, Murray. You know my mother and
stepsister, Pauline.
MURRAY: How do you do.
EDITH: We'd better go. Do try and answer the phone. And let
me know when you go back to the house. And try to get
something to eat.
MURRAY: I'll see she gets something.
EDITH: I wish you would. Thank you.
MURRAY: Goodbye, Mrs – . . .
(*Nobody helps.* EDITH *goes to kiss* PAMELA.)
PAMELA: I haven't cleaned my teeth Mama. (*She lights a
cigarette.*) I'll give you a ring.
(*The other two women go out.*)

You needn't bother to follow up that offer.

MURRAY: Are you sure?

PAMELA: Quite.

MURRAY: Do you think you should be drinking that?

PAMELA: Certainly. It's very good. My agent sent it round as a present. I think he must spend all his commission on it for me. I pay him ten per cent and I seem to get it back in crates.

MURRAY: Was that who you were talking to?

PAMELA: He'd been to Orme's Memorial. He can't resist that sort of thing.

MURRAY: Connie went. I couldn't manage it.

PAMELA: She couldn't resist it either. I saw her all dressed up for it this morning. I went back to sleep.

MURRAY: What was, was that about Ladies' Services?

PAMELA: None of your business. Have some of this.

MURRAY: It is.

PAMELA: It was a private telephone conversation.

MURRAY: I can't pretend I didn't hear it. Come on. What are Ladies' Services?

PAMELA: What do you suppose?

MURRAY: Pamela?

PAMELA: What are you doing here?

MURRAY: Don't be pompous suddenly. I came to see you.

PAMELA: Constance will be here soon. She's only gone to a meeting. It was after Orme's do. I wish you'd go away. This, of course is the, I mean, this is it, the disadvantage, this is why you shouldn't, this is sharing with, with, yes, look, Murray, don't stand there just arrived, I don't need anything, yes I'm in the club, everything's in control, I'm sitting here with a drink, I've got the telephone, I've got friends, I like you quite a lot, but I'd like some, oh, privacy, I guess. Anyway, I'd like to be alone, and not stared at, please go away, ring up Constance, no, waylay her outside and take her to a movie in Westbourne Grove or something. Things . . . are very . . . easy.

MURRAY: Oh, Pamela, what's happened to us?

PAMELA: Don't 'oh Pamela' like that. You're another

Constance. We *aren't* alike. Nothing much has happened. I'm getting out this evening. My Mama decided me.

MURRAY: You mustn't do that.

PAMELA: I'm not getting out of anything that's necessarily happened. I'm just getting back to where I used to live, such as it was. Not very much. But I can warm it up after a day or two.

MURRAY: I'm going to tell Connie, I don't care what you say.

PAMELA: Do what you like. If you do, you're more feeble than I thought.

MURRAY: You think I'm feeble then?

PAMELA: Oh, yes. Don't you?

MURRAY: What do you mean?

PAMELA: You just want to be spoilt and cossetted because you've convinced Constance and I suppose others I don't know about that there's something special about you. What it is I don't know.

MURRAY: And *you* don't want spoiling?

PAMELA: No. And you couldn't do it, anyway.

MURRAY: We could do all sorts of things.

PAMELA: Like?

MURRAY: Like, for instance . . .

PAMELA: Spare me a list . . .

MURRAY: What do you mean: feeble?

PAMELA: Immature, I suppose.

MURRAY: That's what women usually say about men when they can't keep up with them.

PAMELA: I dare say. We don't match up, you see.

MURRAY: What are you going to do?

PAMELA: I wish everyone would just stop asking me: what am I going to do. I am going to get up and I am going to go to sleep, if I've got enough to knock me out. I'm going to speak to Bernard and get his list of Ladies' Services.

MURRAY: And then what?

PAMELA: I shall go back to my little house and one day I shall pick up the telephone when it rings. And if it doesn't ring, never mind. I may have to ring someone else instead. If they're in . . .

MURRAY: I shall come round to the house.

PAMELA: Oh, for God's sake.

MURRAY: I mean it.

PAMELA: Then I suppose I'll have to go and stay with Bernard. He'll look after me and he'll get the police on to you. He'll enjoy that.

MURRAY: I do love you.

PAMELA: Well, even if you do . . .

MURRAY: What is it?

PAMELA: What is what?

MURRAY: Haven't you got anything to say to me?

PAMELA: No, Murray. Not really. We've had a good time together, because we've hardly been together –

MURRAY: We could be . . .

PAMELA: Well, we won't be . . .

MURRAY: Why not?

PAMELA: My nose says so.

MURRAY: Mine says the opposite.

PAMELA: Well, I rely on mine. Not yours. But, anyway, it's had its pleasure. Don't renounce them. I've been looking at Abigail's notices. Before my Mama and little sister arrived.

MURRAY: You want me to stay with Connie?

PAMELA: No.

MURRAY: Well?

PAMELA: You will find each other. Or not. I don't want to talk about it. I won't be involved in your life, or hers. I'm sorry for both of you. *Not* much. A bit. You'll manage, so shall we all. Just remember: what I should do now or at any time is nothing to do with either of you. I owe you no confidence.

MURRAY: Pamela, let's talk about it.

PAMELA: You always want to talk about it. I don't want to, I'm not going to. Now go or talk about something else. Anyway, I'm getting dressed. And I don't like being watched.

MURRAY: You'll change your mind. You will. There's always time for that. I know the handling of you. I really do.

PAMELA: Good. Like a horse. Did you go to Abigail's play? Oh yes, you went with Constance. She didn't seem to like it much. Did you?

MURRAY: Quite. She seemed to enjoy it to me.

PAMELA: Ah! She said it was really about a sort of regional mysticism that didn't, or couldn't, er, engage her, oh, attention, her full interest.

MURRAY: I don't think the play was really about the regional mysticism. Whatever that . . .

PAMELA: Indeed?

MURRAY: No, it was surely about . . .

PAMELA: I can't wait. Tell me.

MURRAY: I don't understand you, Pamela. You seem to treat people as if they weren't there sometimes. As if they were just walk ons. What's happened?

PAMELA: Oh, Murray, do stop.

MURRAY: All these gibes, and immaturity – and your paternalist female ripeness.

PAMELA: Oh, very good, Murray. You sound like the character in your play.

MURRAY: You haven't even read it.

PAMELA: Yes I have. I read very slowly. Like everything else.

MURRAY: You can't be serious about Ladies' Services?

PAMELA: My dear, it's like going to the crimpers. Only more expensive. I may have to borrow some money from you.

MURRAY: I'll give it to you, of course.

PAMELA: You'll lend it to me. No, you won't. I'll borrow it from Bernard. I owe him enough already, but never mind.

MURRAY: You must.

PAMELA: I mustn't anything. I'd go to Wee Willie Wonder –

MURRAY: Wee who?

PAMELA: Wee Willie Wonder. My gynaecologist. But he'd only give me a lecture. Oh, he'd do it.

MURRAY: Is he a moralist too?

PAMELA: Not he. He's not one of those bear down and be joyful queens. He'd just lecture me.

MURRAY: What about?

PAMELA: Like you, like Mama and Constance. Except that he knows me better. Anyway, he's a nice sensitive man. He'll worry about me and reproach himself and I'll have him coming round to the house.

MURRAY: How did it happen?

PAMELA: What? Oh, guess.

MURRAY: Has it . . .?

PAMELA: No, it's never happened before. At least I've not dried up like an old prune after all. You've proved that. That should please you. Still, even Wee Willie nods sometimes. And it's a mysterious, capricious place in there. Especially mine. Not surprising. It feels like a Bosch triptych often enough. It's been better lately, I thought it was odd.

MURRAY: What do you mean: that should please you?

PAMELA: Oh, your eyes. Not just now. I used to see it in my previous gentleman's face sometimes – before he left me. When he was making love to me. He never said anything. He was too reticent. I suppose it's a question of if you become literally substantial they can luxuriate in their abstraction with a nice trailing guide line to mother earth. Trailing guide line, I've said that out of your play. There, you see, I read carefully. Do go, Murray. I want to get undressed and I feel shy with you about the place and Constance will be back and it's quite clear you're longing to tell her. Well, I can't stop you. But I don't want her solicitude and being practical and sustaining all of us. I'm quite practical enough for myself. And I don't want to sustain all of us. Even if you two do, and I know you will. You're all bent on incest or some cosy hysteria. She's bound to blub. You're not above it, and we'll all end up on the floor embracing and comforting and rationalizing and rumpled and snorting and jammed together and performing autopsies and quite disgusting all of it. You both are. Don't indulge her. Just because she demands it.

MURRAY: What?

PAMELA: She was brought up on the principle of fulfilment in as many spheres as possible. As a statutory obligation. I'm only saying don't always give in to her, and not now. There isn't any statutory level of fulfilment we're entitled to. I've tried to explain it to Constance. I've told her it leads to excess and deception. It's difficult to talk to her about a lot of things. She either reduces them to worthy sounding principles or theorizes them so that they relate to any old thing. She's a very coarse woman, I'm afraid.

MURRAY: Have you ever told her?

PAMELA: No. It would hurt her. She'd mind. Besides, I'm fond of her. I used to think we were alike. I take so long to find things out. Dear God, I am always so far behind. She's also rather coarse when she talks about sex. Oh, I know what you think. Lust is O.K. by me. But not when it's ambitious and gluttonous and avaricious. Then it's vulgar. Very vulgar indeed. You shouldn't wear those shirts she gives you. If you want to look really sharp, and you obviously do, you need something a bit more expensive than that. Give me your measurements. I'll go to Jermyn Street in the morning. It'll give me something to do.

MURRAY: Pamela . . .

PAMELA: I haven't cleaned my teeth. Something in silk. A very pale brown I think. And a dark, velvety tie. It would look terribly good. You've not been around long enough. I usually refit most of my gentlemen completely. Pity. Your wardrobe needs a bit of a cast out. Don't let Constance buy too many things for you. And simply remember, you should know by now, you're twenty-nine, you're only a few years older than me: one and one don't make two or three. They sometimes don't even add up to one.
(*Phone rings.*)
Answer that, there's a good boy. If it's my Mother, I've had an enormous bowl of nourishing soup, a boiled egg and gone to bed to sleep it off.

MURRAY: (*On phone*) Yes? Your agent . . .

PAMELA: Darling . . . That's good . . . Please . . . You're quite wrong . . . No, don't come round . . . Listen, could you hang on a minute . . . Murray, are you going?

MURRAY: I suppose I'd better.

PAMELA: You didn't mean that about coming round to my house?

MURRAY: I don't know. Perhaps not, after all.

PAMELA: I wouldn't put it past Constance. Oh, and there's Edith. Cheer up. We'll go out together sometimes. Not the three of us. My nice coloured gentleman will be back soon. You'll like him. He's frightfully New Statesman. Nice though. Fastidious.

MURRAY: 'Bye, Pamela.

PAMELA: 'Bye. (*On phone.*) No, Bernard, it's someone here. Murray . . . Yes, that one. Some of my friends have got real brains, they're not all sex-happy queens like you. Though he's very sexy . . . No, nothing for you, darling. At least, I don't fancy so . . . Actually, I've just read the play he's written. I think you ought to look at it. I know you're not but you might have some ideas. You know everybody. And if you do do anything for him, I want a percentage . . . I'm very poor, Bernard . . . What do you mean, I always . . . He's just going . . . I'll give you his number . . . It'll be worth your while. He's going to be very big. I know it. You know what a success nose I have with people. Didn't I tell you Abigail was going to be the biggest star since Garbo . . . ? I know I told you not to take her on . . . I'd have left you if you had . . . You're not that tasteless. Or greedy. (*To* MURRAY.) What's your number, darling?

(*He looks at her and goes out.*)

(*To* BERNARD *on phone.*) Oh, I think he's gone. I'll give it to you, the play. Look, darling, could you really help me? . . . Could I come and stay with you for a few days? . . . I told you, I'm fine. I just don't want to stay here any longer and I can't face that little house for a bit. My Mama'll only come round and she doesn't know you . . . Well, that's your fortune . . . are you sure, really? . . . I won't stay long and I'll not interfere with your love life, well I know that's impossible . . . Who is he? . . . He sounds divine . . . bless you . . . yes, I've got a paper and pencil. Right, Ladies' Services . . . Dr Gradski . . .

(CONSTANCE *comes in carrying parcels.*)

CONSTANCE: Just missed Murray getting into a taxi.

(PAMELA *blows her a kiss.*)

Oh, sorry.

(*She goes into the kitchen, unwraps parcels of food, coming in and out.*)

PAMELA: (*On phone*) Yes . . . who do I mention . . . how much . . . Dr who? . . . You're kidding . . . yes . . . Don't seem many Smiths or Browns . . . Sure these aren't the names of agents you're giving me? . . . Oh, I know him, I met him with you, the one who procures for you . . . oh come off it . . . Yes . . . another . . . That'll do. I'll try these first . . . and then I'll . . . might as well shop around. No . . . Darling, don't please. I'll make my own way. There's not much to talk . . . Oh, all right . . . half an hour . . . (*To* CONSTANCE.) How are you?

CONSTANCE: I'm fine.

PAMELA: What's all that?

CONSTANCE: Goodies. I've just been to Fortnums. We're all going to have a smashing meal. I bought some Dom Perignon. I've just put it in the fridge. That isn't the one you don't like, is it?

PAMELA: That's fine.

CONSTANCE: I'll ring Murray. I've been thinking about you all day. I rushed away from my meeting. There's some scent for you.

PAMELA: Darling –

CONSTANCE: I'm going to look after you. I've been talking to Murray. He's very worried about you. I've been too soft with you. I wished you'd been there this morning. I think you'd have changed your mind.

PAMELA: I don't need looking after, darling. Lovely scent. I'll put some on.

CONSTANCE: We owe it to one another.

PAMELA: No, we don't. You and Murray should have this place to yourselves.

CONSTANCE: Nonsense. What could be nicer? Besides, Murray's not getting rid of his flat. We both agreed on that.

PAMELA: I must go.

CONSTANCE: He doesn't want it.

PAMELA: Maybe not. I've got a few things packed.

CONSTANCE: But you don't mean you're going tonight? What about dinner?

PAMELA: I'm sorry, but I've got to have dinner with Bernard. He wants me to meet some film producer. It's rather important. I'll have some of the Dom Perignon with a bit of ice in it though. That's sacrilege for you.

CONSTANCE: Pamela, what's wrong? My darling. Tell. Why don't you talk to me?

PAMELA: I've stayed long enough.

CONSTANCE: What is it? I thought you were happy with me. We do get on, don't we?

PAMELA: Sure. But I need to get away for a bit.

CONSTANCE: You mean a holiday? We could all go together, why don't we? What a super idea.

PAMELA: I'm going with Bernard to the South of France. One of his friends has got a villa. I don't think it's what Pauline calls your scene. It's not really mine.

CONSTANCE: Murray would be fascinated I'm sure.

PAMELA: I think Murray might inhibit them a bit. No, I'll just sit by the pool and become a golden girl again. I've been looking at my body . . . look at it. A sort of dirty yellow cigarette stain colour.

CONSTANCE: You look stunning.

PAMELA: Sorry about your dinner. You and Murray can have a nice candlelight session alone together. You don't mind Bernard coming round?

CONSTANCE: No. I'm a bit dazed. I don't know whether I want to cook now.

PAMELA: You must feed up Murray. Spoil him. He likes spoiling. And why not?

CONSTANCE: I'll pack for you, if you must . . .

PAMELA: Don't bother. I'll leave most of it . . . for now. Just talk to me while I undress.

(*She moves between her bedroom and the drawing room dressing and packing in a casual way, talking. At one point, in the bedroom she is naked.* CONSTANCE *wanders about following her, rather helplessly, smoking and watching her every movement.*)

CONSTANCE: I brought you the evening papers.

PAMELA: More rave notices for Lady Tinker-Bell, I suppose?

CONSTANCE: Oh, yes, 'all that's permanently in the air'.

PAMELA: Did you and Murray enjoy it?

CONSTANCE: I think Murray quite liked it. He liked her, anyway, you'll be sorry to hear.

PAMELA: I'm not sorry.

CONSTANCE: I think he thought she'd be good in his play. I think I see what you mean. But she certainly gets the audience and the critics.

PAMELA: You bet. Went out of their frigid little minds. Still, I suppose there's always hope on Sunday.

CONSTANCE: I see you've got all the papers then.

PAMELA: Yes, Mama brought them. She seemed to think I'd want to see them. She's also a great fan of Abigail's too. Natch. Bet she wishes she had a daughter like that.

CONSTANCE: This one says something good about the play too . . . 'Finely wrought and blessedly well constructed'.

PAMELA: That means it's like a travelling clock. You can see all the works. That way you know it must keep the right time. (*She goes into the bedroom.* CONSTANCE *watches her from the doorway with the papers.*)

CONSTANCE: . . . 'What a relief to hear every syllable superbly and uniquely delivered.'

PAMELA: Why doesn't he own up he's deaf? He was the only critic who couldn't hear Orme. And he had a voice like a ton of Welsh nuts. I don't mind people being old as long as they're not bullying with it.

CONSTANCE: I think there's actually one with 'mystery behind the eyes'. Yes, here it is: 'a fugitive, self-scrutinizing mystery'.

PAMELA: Self-absorbed he means. He's hardly taken his eyes off the leading man all evening. He's the one who made that little play I was in sound so worthy and full of painful silences and hauntingly expressed, delicate agonies or something. Kept them away in droves. Mind you, it *was* a bit worthy, all greys and browns and sort of obsessed wit being rarefied and staring you out with austerity. I got good notices, specially from him. I knew I would. It was a sympathetic, bearing down part. All I had to do was upstage myself and keep a straight back. Sounds like cricket doesn't it. I got stuff about my repose and troubled enchantment and the impression of a powerful intelligence in perfect unison with heartaching turmoil. Something like that.

CONSTANCE: Well, you remembered it.

PAMELA: Even I remember some jokes. Actually, I wasn't really thinking about anything. I just kept trying to think what Orme would have done. He didn't think too much of it. He said you're giving your critics' performance. So, I said I know, but I've got to get on sometimes. And he didn't say anything. Except: that's all right. As long as you know it. Try and give the audience the real thing sometimes. Would you like me to do Abigail for you?

(CONSTANCE *laughs*.)

You can't miss if you do that. They go off their heads.

CONSTANCE: Gosh, you've got a beautiful body.

PAMELA: As I say, you have to be frigid to be one of them.

CONSTANCE: You really are permanently brown all over. You haven't got those awful bra cup marks.

PAMELA: You need to be three things: timid, aggressive and frigid. T.A.F. Like Welsh.

CONSTANCE: This one seems to have lost the point completely.

PAMELA: Probably wasn't listening, poor darling. Who is it? Oh, he's the one who sends me those dreadful telly plays he writes. Takes the part for the whole – as the actress said to the critic. Don't look so glum. I've just made a joke. I thought you were mad about jokes?

CONSTANCE: I hate to see you go. Do these upset you?

PAMELA: It takes more than an Abigail to make me give up. It's all like the weather. As for them, there's something fundamentally wrong with you if you want to do that. Something missing. I've noticed it. When you meet them. Impotence. That's why when they've been really nasty, they try to ingratiate if you're ever unlucky enough to meet one. 'Oh, did I say that? I'm sure I've said other things. I've always admired your work'.

CONSTANCE: You're looking better.

PAMELA: I feel it. Thinking of Abigail and all those people being hoaxed. Put some ice in that lovely Dom Perignon.

CONSTANCE: Good idea. You seem almost superstitious about her.

PAMELA: How?

CONSTANCE: Well, it's as if she didn't take everybody in, you'd be disappointed.

PAMELA: I suppose I would; they might have taste.

CONSTANCE: Wouldn't it be better if they did?

PAMELA: It would. But they haven't.

CONSTANCE: It seems to give you back your energy. You're so afraid of losing it.

PAMELA: So would you. It's a delicate plant. Not like your great climbing tree.

CONSTANCE: No. I have to flog mine. You're right. But good fortune, if you like, seems to fill you with dread.

PAMELA: Dread never is very far away, is it? Here's to success! Um. Delicious.

CONSTANCE: It'll seem strange not having you drink champagne about the place. We usually drink whisky when we're together. Murray, I mean. It's only when we're with you. Perhaps you've converted us. He really loves you.

PAMELA: You can't afford it. Champagne I mean. Well, not Dom Perignon.

CONSTANCE: Darling, please stay. You need love more than anyone I've ever known. And looking after. We'll both do it.

PAMELA: You look after Murray. He's the sort who needs it. Clever men need a lot of pampering. They have a hard time in some ways, I think.

CONSTANCE: Pamela, why don't you play the part in his play?

PAMELA: I thought he liked the idea of Abigail? If he can get her.

CONSTANCE: I think you'd be much better.

PAMELA: Tell a management that.

CONSTANCE: Gosh, actresses get ready quickly.

PAMELA: We have to.

CONSTANCE: You did like it, didn't you?

PAMELA: Yes. I'm giving it to Bernard. He might have some ideas.

CONSTANCE: What did you think of it?

PAMELA: Actually, he did ask me if I'd do it.

CONSTANCE: Well?

PAMELA: I don't really understand it, Constance. Perhaps I'm not clever enough.

CONSTANCE: You don't mean it. You don't like it. Did you tell him?

PAMELA: No. Why? What's my opinion! You like it. I'm sure a lot of people will.

CONSTANCE: But why? He respects your opinion.

PAMELA: Well, tell him not to.

CONSTANCE: What's wrong with it?

PAMELA: Oh, please. Don't hedge me in. Authors should never go peddling in the market place.

CONSTANCE: I know. It's vulgar.

PAMELA: Quite. Oh, all right, if you must. I think it's, yes, clever. It's full of erudite banalities. It's not a play, it's a posture by a clever annotator, a labeller. People sit around and make up Freudian epigrams about one another. It's written by someone thinking about writing it instead of thinking about whatever it's about. Do I make myself incomprehensible? I'm afraid it's catching from that script. I'm sorry, darling.

CONSTANCE: It seems as if just everything is over. You're going away. The recess'll be over soon.

PAMELA: It was never to be a permanent arrangement.

CONSTANCE: No. Perhaps I had deluded myself that it would be somehow.

PAMELA: It's always tempting but one must guard against the more likely possibilities.

CONSTANCE: Pamela, why were you taking down those phone numbers?

PAMELA: Oh, my God. I must ring them before I go. Ladies' Services, darling. Somebody in need.

CONSTANCE: Who?

PAMELA: No one you know.

CONSTANCE: Who?

PAMELA: Audrey – the girl in the crimpers. Silly girl. I thought they all took the pill those girls now.

CONSTANCE: Aren't you taking a risk?

PAMELA: Darling, I'm just helping the poor girl out. Hope she can afford it. Oh, don't look like that. What does one do – wait for the third reading in the Lords?

CONSTANCE: Darling, you will keep in touch, won't you?

PAMELA: Of course. I always do. Don't blub, darling. Have a nice dinner and a cuddle with Murray.

CONSTANCE: Sorry. I blub too easily.

PAMELA: Yes. You do. You must learn to do it without letting your mascara run. It's quite an easy trick. I'll show you. (*Doorbell rings.*)

CONSTANCE: Damn! Don't go yet. Please. When's Bernard coming?

PAMELA: I said half an hour. He'll be late.

CONSTANCE: Might be Murray. Hope so. I'll make *him* talk you out of it.

(*She goes to the door.* EDWARD *stands there, slightly drunk with* ABIGAIL *beside him. She is dressed in Men's Carnaby Street clothes. She also wears a theatrical moustache. It is almost possible to mistake her for a man at first glance, but only just. It is just the starlit* ABIGAIL.)

EDWARD: Hi.

CONSTANCE: Edward. Come in. What –?

EDWARD: Is Pamela up?

CONSTANCE: She's just dressing. I don't know . . . Is it . . . Why Abigail!

ABIGAIL: Constance, love!

CONSTANCE: Do you know, I really didn't recognize you. Good heavens. You look, you look marvellous. What, what happened?

EDWARD: She looks a gas doesn't she? Pamela! Don't say anything – (*To* CONSTANCE.)
(*They come in.*)
How are you, darling? Better?

PAMELA: Hello, Eddie. I'm all right darling. Just coming.
Constance, give him some of your expensive champagne.
CONSTANCE: I'll get it.
(PAMELA *appears. She stares at* ABIGAIL, *who is seated in the centre of the room.*)
PAMELA: Who's your friend? Good God! . . .
CONSTANCE: I was wondering if you'd be taken in. I was. Just for a moment. Doesn't she look marvellous.
EDWARD: We thought it was fun.
PAMELA: Hilarious. Where have you been like that?
ABIGAIL: Well, darling, how are you, you look really beautiful, honestly more than ever. I adore your hair.
PAMELA: I haven't been to the crimpers for two weeks.
ABIGAIL: Well, we had this night last night, you see, what with everything.
CONSTANCE: Oh, congratulations.
PAMELA: Yes.
ABIGAIL: Thank you, my darlings.
PAMELA: Did you get my telegram?
ABIGAIL: Yes, darling. Bless you. Isn't it marvellous? I can't believe it.
PAMELA: I don't know why. I find it only too believable. I thought I'd forgotten to send that telegram.
ABIGAIL: Eddie's been super. We had an absolute rave night. The management gave a party. That looked like being a bit draggy.
EDWARD: I'll say.
ABIGAIL: No, but darling, everyone was so sweet. And, you know, all the old excitement, and, oh well, you know what it's like, Pamela.
EDWARD: Hey, Connie, where's your record player. We just bought a fabulous record.
ABIGAIL: Oh, yes, Eddie. Do play it for them. Pamela will adore it. I'm mad about it.
PAMELA: So you did what?
ABIGAIL: Oh, yes, well there was the first night, and, well it was extraordinary. I don't remember much. I know I cried at the call.

EDWARD: They were hanging from the ceiling. It was a cert. You could tell.

ABIGAIL: You know that feeling?

PAMELA: Yes.

ABIGAIL: Well, I couldn't get out of my dressing room for hours. Then we finally got to this party. They were getting a bit narked I think, but it was lovely when we got there. Oh, everyone was so happy. Somehow, good things, well they simply change everyone, don't they? I mean they do. Everyone was just pleased and happy and I didn't care what happened. Then we left finally. Eddie drove us down to get the papers. Though everyone said we needn't bother. And, of course, it was super. We all went back, well, some of us, to Eddie's and we just went dotty all night. Eddie and I didn't go to bed at all.

CONSTANCE: How do you feel?

ABIGAIL: Wonderful! Oh, I do think people are really *it*. Absolutely. I do! Oh, champagne, how delicious. So, yes we had champagne and Eddie cooked bacon and eggs with it for breakfast. And he said let's go out and buy anything we want. We're loaded. We bought pictures and rugs and I bought a lovely ring and Eddie bought a fabulous cigarette lighter. Oh, we went to galleries and I bought some clothes. Then Eddie said we must have lunch at the Caprice. We hadn't booked a table and it was packed but we just walked in. We saw loads of people, didn't we, Eddie?

EDWARD: Yeh.

ABIGAIL: Then we saw a bit of some Swedish movie. It had some thrilling things with a girl having a baby.

PAMELA: Really?

ABIGAIL: I thought it was rather beautiful. But Eddie got bored and fell asleep and I woke him up, and we bought these super records. And, oh, yes this, well, we thought it would be fun if I changed. You know, there's a picture of me in every paper today. So we dropped in at Wig Creations for the moustache, then got a taxi to Carnaby Street. Walked all the way to Charing Cross Road. Not a head turned. Isn't it marvellous?

PAMELA: Fantastic.

ABIGAIL: That's right, Eddie. Oh, it's marvellous, Listen to this, Pamela. You'll go dotty. Constance . . . Eddie. (EDDIE *and* ABIGAIL *dance to the record.* CONSTANCE *and* PAMELA *watch.*)

EDWARD: (*Presently*) How are you, Pamela?

ABIGAIL: Isn't it divine? Yes, are you all right, darling?

PAMELA: Sure.

ABIGAIL: Oh, my God!

EDWARD: What is it?

ABIGAIL: Oh my God. Pamela! What have I done?

PAMELA: Tell me.

ABIGAIL: I should have gone to your father's Memorial!

PAMELA: I shouldn't worry. You had a better time.

ABIGAIL: But I should have gone.

PAMELA: Why? He didn't want anyone to go. I'm sure he would have approved of your day, Abigail.

ABIGAIL: But don't you understand. I was supposed to read one of the lessons.

CONSTANCE: Abigail –

PAMELA: I'm sure there were too many.

ABIGAIL: How *awful*. Pamela, what can I say?

PAMELA: Don't.

ABIGAIL: But I was asked.

PAMELA: They must have managed. No one mentioned it to me.

ABIGAIL: Darling. Eddie, turn that off. He really was the most marvellous actor. My Father was mad about him. I scarcely saw him.

PAMELA: No.

ABIGAIL: Are you all right, darling?

PAMELA: Fine.

CONSTANCE: She's a bit done in.

ABIGAIL: Eddie. Darlings, I must go. Look at the time. I've got a performance. Can we get a taxi here?

CONSTANCE: You'll get one in the street.

PAMELA: I should take your moustache off.

ABIGAIL: Darling. Bless you.

(Embraces all round.)

Sorry we barged in. Just wanted to see if you were all right.

EDWARD: My idea really.

PAMELA: I know. Thanks, Edward.

ABIGAIL: 'Bye, darling.

(She and EDWARD *do a musical exit. Then he comes back for the record.)*

(Pause.)

CONSTANCE: I think they've finished off the champagne.

PAMELA: I've got a last bottle. At the back at the bottom.

CONSTANCE: I'll get it. Can't you put Bernard off? I'll ring Murray.

PAMELA: I'm all ready.

CONSTANCE: Don't let Abigail break everything up.

PAMELA: I don't think she has.

CONSTANCE: Don't be hurt by it.

PAMELA: My dear girl, I promise you I'm not. Bernard's bound to be late.

CONSTANCE: There: here's to us.

PAMELA: To us all.

CONSTANCE: Are you taking the books with you? Orme's?

PAMELA: Oh, they'll go in Bernard's car. In the back somewhere.

CONSTANCE: Why do you suppose he goes around with Abigail?

PAMELA: Why do you think? Why does Murray want her for his play? At least she's alive in her way. Even he gets bored with his dollies. The thing about them is they really are mostly wooden. Abigail isn't wooden.

CONSTANCE: Please ring him up. Stay tonight.

PAMELA: It's too late. He'll be on his way. Look at that: Portia's solicitude for Brutus.

CONSTANCE: It looks a bit more than solicitude.

PAMELA: Oh, Orme couldn't bear her. He said her underwear was never clean. I can quite believe it.

CONSTANCE: What does he say about Abigail?

PAMELA: We don't talk about it. We didn't talk about it. Kingsway Theatre. Founded on the French of Gabriel Vardie. Queens Theatre. Meggie Albenesi. He knew all about her. Remembrance. That sounds good. Oh, he's playing a wog here. Count Stefano Ciffoni. He liked that. There he is on the West coast of Scotland. That's his place. His bleeding piece of earth, he called it. Well, *he* thought it was funny.

CONSTANCE: What were his big roles, really?

PAMELA: He was big in all of them. Even when he was bad. Oh, I suppose you mean, well, Shylock, Macbeth of course, Brutus oh yes, Hotspur and a very funny Malvolio.

CONSTANCE: What was *that* called?

PAMELA: 'The Real Thing'. Aah, here we are. The Countess lights upon – lights upon already – the Count in a compromising situation. Oh, Orme. She looks het up all right. Drunk I expect. Yes, look, see he's having to hold her up. He always did. Yes, it's the last act. What's new in the next session?

CONSTANCE: Oh, pretty heavy.

PAMELA: You won't have much time then?

CONSTANCE: No, what about your film?

PAMELA: Don't know yet. I expect I'll do a telly. Here we are: 'The Real Thing.' 'Think, Ella, there *is* no inheritance, nothing, only my debts and no career. Just the poor son of a parson, an ex-captain. Now that Jock Crawley has deprived me of my one chance, my one hope of happiness and redeeming myself, there is nothing left for me to do. Only go out of your life. No, I want you. I want you to be my wife. That is not possible. I *want* your life. Ella, Oh Ella, you are a magnificent woman. A gem.' *She* had mystery behind the eyes even then. 'And so are you David. All that a woman could ever want. A real gem. Not paste. But the real thing, David. The real thing.'

CONSTANCE: Perhaps it should have been called 'A Real Gem'.

PAMELA: No. 'The Real Thing' was better. Oh, here's one of his great flops. His own adaptation of 'The Brothers Karamazov.' Lost all his savings in that. Here we are, here's the critics: 'A gloomy piece, which will only, we confidently predict, achieve a limited hold on the public.' It certainly did. Lost all his savings. His own management, you see. And his own wife dunning him for money all the time. He was always having affairs with actresses.

CONSTANCE: Oh, Pamela . . . what are we all going to do?

PAMELA: You'll go back after the recess. That's what you'll do. It's getting better all the time.

CONSTANCE: Is it? I don't know.

PAMELA: Anyway, someone said, I think: 'The worst has already happened'. Or something. He adored actresses. But he didn't like the idea of marrying them. At least, I think he did, but he didn't meet her. That was the trouble with Mama. Just because she was always on about Kokoschka and Thomas Mann and the texture of life in a Socialist society, he was taken in by it. He thought she was not only cleverer than his other ladies, but cleverer than him.

CONSTANCE: What's she really like?

PAMELA: Daft as a brush. The old man had more in the way he held a tennis racket than every letter she ever wrote to the papers. From unemployment in the Highlands to bed wetting. Thank God for Orme, I was born before Dr Spock. He was through that. Please don't cry, dear. Or I'll have to go before Bernard turns up.

CONSTANCE: It all seems so wrong.

(*Bell rings.*)

PAMELA: I'll go.

(*She goes.* CONSTANCE *can't move. The door reveals* BERNARD.)

Darling, you're on time.

BERNARD: Darling – for you, anything. What are you up to, you naughty girl? I'm going to give you a tough evening.

PAMELA: Oh no, you're not. You can just tell me the news and then I'm going to bed early. You'll have things to do anyway. You know Constance.

BERNARD: Hello. Where do you want to eat? Is that all the stuff you've got?

PAMELA: I'm sending back for the rest. How about the Armpit Restaurant?

BERNARD: My dear, I've got so much to *tell* you. How about Abigail Ratatouilles?

PAMELA: Don't tell me.

BERNARD: Shall I take these?

PAMELA: Darling, would you? I'll get my fur coats. Always need *them*. It gets cold, even in the South of France.

CONSTANCE: Won't you have a drink before you go?

PAMELA: Bernard doesn't drink, isn't it dreary? He's so obsessed with his figure, which isn't so hot anyway. And also his performance. About which who knows.

BERNARD: You might find out one day, darling. Don't think I can't. You're looking fabulous. Doesn't she?

CONSTANCE: She does. Pamela?

PAMELA: Could you take these, Bernard? I'll just say goodbye to Constance.

BERNARD: Right, I'll be downstairs. 'Night, Constance.

CONSTANCE: Goodnight, Bernard.

(*He goes.*)

Oh, my dear. It isn't right.

PAMELA: Sh. There. I'll teach you that trick the next time. Take care.

CONSTANCE: Take care.

(*They embrace.*)

PAMELA: Oh, Bernard will look after me.

(*She goes out.* CONSTANCE *drinks the rest of her champagne. She goes to the telephone and dials.*)

CONSTANCE: (*On phone*) Darling? You're there . . . No, I'm O.K. . . . I arranged a dinner for Pamela and she's gone . . . Yes, left . . . I don't know . . . How do I know . . . I don't know what she's bent on or anything . . . come on over . . . yes, now, please . . . I love you . . . I ache for you . . . Do you? Thank heaven for that . . . Darling . . . oh, my darling . . . Pamela's going to give me a lesson . . . yes, right . . . Don't be long . . .

(*Curtain.*)